JOHN ROBERTSON – SUPER TRAMP

John Robertson's football journey took him from the Glasgow suburbs to European heights with Forest. On the international front he won 28 Scotland caps and experienced the ecstasy of scoring the winning goal against England at Wembley.

John Lawson is a journalist of more than 40 years' standing and has specialised for the most part of his career in football and cricket writing.

JOHN ROBERTSON
SUPER TRAMP

My Autobiography

WITH JOHN LAWSON

MAINSTREAM
PUBLISHING

EDINBURGH AND LONDON

This edition, 2012

Copyright © John Robertson, 2011
All rights reserved
The moral right of the author has been asserted

First published in Great Britain in 2011 by
MAINSTREAM PUBLISHING COMPANY
(EDINBURGH) LTD
7 Albany Street
Edinburgh EH1 3UG

ISBN 9781780575339

The author has made every effort to clear all copyright permissions, but where this
has not been possible and amendments are required, the publisher will be pleased to
make any necessary arrangements at the earliest opportunity

A catalogue record for this book is available
from the British Library

Printed in Great Britain by
CPI Group (UK) Ltd, Croydon, CR0 4YY

1 3 5 7 9 10 8 6 4 2

Dedication

I WOULD NEVER PRETEND THAT I have been a saintly character. There are a few skeletons around and I've done one or two things that I have regretted and three or four things of which I am not particularly proud. But throughout the ups and downs, the delight and the despair, I would like to think I have done my very best to be a good father.

I'm privileged to have played a part in bringing four wonderful children into the world and to them I would like to dedicate this book. Only three remain, following the heart-wrenching death of my eldest child Jessica in September 1996 at the tender age of 13. But Jessica is in my thoughts every day and as much a part of my life as my lovely daughter Elisabeth and wonderful sons Andrew and Mark.

As everyone knows I have been fortunate to win a number of medals after somehow being blessed with the talent to have a successful and memorable career in football. My medals and football memories are precious to me but my real jewels are my wife Sharyl and the kids. I love them all dearly and I can't pay Sharyl any bigger compliment than to say that I am happier now than at any stage of my life. Undoubtedly, that's all down to her, the love we have for each other and the positive influence she has had on my life.

No matter what people think of me I hope they see that first and foremost I am a family man. I have a wonderful family behind me and at times like this, when I'm reflecting on the best part of 60 years of my life, I cannot help but spare a thought for those loved ones who are no longer with me. I miss them every hour of every day.

Contents

Foreword

IT WAS HALF-TIME IN THE home dressing-room. Nottingham Forest were playing Leeds United in the old First Division, early 1979. It had been a poor first half for us and Brian Clough was angry. Really, really angry. And particularly with me.

'Son,' he shouted, 'you and I are going to fall out very soon. You haven't had a bloody kick first half.'

It was true, I couldn't deny. I was playing down the right-hand side for Forest and hadn't seen very much of the ball that afternoon. I tried to explain to the manager glaring straight into my face from less than two feet away that it was hard to get a kick if the ball was continually going down the left-hand side of the pitch, where, incidentally, it seemed it had been going for prolonged periods over the last three seasons.

I was trying my very best to reason with the manager but seemingly only succeeded in riling him further. 'And so it should go down the left-hand side,' he roared at me. 'Because that lad's a bloody genius,' pointing to the player sitting quietly on my left shoulder. The genius Clough was referring to was John Robertson, who had just been paid the highest compliment by one of football's greatest ever managers. There was no doubt about it . . . he deserved the accolade.

Forest were, at that very moment, champions of England and soon to be crowned champions of Europe. And 'the genius' was in the middle of a golden period of his footballing life, mesmerising opponents with his magical left-wing play and influencing games in the most incredible fashion. It didn't seem so just then but it had been a tough struggle for him to reach such a pinnacle.

I first met John in October 1971. I was 19 years old, a full-time student at university in Belfast, playing part-time football with Irish League club Distillery, with no experience of the professional game in England until I arrived at Forest. John, on the other hand, despite being a year younger than me, had been at the club for more than three years, signing as an apprentice straight from school in Glasgow. He was just breaking into the first team at the time, emerging, at least within the confines of the club, with a burgeoning reputation as a gifted two-footed central midfielder who could spray passes all over the pitch. He unfortunately also possessed a calculated penchant for laziness.

Still, it was strongly felt among the senior players that it was only a matter of time before John would make the grade. But Nottingham Forest were in decline. The wonderful team that had finished runners-up to Manchester United less than five years earlier no longer existed and with the transfer of Ian Storey-Moore to Old Trafford in March 1972, all hope would evaporate and relegation would soon, inevitably, follow.

Against this backdrop, both John and I were struggling to make an impact on the game. The club would remain in the Second Division for five years and John's early promise flickered briefly but never really ignited. Managerial changes seemed to reflect John's moods. Dave Mackay and Des Anderson arrived from Swindon to manage the club and for a spell John thrived, turning in some masterful displays in midfield to much approval. All too soon Dave and Des left for Derby County, leaving us both with a great, almost self-pitying sense of loss and injustice. Allan Brown's arrival as the next manager of Nottingham Forest saw dark days ahead for both of us. Despair set in.

Looking back, we were quick to blame the manager for some of our ailments but nevertheless the future looked far from rosy. John, often sullen, was in desperate need of some manager to come along and extract this undoubted natural talent and put it on show. I think back now on the innumerable times in the King John public house in Nottingham city centre when Tony Woodcock, Viv Anderson and I had to listen to John's tale of woe. As if he were the only one with problems. Ah, selfishness does have a place in this world. His diatribe was a familiar story each Saturday evening. John should be in Forest's first team, Brown had no idea how to manage and he would tell him so at training on Monday and his football renaissance would start all over again for another week. But, in truth, the Roxy Music-loving Robertson was on his footballing uppers.

What he didn't realise was that the next managerial change was to herald the sea change that the club so desperately sought and that John Robertson's career would be propelled to stratospheric heights, culminating in League and European Cup triumphs and acclaim as the best wide player in Europe. Brian Clough, immediately, and Peter Taylor, a little later, would be the catalysts for this amazing change from gifted but lazy midfielder to world-class winger.

From a playing point of view, the rest, as they say is beautiful history . . .

Several years later I wanted to break into football management but had little joy with most applications until Grantham Town, in the Beazer Homes Midland Division, took a chance with me. John was running a pub in a nearby village and I asked him to play on Saturdays. Despite working in the pub and having personal issues that carried many impediments, he agreed to come along and play but one day the lure of the big stage captured his attention.

He decided to abandon playing for me to watch Manchester United at Old Trafford instead. I was pretty infuriated by his actions because I needed commitment and we didn't speak for quite a while afterwards. But as time went on I enjoyed and appreciated his input when analysing players' performances and the incident was swept under the carpet.

Eventually we got together again, spending the last 15 years as manager and assistant manager. Along with Steve Walford and intermittently Seamus McDonagh we have remained together at Leicester, Celtic and Aston Villa. Throughout that time John was very astute, particularly when it came to judging players and their attitudes.

With the odd exception, he got on very well with the players in the dressing-room and never betrayed the trust they seemed to have in him. Our own relationship is based on the same respect and loyalty that now encompasses some 40 years (where have they all gone?). I need pay him no higher compliment than to say I trust him implicitly. He has been a good friend, an excellent confidant

11

and very much more than a self-confessed sounding board.

John Robertson has many qualities. A genius on the pitch? Absolutely. The perfect No. 2? Absolutely.

Just one thing . . . I only wish, at least for my own health, he would stop smoking.

Martin O'Neill

1

In the footsteps of Jimmy Johnstone

MILLIONS OF PEOPLE A YEAR drive past Uddingston probably without realising it's even there, sitting just south of the M74 on the main motorway route from England into Glasgow. I think it's officially classified as a village but, with a population of around 5,000, perhaps it's time it reached out for 'town' status.

For a little dot on the map it has a fair bit of notoriety – not least for the Tunnock's factory that has been producing those caramel wafer biscuits and teacakes for well over a century and attracts visitors by the busload. It's also the birthplace of James W. Black, a Scottish doctor who won a Nobel Prize in Physiology in 1988 for his work in medicine.

And this is where I come in, because it's also the starting point in the lives of a long list of footballers who kicked balls around the View Park area of Uddingston and ended up in the professional game. I'm unbelievably proud to be one of them and I don't mind a jot that someone recently described me as the second-best player to come out of View Park. The man they – and I – hold in such high esteem is a player who went to his grave in 2006 knowing he had earned the respect and adulation that goes with being labelled Glasgow Celtic's greatest ever player.

Jimmy Johnstone was that man – a player christened 'Jinky' by the Parkhead faithful for the endless hours of entertainment he provided for the Celtic hordes, weaving his magic this way and that through beleaguered opposition defences. He was one of the Lisbon Lions – the famous Celtic team of 1967 that won the European Cup under Jock Stein. But whether in the green and white hoops or the Scotland blue, Johnstone was revered for the

13

sheer pleasure he brought to so many on a football field.

Little Jimmy gave Uddingston identity long before I arrived and his huge reputation will make sure it stays that way for many generations to come.

I came along nine years after Jimmy, born as John Neilson Robertson on 20 January 1953 and to be perfectly honest I think I was a mistake. My mum and dad already had two children – Caroline, who was eleven and Hughie, who was a couple of years younger – and I think they thought two children – one of each – was probably enough. Then I came along. The 'Neilson', by the way, was from my grannie, another Caroline, who, as I will explain later, had an influential part to play in me arriving at Nottingham Forest. In those days it was a bit of a tradition in Scotland that middle names were often taken from the wife's maiden name and for all you Wikipedia readers, you now know the answer to that particular poser.

I came into a loving household but one that had no pretensions to be anything other than a very honest, caring, working-class family. My dad Hughie spent most of his life working as a miner before he got a job as a gateman with the electricity board in his later years. He was a quiet, unobtrusive man who just went about his life in a methodical but fairly basic manner, caring for his wife and family and not demanding too much out of his time on earth. To my knowledge he had no great talents as a footballer or as any other potential sportsman. He enjoyed watching the game, mainly from his seat in front of the telly, but that was about the sum total of his interest in football and it was left for my brother and me to try and make a few inroads in that direction.

In fact, my parents always reckoned that I first showed an inclination to be a footballer when I was in my pram. They swear I used to play keepy-uppy with a rattle from a very early age . . . and with both feet you understand! I'm not sure I can go along with that tale but what is factual is my mother's claim that in future years it cost her an absolute fortune in new football boots. When you are growing quickly your foot size changes all the time but like all football-mad kids I always wanted the latest boots to appear in the sports shops. I'm sure it was a severe drain on their finances but Mum and Dad did their best to keep me abreast with the latest gear.

The fact that my parents were a bit older than the average must have hit home one day in the back yard of our council house at 12 Woodview, Uddingston, where we had moved to after I spent the first ten months of my life in a tenement block in Tannochside View Park. Moving into a proper house was a big step and one of the first things I remember as a wee laddie was standing on the back step and shouting out to a neighbour, who was hanging out her washing, 'Mrs Coakley, my mammy is 40 today.' I can't remember whether or not I got a clip round the ear for broadcasting that bit of news but it's something that sticks in my memory from childhood. Incidentally, Mrs Coakley's son Tommy went on to become manager of Walsall . . . another Uddingston product in a small world.

I also remember ending up in York Hill Hospital, Glasgow, on a couple of occasions after getting bangs on the head. The first, I'm embarrassed to say, came after I trod on a football and fell over and the second was playing a game of 'hide and seek' and poking my head round a corner and somebody running the other way came banging into me at full pelt. On that occasion I was apparently talking gibberish for ages and my sister, who was looking after me at the time, said my language was appalling. Can't believe that.

There was no lasting harm done and it wasn't long before football started to dominate my life without ever thinking of what was to come. I never particularly liked school and the best part of the day was to hear the bell ringing, signifying school was out and I could get home and start kicking a ball around with my mates.

We were fortunate in that the school was about 20 yards from my house and equally nearby was a strip of grass that was our pitch and the nearest we were likely to get to Hampden Park. Two trees were perfectly positioned to act as goalposts at one end but at the other we had to find a coat or some other piece of clothing to line up alongside a solitary tree. That, I can assure you, was a recipe for many a decision – oh for goal-line technology! Me and my mates, who included Iain Munro who went on to play for Stoke City, Sunderland and Scotland, would race out of school to get as much time playing before the light went or we were called in for tea.

I used to look forward to the rare nights when my mum and dad had a night out because my sister Caroline would bring her boyfriend Jimmy Rooney round to the house and we would have an indoor football game of some description, more often than not using those decorative wax fruit things as footballs. I think a doorway in the front room was one goal and a display cabinet the other – thankfully we largely escaped any serious damage. Jimmy went on to marry my sister and down the years he has been a very important figure in my life. Like most people I've had moments of trauma and sadness but Jimmy and Caroline have always been there for me – right on the battle front if you like – and I've got to thank them for that and the many other influences they've had on me over many years. I owe them so much.

My interest in football took a major step forward in 1960 when I saw Real Madrid play Eintracht Frankfurt in one of the all-time great European Cup finals. Real won 7–3 and Ferenc Puskás, a Hungarian striker who had humbled England at Wembley in the year I was born, scored four of the goals. Watching the game on telly, I couldn't get my head round the fact that this supremely gifted footballer Puskás and his Real Madrid team in all their glory and glamour were playing a few miles down the road at Hampden in what was to be labelled one of the best matches of all time. Puskás was magnificent, all left foot, but even though I was very right-footed all I wanted to be was him. I used to smack balls into a fence and pretend I was this great player who was a world away from my life. 'It's Puskás in for the kill . . . and it's 1–0 to Real Madrid.' Little did I know then that some 19 years on I would be playing against a side he managed. But more of that later.

I was only seven but it was around that time that my brother Hughie started to make a bit of a name for himself with a local football club called Larkhall Thistle. He was a left-winger-cum-centre-forward and on one occasion he scored all six goals for them in a match. His promise led to the offer of trials at Wolves and Celtic and, although in time he went on to play a few games in the first team at Berwick Rangers, he never really made the most of his ability.

The age difference between us meant he wanted to spend his time with his mates but one thing I have always remembered is that he used to sing me to sleep at night. I've always been a music lover, enjoyed listening to ballads and he would get me off to sleep singing 'Nobody's Child', 'Old Shep', which was an old Elvis

Presley song, or 'Geisha Girl', and by the time he had got to the third one I was away.

As far as football was concerned he helped me with the basics of the game and I used to thoroughly enjoy just kicking the ball to and fro between us with him wanting the ball to his feet all the time. Looking back, that's probably where I got that part of my game from.

I just kept on playing as much as I could with my mates until I got my first bit of recognition when I was eight. The school team (Burnhead Primary) had reached a cup final at Brandon Park, which was the home of Belshill Athletic, and although I was nowhere near being picked, Iain Munro suggested to the teacher that I was good enough to go along as a reserve. Iain was the best player in the school and I've got him to thank for tipping off the head teacher about me. I was really chuffed and if memory serves me right I think I got a runners-up medal in one cup final even though I never got a kick of the ball.

I went on to play for the school team and football continued to be a lot more important to me than my education. Predictably, I failed the 11-plus but I don't think my mum was too worried or surprised. By that time she had taken up a factory job at the aforementioned Tunnock's Caramel Wafers and had I passed for Uddingston Grammar School I would have had to catch the same bus as her. She always complained about the rowdiness on the bus and although that was perhaps not the best reason for ending up at Hozier Secondary School, that became my seat of education for the next three years – or should I say most of it.

It was a source of satisfaction that I was in the Hozier school team that beat Uddingston Grammar 5–0 on one occasion and football continued to be a big part of my life. By contrast, my education took second place and if I could get out of going to school, make no mistake I did. I used to be spoilt at home and early on a morning my dad used to bring me toast and marmalade upstairs to have breakfast in bed before he went off to work. Little did he know what I used to get up to after he and my mum had shut the door behind them.

Depending on what subjects were on that day I used to 'dog' it, as we used to call it, by writing a letter to school and making sure that at the end of it I put 'Much obliged – Mrs Robertson' because

I remembered that on the occasions my mum sent in a genuine note, she always ended with those words. There's a good chance the music teacher David Main and Jack Scott, who was in charge of metalwork, woodwork, technical drawing and that sort of thing, knew what was going on but turned a bit of a blind eye as long I was there for the football teams they both ran in the school. Jack, in particular, was a big help to me in those years and it was he – not Brian Clough and Peter Taylor – who got me playing as an outside-left for the first time. For some reason I had become a centre-forward but he figured that I was a bit on the small side and would benefit from getting wide and able to work in a bit of space.

The school team became the hub for my football and we not only reached the County Cup final but also got through to the quarter-finals of the Scottish School Cup which was quite an achievement.

It was a time when my football games were all about the possibles and the probables. I went for a series of trials, starting when Iain Munro took me and Johnny Stevenson, another of our pals, along to the famous junior club Drumchapel Amateurs. I started off in the possibles but it was all about attempting to graduate into the probables and then eventually making the team. I achieved that with Drumchapel, then Jack thought I was good enough to go forward for the Motherwell and District Schools side and then the county side Lanarkshire Schools. Things were happening at a pace for me and after I had played for Lanarkshire against Dumfries and Galloway, I got myself within striking distance of the Under-15s Scotland schoolboy squad. Forty-four of us young hopefuls turned up at Stenhousemuir's ground and after I had scored a couple of goals in a match, I made the final twenty-two.

There was a big friendly coming up against England at White Hart Lane and I was thrilled to bits when I heard that I had been picked in the starting XI for that game. It got better. I was lucky enough to send over the cross from which Brian Laing, an Edinburgh boy who joined Liverpool without quite making it, headed home. Graeme Souness, who went on to have a magnificent career in the game, and Ally Robertson, who played at the heart of West Brom's defence for many years, were in the same Scotland side. There was also another Drumchapel lad in there called Tommy Sinclair, who everyone who knew anything about the game predicted would be a top player but sadly he died in his teens from leukaemia and that was a tragic loss.

After the England game we also beat Wales 2–0 in Swansea and then there were more national trials to give other lads a chance of progressing into the side.

Souness, who was already looking a million dollars as a player, was involved in the trials and at the first session we got an insight into the self-belief that he possessed back then and which guided him through his tremendous playing career with Tottenham, Middlesbrough, Liverpool, Sampdoria and Glasgow Rangers. Even at that age he was strong, talented and oozed confidence. He was certainly not afraid to stand his corner and speak his mind – even at a cost to himself.

One day I remember the coach telling Dougie Devlin, who ended up at Wolves, to wear the No. 4 bib and Graeme the No. 8. 'I always wear 4,' said Graeme. 'Well you're not now,' answered the coach. 'And if you don't want to wear the No. 8 you may as well go home.' With that Graeme simply walked off and I didn't see him for another three years. I thought at the time it was a big gamble to take so early in your career but he clearly had enough confidence in his ability to know that he would come back into the picture sooner rather than later.

I often wished to myself as a youngster that I had the same self-belief. Throughout my life I've always taken things steadily, not wanted to jump into anything and, if not exactly being shy, was nevertheless always likely to err on the cautious side. That was particularly the case in my earlier school days but the call-up for Scotland schoolboys certainly gave me a lot more confidence, certainly in my footballing ability, and I stayed in the international picture.

The next game was against Northern Ireland schoolboys over in the province just before the serious troubles started. The game was played at the Brandywell Stadium, home of Derry City, and we lost 3–1. I don't know why but I always remember buying the Love Affair's record 'Rainbow Valley' during the trip.

Back in Scotland we had a re-match with England at Ibrox Park but this game was for the Victory Shield and we were determined to do everything we could to win it. Thankfully, we did by the same 1–0 margin and it was a bit of déjà vu as far as the goal was concerned. I was involved in a short corner on the left, managed to side-step the England full-back and cross for Brian Laing to get in another header past the English keeper – a lad called Mick Dilnot, who I was later to meet up with on the staff at Nottingham Forest.

By this time what academic education I had was well and truly over. Football was all that mattered and I was determined to go one step further than my brother and make the most of any opportunity that came along. I talked about it with my family and told them, 'If I ever get the chance to go to England, I'm off because that's where the future and the money is in the game.' But despite doing well for Scotland schoolboys, the choices that I was looking at initially were staying north of the border or going to Wales. There was talk of Partick Thistle, who were managed by Willie Thornton, the ex-Rangers centre-forward, offering me terms and there was a fair bit of interest from Cardiff City, whose manager at the time was Jimmy Scoular, the old Newcastle wing-half.

Then Nottingham Forest representatives arrived on the scene – first of all in the shape of Bill Anderson, a jovial Geordie who was assistant manager to Johnny Carey. He came to my house to talk to my dad and, in line with my reticence to get involved with men talk, I went out for a walk while Bill had his say. He paid us another visit soon afterwards and brought with him Bob McKinlay, whose career as Forest's record appearance maker of all time was coming to an end. He was still playing but preparing himself for life on the City Ground backroom staff. Bob, who was a gentleman off the field as well as on it, was from Lochgelly and I'm sure that Forest thought if they could get a Scotsman inside our house it might help persuade me to make the big move.

They talked it all over with my parents but it was my grannie, who was known as 'Carry', who swung it. Apparently she fell for the charm of Bill and Bob and piped up, 'Don't know why you don't go for it – they're lovely people.' By that time I had involved myself in the talks and whether it was bravado or not I announced, 'Yes, I'm going to do it.' In fairness it was the kind of opportunity I had hoped would come along but in line with my usual apprehension I still needed a nudge.

Only a year before, the 1966–67 season, Forest had proved themselves one of the best teams in England, finishing as runners-up to Manchester United in the old First Division and reaching the semi-final of the FA Cup before losing to Tottenham Hotspur at Hillsborough. I knew I was joining a club that wasn't one of the giants of the game but nevertheless they were still a major force and had a reputation for playing good football. They had players like Joe Baker and Ian Storey-Moore in the side and although the team was showing signs of breaking up it was still one that upheld the best traditions of Nottingham Forest in being a club who always played the game the right way.

It was a whole new big wide world that was opening up in front of me but I had a bit of Scottish companionship with Forest taking Maitland Pollock along as well. I had come up against Maitland when he played for Dumfries and Galloway Schools and I think that Forest thought that we would be good for each other.

It was in the late spring of 1968 that I was invited down to Nottingham for the first time to get a feel of the place and have my first days away from my family. The only previous occasion I had not slept in my own bed was when I was on holiday so it was a strange feeling. I had a bit of a lump in my throat the day I left. My mum and auntie Mattie came to the railway station to see me off and there I was resplendent in a smart, new suit ready for the trip south. We were all a bit upset and I just said to them, 'Off you go, just get off home, no waving – I'll be all right.'

When I arrived in Nottingham Maitland and I were put in digs with a Mrs Williams, who was already looking after other players, including Duncan McKenzie. Even in those days Duncan was a bit of a motor-mouth. He just couldn't stop talking and had opinions on everything and nothing, but all the same he was a likeable lad. While we were there I remember settling down to watch the European Cup final between Manchester United and Benfica at Wembley which United won 4–1 after extra-time but, as is his wont, Duncan blabbed his way through it.

Maitland and I had been invited down specifically to travel with the youth team who were taking part in the end of season Blau-Wit Tournament in Holland. We were not playing, just going along for the ride to get a taste of things before reporting for pre-season training a couple of months later. We went from East Midlands Airport to Amsterdam and it was the first time I had ever flown in an aeroplane but, unlike a lot of footballers, I took to the experience pretty well, which wasn't always the case as the years passed and travelling by air became such a regular thing for me.

When we arrived back in Nottingham, we were soon on our way north to prepare to return for pre-season training and the start of an era that was to be beyond my wildest dreams. But there was a lot of soul-searching to go through before I reached those days.

2
Into the Forest

I ARRIVED AT THE CITY Ground, home of Nottingham Forest, in the summer of 1968 and there were occasions when I thought it would all end as quickly as it started. I was only 15 and away from home for the first time in my life so I knew it was not going to be easy. The whole thing was a bit of a culture shock to me. I was used to being a kingpin in schools football in Scotland but here I was just one of the young boys – a small cog in a very big wheel with very distant hopes of getting to the top.

As a kid on the staff you never got any special treatment, you had to muck in and do jobs that you didn't really fancy. In the very early days I remember saying to my dad, 'I don't think I will be able to do this.' But he sat me down and said reassuringly, 'Let's not be too hasty, son. Give it a chance and if you don't like it you can always come home. But, one thing, don't come home with regrets.' I took his words on board and slowly but surely, the homesickness became less of an issue and I began to settle into a very different way of life in Nottingham.

I even got a job away from football because I think I am right in saying that boys coming down from Scotland had to sign on as amateurs initially. The only way clubs got round the problem was to find them a job and mix that with training. I was assigned – along with Maitland – to a printing works in the Meadows area of the city. It was Temple Printing, whose business was built around producing the matchday programme at Forest but they were also known as a jobbing printer, specialising in short print runs to local firms. They even gave me a bicycle to make deliveries and I had the added bonus of being able to use it to get back to my digs at night.

Barry ('Baz'), the boss's nephew, ran the factory and was a Nottingham bloke through and through. I picked up a lot of the local lingo from him . . . and a few choice swear words that I'd not even heard of in Scotland. To be perfectly honest I wasn't really interested in working there. All I wanted to do was play football and couldn't get my head round the fact that I was ending up in a printing works every afternoon after training. I got on the wrong side of Baz on a lot of occasions and more than once he said to me, 'You think work is a dirty word, don't you?'

While I was at Temple I made a very good friend called Trevor Waldran. We hit it off straight away. Like me, he became a massive fan of Bryan Ferry and Roxy Music. I've always liked my music and I don't think I was terribly popular with other lads in the digs who didn't share my taste, particularly when it came to Roxy Music.

Trevor became a really good mate but sadly his life ended early in tragic circumstances. First of all he was the only survivor in a huge car crash that killed three people in Clifton on the outskirts of Nottingham but then he lost his life in another car accident not long afterwards . . . terrible. In the time that I knew him Trevor helped me get used to life in Nottingham and he helped me come to terms with the homesickness I had.

When I joined the full-time staff I was in digs with Bernice and Doug Johnson, who were a really friendly couple who did everything to help us settle in. They actually went on to run the club hostel and I moved in there with Duncan McKenzie, Bill Styles, Dave Serella, Jimmy McCaffrey, Melvyn Johnson and Jimmy McCann and we had some good times together as we set about trying to get down to the serious business of proving ourselves good enough to have a career in the game.

As young apprentices we were not around the first team scene much but we did get to clean their boots, which was a normal task for the young kids in those days. I wasn't into the mundane sort of jobs but when you are cleaning mud off boots worn by the likes of Jim Baxter and Joe Baker, it's no great hardship.

Being a Scotsman who lived and breathed football, the name Baxter meant something special to me. I was brought up as a Rangers fan and Baxter, a legendary figure north of the border, was one of my heroes. He was known as 'Slim Jim' Baxter during his marvellous days with Glasgow Rangers, had a wonderful left foot and his natural talent stood comparison with anyone. By the time I saw him at Forest he had been at Sunderland and had certainly lost some of the slimness but even though his best days were behind him I was still gobsmacked to be at the same club as him. When we spoke he was a perfect gent, had no edge and was just very pleasant.

In football terms he was right at the top of the tree when he was at his best and Baker had attracted the same kind of adulation at Forest where he was a cult figure with supporters who idolised his every move.

At the age of 15 I used to think I knew what made a good player but in reality I hadn't a clue. My game was all about having a bit of a dribble and trying to go past people but I didn't understand back then about what it took, for example, to be a centre-forward with your back to goal and being kicked from pillar to post while you held up play for your team-mates to join in. A lot of the game's terminology was a foreign language to me and when I heard things shouted on the training ground I couldn't help but laugh at times. When somebody first shouted, 'Get back,' at me, I thought they were referring to an old Beatles record; the only tackle I knew was in fishing and I thought work rate meant that somebody wasn't being paid enough. I must admit I've made the odd reference to things like that when I've done the occasional after-dinner speech.

For the most part we were well away from first team players and apart from the boot room, the nearest we got to them was cleaning out the toilets and showers they used in the dressing-room. Dave Serella was working in there one day – he was cleaning the bath area, which contained one of those big communal football baths that you don't see these days – while I was cleaning out the main dressing-room area. I asked if I could borrow his water bucket and Dave's only comment was, 'Make sure you bring it back.' Predictably, I didn't so Dave, who was not very happy, taught me a lesson by squeezing his mop out all over the area I was cleaning. There was water everywhere and it wasn't even clean water. It didn't end there, we carried on a stand-up argument and I said something like, 'If you want to land me one, go on and do it.' Dave was a centre-half, was a fair bit bigger than me and didn't need a second invitation. He smacked me one across the face and I suppose I deserved it.

25

The upshot of that little disagreement was that Dave and I, who had not had that much to do with each other apart from sharing digs in the hostel, became really big friends – and have remained so right through to this day. As well as being a really good mate he used to specialise in the unexpected in his earlier years. On one occasion he clambered up one of the pylons at The City Ground and swung off it with one hand, gorilla-style. In another barmy act he decided he would suspend himself from Trent Bridge, which is a Nottingham landmark and a place where a number of people have committed suicide in the past. Dave just wanted to have a laugh and climbed over the side of the bridge and clung on to a ledge with the water flowing beneath. Fortunately, he came away unscathed from both incidents but his stunts could easily have gone horribly wrong.

Us lads in the youth team were no more than 15 or 16 and used to play in a Thursday league where we were up against men, but it was a great experience and certainly helped us grow up quickly. We also played 'A' team football – Len Beaumont, a former Forest player who is sadly no longer with us, used to run the side – on a Saturday morning and then had to report to The City Ground when there was a home match to help out in the dressing-room area.

And five matches into the 1968–69 season, on 24 August to be exact, there was an incident at The City Ground when there was literally no smoke without fire. Forest were playing Leeds United in the First Division and were drawing 1–1 when smoke started appearing from the Main Stand. It didn't seem much of an issue at the time and to be perfectly honest there wasn't a great deal of concern initially. There couldn't have been because Dermot O'Shea, who was one of the other groundstaff lads, and I were told to go into the home dressing-room and get the players' suits and other belongings off the pegs. We were doing that when someone came in to say, 'Get yourselves out of here now, it could go up.' And up it went . . . the whole bloody stand! Everyone was ushered out of the Main Stand onto the pitch for safety and from a seemingly innocuous situation, the entire stand was up in flames.

When you think of the terrible disaster that hit Bradford City's Valley Parade ground in 1985, when 56 people lost their lives and 265 were injured, you look back now and wonder how close the

Forest fire came to claiming victims. Thankfully, everyone got out safely and if there were any injuries they were only minor ones.

The match was abandoned at half-time and Forest temporarily played home matches across the river at Meadow Lane while the ground was made secure and the Main Stand later rebuilt. We used to get changed at nearby Trent Bridge cricket ground before training sessions.

It didn't really affect us youngsters too much but soon afterwards I was making my first appearance for Forest Reserves in the old Central League at the reopened City Ground. I was only 15 at the time so it was a big occasion for me and I couldn't wait to get going in the match against Manchester City. I played outside-right and was up against Bobby Kennedy, who was quite an experienced full-back, but I looked upon it as a great experience.

We won the game 1–0 and according to the report in the *Nottingham Evening Post* I did pretty well. I played in the next game, too, against Newcastle United at The City Ground and we won 3–1 and I scored one of the goals, smacking a shot into the roof of the net.

I was pretty pleased with myself at the time and couldn't wait to call my dad and tell him I had scored but in football terms it was a case of not trying to run before I could walk. I was embroiled in my own future, desperate to play as much as I could and get the chance to impress, but from a Forest point of view we didn't go through the happiest of periods.

Most people at the club, and certainly the fans, thought Forest would kick on after their marvellous season of 1966–67 when they came so close to winning a trophy. But someone of influence decided that Forest were a selling club and there seemed to be a never-ending trail of top players being prised away to more ambitious rivals. Brian Clough played a significant part in it all, luring the likes of Alan Hinton and Terry Hennessey to The Baseball Ground; Joe Baker was allowed to leave for Sunderland, Peter Grummitt joined Sheffield Wednesday and on the day I made my first-team debut, Henry Newton played his last game before signing for Everton.

I was 17 years and 263 days old when I made my first appearance as a substitute against Blackpool at The City Ground . . . and I don't mind admitting I was shit scared. I don't know whether it was the occasion, the fact that I was relatively young or whether my problems of lacking self-belief had come back to the fore. By that time I had been playing regularly for the reserves and thought I was doing OK and might get a look in at some stage but when you get the call it's always a bit nerve-racking. I found out on the Friday lunchtime that I was substitute. Matt Gillies, who had taken over from Johnny Carey as manager, had named the team and I was on the bench. During the match Paul Richardson, who became one of my rivals for a place in the side, came off and Gillies just said to me, 'Get on and enjoy yourself.'

I took Paul's place in central midfield and I was happy about that because it was where I always saw myself playing permanently. I had been a winger but they weren't fashionable after Sir Alf Ramsey started picking England teams without them and in any event, playing in the middle meant, in theory at least, that you saw more of the ball.

There was a crowd of only 16,618 at the game but it was one hell of an occasion for me and we ended up beating Blackpool 3–1 with goals by Peter Cormack, Barry Lyons and Ronnie Rees.

Newton's departure to Goodison Park caused another stir among supporters but they had become used to an exodus of the club's best players by now and at least his sale was tempered by the fact that Tommy Jackson, a Northern Ireland international, was joining us in part exchange. He made his debut in the following match against Coventry at Highfield Road but he was injured in the game and that gave me a chance to make my full debut in a goalless draw with Huddersfield Town at Leeds Road in the next match. But with Jackson fit again to return the game after, I stood down and didn't get another look in that season. It wasn't easy to take but I kept telling myself, 'Robbo, you're still young and your time will come again.'

My mood wasn't exactly helped by Tommy Cavanagh, who was a first team coach under both Johnny Carey and Matt Gillies. He wasn't my cup of tea as a bloke and not one of those people who had any time for putting a comforting arm around young players like me. I didn't like being anywhere near him. I was a bit run down when I went into training one day and cold sores had broken out all over one side of my face. He just took one look at me and said, 'You look like a sack of shit!' I wasn't sure how I was supposed to react to that but I kept my thoughts to myself, until one day he

28

just went one step too far. He kept nagging away at me and in the end I snapped back at him, 'What do you want for seven quid a week, fucking Pelé?'

I'm sure Cavanagh used to shout for the sake of shouting at times and he was always ready to explode but I suppose he felt it was his way of trying to get the best out of players. It might have worked for seasoned pros but not for kids; Duncan McKenzie tells the story that Mel Johnson, who, like Duncan, came from Grimsby, was destroyed by Cavanagh's rants to such an extent that he went home to the east coast, gave up football and became a lorry driver.

One player who went undeterred about his business in a magnificent way was Ian Storey-Moore, who was an established star by that stage. With due respect to the players who represented Forest between the 'nearly' season of 1966–67 to the relegation campaign of 1971–72, it was Ian's goals that kept us in the First Division. I consider myself privileged to have played with him for Forest and what an outstanding player he was. He was skilful, quick, powerful on the ball . . . and could score goals from any position or angle.

Ian was, without doubt, one of the most talented forward players of his generation and it's amazing for someone bristling with so much ability that he won only one cap in 1970. I remember the game, too. It was against Holland and England won 2–0 and he scored a 'goal' with a header but it was disallowed. He picked up an injury that prevented him being selected the next time and amazingly didn't figure in an England squad again.

He used to wear the No. 11 shirt at Forest but he wasn't a winger by any stretch of the imagination. He was given a roving role and used to pop up here, there and everywhere and more often than not he made an impact. One goal he scored against Arsenal at The City Ground in the relegation season was one of those once in a lifetime efforts. I don't know how but someone calculated that he had picked up the ball 74 yards from their goal and just kept going, evading desperate challenges as only he could before thumping the ball home in typical style. It really was an unbelievable effort.

I remember another game earlier in that season when we were 3–1 down to Liverpool at The City Ground and I went on as a substitute for Tommy Jackson. I stood the ball over the top for Ian and although his shooting angle was almost impossible he managed to get his body in the perfect position to score from an acute angle. It was a magnificent strike and owed everything to his individual talent but I used to rib him about how I made the goal for him. In reality he had to perform contortions before producing the superb technique needed to score from the situation he was in.

Ian was one of so many outstanding talents in the game at the time – every club seemed to have players of exceptional skill. Manchester United had George Best, Bobby Charlton and Denis Law; Chelsea had Peter Osgood and Alan Hudson; Kevin Keegan and John Toshack were creating goals and mayhem at Liverpool . . . the list is endless. It was an era of wonderful players, who played the game hard but managed to produce fantastic entertainment.

I've always maintained that the Leeds United team of that time was as good as any team the game has known. I felt that if Don Revie had let them off the leash and allowed them to express themselves without dossiers and things, they could have been something extra special. I know they were not everyone's cup of tea (as Brian Clough never tired of pointing out in the only way he could) but you could not fail to appreciate the talents of players like Johnny Giles, Billy Bremner, Norman Hunter, Eddie Gray, Terry Cooper and all the others.

I remember one day at The City Ground playing against Leeds and Bob McKinlay, who was our coach, told me to follow Giles all over the pitch wherever he went. 'Stick to him like glue' was my last instructions before I went onto the field. Anyone who knew me will tell you that man-to-man marking wasn't my game at all. I did my best to carry out my instructions but after about ten minutes Giles decided he would sort out this little problem. He went and literally positioned himself on the left wing and, true enough, I stood there beside him doing absolutely nothing. I heard him say to Eddie Gray, 'You go and play midfield Eddie and I'll stay here.' And with me and Peter Hindley, who was our right-back, stuck in the same position, Eddie ran the show from the middle of the park. Another lesson learnt the hard way.

As I said, every team had stars and it was imperative that we hung on to our top performer, Storey-Moore, or 'Muggsy', as everyone in football knows him. But in March 1972 the player who had almost single-handedly kept Forest in the First Division was on his way out of Nottingham Forest. We all thought he was set to join Derby County, who were managed by Brian Clough and Peter Taylor. They had already snaffled Hinton and Hennessey from The City Ground in pursuit of turning Derby into a major force and getting Muggsy would have been a real coup.

Someone at Forest had given him permission to go and talk to Derby and Cloughie must have thought he had pulled off a master stroke when he agreed terms with Muggsy and Taylor paraded him on the pitch as 'their new signing'. It was then that Forest, mindful that Manchester United were also interested, called off the deal and Frank O'Farrell, who was manager at Old Trafford, claimed they had agreed a transfer.

For a few days it was crazy as the claims and counter claims went on between Forest, Derby and Manchester but in the end Forest, who were run by committee at the time, called off the transfer to Derby following an emergency meeting. Ian then went on to join United, leaving Cloughie fuming and I can only imagine the fall-out there would have been at The Baseball Ground as he lamented the loss of a player he thought he had got in the bag. For years he didn't speak to Muggsy because he felt he should have dug his heels in over a move to Derby but Ian was in a totally invidious position – one I was about to find myself in some years later.

Ian's loss was huge for Forest. His goals were all-important, of course, but he also had the ability to inspire the players around him and lift the fans out of their seats with one of those electric bursts that became his trademark.

There was no doubt that Forest were in free fall and one of the players they brought in to help stabilise them was Scotland full-back Tommy Gemmell, who came from Celtic in what was something of a stellar signing. Tommy was one of Celtic's Lisbon Lions, who had captured the European Cup for a British team for the first time, and he was still the younger side of 30 with plenty of football left in him. He was a good bloke too and although he had been principally signed to fill a void at the back when Liam O'Kane broke his leg against Everton, he showed what he was all about as an attacking force. He scored twice to give us a vital 2–1 win over Chelsea and thumped one in from the best part of forty yards to set us on the way to a 4–0 win over Coventry City.

We only lost one of our last five games but in the end there was too much to do and the inevitability of relegation became a reality. The doom and gloom descended and when Peter Cormack, a gifted Scottish midfielder who had joined Forest from Hibernian, was sold to Liverpool during the summer it did not look good for an instant return to the top flight. We still had some old pros like Peter Hindley, John Winfield and Sammy Chapman, who had all figured in the 1966–67 team, and it must have been galling for them to have witnessed the demise of Forest as a top-class side in a small matter of five years.

I was one of several young players still trying to find their way in the game amid the depression that had come over The City Ground but, believe it or not, we started the following season in Division Two pretty well, winning three and drawing the other two of our opening five games.

But if there was a renewed optimism it didn't last for long. Gates dropped to four figures and for one match against Cardiff City there were only 6,414 in the ground. We won the game 2–1 but you could have heard a pin drop for most of the night.

Supporters, who had been used to seeing Liverpool, United and Arsenal turn up, became increasingly restless and the manager Matt Gillies, a mild-mannered Scot who had enjoyed good times at his previous club Leicester City, was under all sorts of pressure. Crowd demonstrations were commonplace inside and outside the ground and the writing was on the wall for him when fans started to turn their abuse on club officials. The committee box was in the centre of the Main Stand and supporters could get close, and at one match there were reports of fans spitting at officials.

Something had to give and sure enough after a game against Bristol City at Ashton Gate in October 1972 Gillies resigned. Where would we go from here? No one really had any ideas on the playing staff and we waited to see where the club would turn next for their salvation.

Bill Anderson, who had brought me down from Scotland in the first place, was put in caretaker charge but in the next game at home we found ourselves two goals down to Swindon Town. There were only two minutes left when I managed to pull one back and before the end Martin O'Neill snatched an equaliser to give us a bit of a boost – and goodness knows we needed it.

Dave Mackay, who had become a legend during his playing days spent largely with Tottenham – he was a highly influential member of their double-winning team of 1960–61 – was in charge of Swindon and still finding his way as a fledgling manager after ending his magnificent playing career at Derby and then Swindon. Whether or not it was his presence that day that jerked some reaction from Forest officials to think of him as a successor to Gillies I don't know, but within a couple of games he was on his way to The City Ground as our new boss.

His first game in charge was against Millwall at The City Ground and I scored the winner at the Bridgford End after cutting in from the left. I thought at the time that scoring that goal would do me a favour or two – at least it got me noticed by him. I liked Dave because he believed in encouraging players to get the best out of them. I was going along quite nicely and had a new sense of purpose.

During his playing days Dave had built himself a reputation as a hard man but that did not detract from the immense natural ability he possessed. He was an old-fashioned wing-half but even in training you could see that he had a wonderful left foot and a touch that was soft and easy on the eye. He could play keepy-uppy all day long and even though his playing days were well and truly over he oozed skill and charisma. There was no doubt he was one of the top players of his generation. He won loads of silverware at Spurs and after all his marvellous success in ten years in North London, Brian Clough yet again showed his foresight in recruiting Dave to add the final touches to his Derby side that won promotion to the First Division in 1969. Years later I remember talking to Bertie Auld, the old Celtic player, about the legends of the game and Dave's name was the first one he came up with.

We wondered whether the hard-man image would be evident as a manager but nothing was further from the truth. Don't get me wrong, you didn't mess with Dave but he had a great sense of humour and a fairness that endeared him to the players.

His assistant was a bloke called Des Anderson and he had the kind of outgoing personality that players liked. It would be frowned upon now – and probably would have been then – but I regularly remember Des and his wife Lesley, who was a lovely lady, coming for a drink with the players at The Trent Bridge Inn after home games. It's perhaps not the done thing for management and players to mix in that way but we enjoyed Des's company and he clearly was very comfortable with the players.

I loved playing for Dave. 'Just go out and play, son, and enjoy yourself,' he would say in that Scottish brogue that was still as strong as it was in his Edinburgh youth. It was the kind of encouragement I wanted to hear from a manager and although he spent barely a year at The City Ground, it seemed like we had turned the corner with him. It was a pleasure to come into work and train and although results weren't fantastic, there was a feel-good factor and a genuine belief among the players that we were heading in the right direction.

From a personal point of view I was really enjoying my football and for the remainder of the season I was virtually a regular in the side. We finished 14th in the table and had a very tight FA Cup third round tie with West Brom, drawing at The Hawthorns and The City Ground before going out 3–1 on neutral territory in the mud of Filbert Street, where I thought I had done really well.

I did drop a clanger with Dave before the next match with Queens Park Rangers. I was picked in the team for the weekend game but overslept on Friday and was late for training. It was a sin really, I had to hold my hands up and quite rightly got dropped. But I was back in for the next game.

At the end of the season Dave took the players off to Portugal for an end of season tour that included matches against Benfica and Oporto – and that's where I got a sharp reminder that football can kick you in the teeth when you think things are going your way. We played Benfica in the first match at the magnificent Stadium of Light and although there were only 5,500 in what was a vast ground, it was a great experience for me and the other younger lads.

Then disaster struck. I lunged into a tackle with one of their players, stretched for the ball and when he turned I tried to go with him only for my studs to stick in the ground and wrench my knee. It was the worst pain I had ever felt in my life. I knew straight away that I had done something fairly serious and although I did eventually try to play on I knew it was hopeless, I could hardly stand up and had to get off the field. It was the early part of the trip and although clearly that was the end of me figuring in the games, I limped along with a view to getting the problem looked at when I got back to Nottingham.

Unfortunately for me, the knee decided it was going to cause me more immediate problems and the swelling kept going up and up, the pain was getting to the point of being unbearable and the physio decided we ought to go to hospital. That was fine because I wanted someone to end the pain, but when I saw the size of the needle the doctor had in his hand, I began to have second thoughts. I can remember muttering under my breath, 'For Christ's sake, you're never going to stick that into my knee, are you?' I had never seen anything like it in all my life but he managed to drain blood or fluid, whatever, out of the knee and I must admit it did calm things down a bit without getting rid of the pain altogether.

I limped through the rest of the trip – we lost 3–0 to Benfica and drew 1–1 with Oporto – but I was glad to get back home and get the knee seen to. It turned out to be a torn cartilage but I'm sure there was a lot more to it than that because Des Anderson said he had come back inside five weeks after a cartilage injury and I had a bet with him that I would be back sooner. But I broke down in training one day and had to start from scratch.

Although I was a long way out of the picture, the 1973–74 season didn't start great, we drew a lot of games but there was still confidence in the dressing-room that we could push forward. And Dave made what we all thought was a good signing in October 1973 when he bought Ian Bowyer from Leyton Orient, where he had gone to get regular first team football after starting his career at Manchester City. He scored on his debut in a 2–2 draw at Blackpool and after that game all hell broke loose down the A52 at Derby, where Clough and Taylor had walked out and left the place in total disarray.

We looked on from a distance but the players were almost in revolt, there was talk at one stage of them refusing to play and Derby chairman Sam Longson and his directors seemingly didn't know which way to turn. With the rivalry between Forest and Derby I think everyone in Nottingham was having a bit of a laugh about things, particularly when Clough had exploited Forest's willingness to sell their better players in preceding years. But the smiles were about to change. Derby realised they had to get someone on board who could settle things down and bring some semblance of order to the place – and that someone was Dave Mackay. He had barely been with us a year and he was off but you could not deny that he was the best man for the situation at Derby, having known most of the players from the end of his playing days.

It was a sad day for me when he left and we were again looking for a new manager with Bill Anderson, the eternal caretaker boss, again stepping in for a few games while the club made their move for someone to succeed Dave. Nearly a month went by without an appointment being made and when they announced that the new man would be Allan Brown it didn't exactly leave us ecstatic. He had had a good playing career, mainly with Blackpool and Luton Town, and was actually in the Luton side that lost to Forest in the 1959 FA Cup final. But his managerial career had taken him from Wigan, Luton, Torquay and Bury to The City Ground and we weren't quite sure what to make of it.

I must admit he and I didn't get off to the best of starts because on our first meeting he turned to me and said, 'How are you, Jimmy?' Jimmy? Maybe he was giving me the 'Jimmy' tag because I was Scottish or confused me with Jimmy Robertson, the old Tottenham winger, but I just felt he had got my name wrong and that was a bit upsetting to me because I thought I was beginning to become known. I was feeling very low, the knee wasn't fixed and my new manager didn't even know my name. After the good days under Dave I started feeling sorry for myself again and I've got to confess I had a bit of the big-time Charlie about me, which certainly didn't help, and I was probably not looking after myself as well as I could in terms of diet and general fitness. When I got myself fit again Brown made it clear that he didn't think I worked hard enough. He wanted grafters in his side whereas my first thoughts were on being able to play the ball.

Results-wise we were not doing too badly and early in 1974 we started to put together a run in the FA Cup that threatened to take us a long way down the road to Wembley. Our run coincided with games being played on a Sunday and the first ever match to be staged at The City Ground on the sabbath was our third round meeting with Bristol Rovers. We won what turned out to be a thrilling match 4–3 but, just as significantly, more than 23,000 came to see it and that was more than double some of the gates we had been getting in the league.

We got a plum draw in the next round when we were at home to Manchester City . . . Rodney Marsh, Colin Bell, Francis Lee and all. Nobody really gave us a chance but in one of the most thrilling games The City Ground has seen we beat them 4–1 and deserved all the praise that came our way. Most of it fell on Duncan McKenzie . . . and quite rightly so. He was absolutely unplayable on the day and although there have been victories that carried a lot more importance down the years, for sheer entertainment this took a hell of a lot of beating.

Duncan loved a trick – I swear he got more pleasure from nutmegging opponents than he did scoring goals – and on the day everything worked for him. He was breathtaking, dancing his way through a team who boasted some of the best players of the day. They just could not come up with a way to stop him. Duncan scored one of the goals, made two for 'Bomber' (Ian Bowyer) and George Lyall got the other.

I was still out of the picture and looking on from the stands but Forest fans had got a dose of cup fever and they wanted more. A crowd of 38,589 crammed into The City Ground to see us defeat Portsmouth 1–0 with a McKenzie penalty in the fifth round and that set us up for a sixth-round trip to face Newcastle United.

I was in with a good shout of playing in the game because I had made my comeback a few days earlier against Notts County and we all looked forward to turning out in front of 50-odd thousand at St James' Park. We had nothing to lose and just went out and played with a lot of freedom and caused Newcastle all manner of problems. Bomber scored to put us ahead, Liam O'Kane scored the only senior goal in his career and George Lyall added a penalty. We were leading 3–1 and were given another helping hand when Newcastle defender Pat Howard was sent off for dissent.

But then it happened. Newcastle fans let their frustration get the better of them and poured onto the pitch at the Leazes End, there was a lot of commotion and in the confusion that followed my mate Dave Serella got a smack around the head. It was quite intimidating to say the least and we didn't have a clue what to do. Liam showed a lot of initiative though. He knew Newcastle players Willie McFaul and David Craig from his days with Northern

Ireland and went to stand by them as the fans continued their riot. It was one of the smarter moves Liam made in his career. The referee Gordon Kew eventually took the players off for more than ten minutes while some sort of order was restored; despite all the trouble, we felt that with the game well into the second half we just wanted to get back out there and finish the job. Unfortunately, it didn't work out that way. From being totally in control and relaxed we were tentative and nervous and Newcastle, roared on by the fans who were now concentrating on supporting their team, came back to win the game 4–3.

On the way back to Nottingham we were all complaining bitterly about the unfairness of it all and Brown went down further in my estimation for something he said. We stopped at Wetherby on the A1 for a break and I happened to be in the next urinal to the manager. It's normally a place where us men pass the time of day in an amiable fashion but he muttered to me how he felt that the inexperience of Martin O'Neill and myself had let Forest down. I felt like saying, 'Are you taking the piss?' I was livid and when I told Martin he wanted to go back into the hotel and have it out with the manager there and then. Somehow we calmed down sufficiently to keep our thoughts and feelings to ourselves.

Of course, it wasn't the end of the matter as far as the tie was concerned. Forest put in an appeal over the weekend and the FA decided that the match would be replayed on a neutral ground – Everton's Goodison Park. We were miffed about that because Newcastle had had their turn and it seemed only right that any replay should be at The City Ground. We drew that game 0–0 and naturally assumed at long last that we would get a home match but the FA, worried about potential trouble between rival fans, decided that the third game would again be at Goodison Park. We had kept their match-winner Malcolm Macdonald quiet in the first two games but he got away once in the third game, scored the winner, sent Newcastle through to a semi-final against Burnley and left us to reflect on what could – and should – have been. We were two steps from Wembley and for Forest at that time, it would have been a massive achievement to figure in an FA Cup final.

It wasn't the last time that I wasn't happy with what the manager said to me. He was keen on signing a lad called Ronnie Glavin, an attacking midfield player from Partick Thistle, and called me into his office one day. I thought he was going to ask me about Ronnie but instead said, 'I'm going to offer you in part exchange.' You could have knocked me over with the proverbial feather. Leaving Forest was something I hadn't even contemplated and with due respect to Partick I thought I had shown enough promise to stay at The City Ground or at least attract some interest from another English club. I was flabbergasted but wanted to get out of his office as quickly as possible and said, 'Let me think about it.' I had no intention of going back up the road to Scotland and in the meantime Glavin moved on to Celtic and had a good few years at Parkhead.

That summer our prospects of raising a promotion effort receded still further when McKenzie, who had scored 28 goals – 26 of them in the league – became the latest in a long line of departing players when Cloughie took him to Leeds during his eventful 44 days in charge at Elland Road. It was almost inevitable that Duncan would leave after having had such a productive season but it was yet another sign that we were settling in to become a middle-of-the-road Second Division side.

I was in need of a pick-me-up and I got one from the most unlikely of sources – I was called into an England squad! Me, a Scotsman through and through, being recognised by England – could you believe it? Brown arrived on the training ground one day and stunned me and the other lads when he looked at me and said, 'You've been picked for England.' Don Revie, who had taken over the England job, had named something like 90 players for a get together to introduce himself and get to know as many present and potential internationals as possible. I thought it was a bit of a wind-up but it turned out to be true. In a daft sort of way it gave me a lift to know that Revie had clearly remembered me from games against Leeds and that somebody of his status thought enough about me to pencil my name into a squad no matter how big it was.

Would I have considered going? Not a prayer – I was Scottish and proud of it. But it was a bit of light relief because whether it was because I had shown no interest in the Partick business or not, Brown hardly spoke to me at the beginning of the 1974–75 season and apart from a couple of games at the start of the campaign, I was right out of the first team picture. I was at a low ebb, my confidence shattered and I must admit I got a bit disillusioned about my future prospects.

The team were not setting the world alight either, winning the odd game here and there to keep our heads above water, but the fans were beginning to get restless again and you sensed there was something about to happen. Sure enough, right at the end of December we lost 2–0 at home to our city neighbours Notts County and the Forest Committee decided the time was right to look for a new manager. Allan Brown was on his way from The City Ground and I didn't shed any tears that night.

3
Life of Brian

WHEN BRIAN CLOUGH COMES INTO your life, believe me . . . you know about it. That day for me was 6 January 1975 . . . and life, not just the football side of it, was never quite the same again. He seemed to influence you for every waking hour and dreaming about him became fairly commonplace too.

He had been out of work since leaving Leeds United after his infamous 44 days at Elland Road, where by his own admission he had gone in like a whirlwind and met so much resistance from a squad of players moulded into the Don Revie way of things. By all accounts he had left Leeds a very wealthy man but he was still young for a football manager and wanted to get back into the game.

We didn't realise it at the time but Forest, even before they sacked Allan Brown, were working feverishly at trying to open the way for him to take on the job of reviving their fortunes. Stuart Dryden, a local postmaster who had joined the Forest Committee, was at the forefront of that bid to get Mr Clough on board but there was a general feeling about the place of whether the Brian Clough that we used to watch on television would fancy the idea of joining a Second Division club that had lost its way. He was a household name and a man who had won the First Division title with Derby less than three years earlier. It wasn't as if there was a treasure chest of transfer funds awaiting him either. Forest had no rich benefactor sitting in the wings ready to fund the kind of instant revolution he would have wanted. But credit to Mr Dryden for getting the big man to say 'Yes' despite there being a fair bit of 'anti' among his fellow Committee members, and life at Nottingham Forest was never quite the same again.

On his first day Clough burst into the home dressing-room at The City Ground like a tornado. I was sitting in there with the other lads when he stormed through the door, took off his jacket, hung it on the peg and, rubbing his hands together, said to Sammy Chapman, 'It's cold enough to freeze the balls off a brass monkey, isn't it, Sam?' It wasn't so much what he said but how he just exploded on the scene that left me thinking, 'God, this bloke means business.' His entrance stunned us and it took just a few seconds to know that this guy wasn't here just for the ride.

After that he took us training with Jimmy Gordon, who he had recruited as his first team coach over the previous weekend, persuading him to come out of retirement to give him support. At that stage – and for the best part of 18 months – there was no suggestion that Peter Taylor was joining him.

Apparently, the press conference, which he went into after training, was something special too. He was so media savvy that he had them eating out of his hand and was lining up a series of articles for various newspapers with payments for fridges, washers, ovens and anything else that was needed behind the scenes at the club.

Like a lot of the lads I didn't really know what his arrival was going to do for me. But I knew one thing . . . after Allan Brown I had nothing to lose. My career might take off but the worst-case scenario was that he would bomb me out of the club and I would have to start again elsewhere.

For a while I had no opportunity to impress him. He was focused on a third round FA Cup replay with Tottenham at White Hart Lane on the Wednesday following his appointment and he was soon whisking the players off to Bisham Abbey, a retreat in Buckinghamshire that had been frequented by the England team from time to time. He didn't have time to think about the likes of me but just picked up the pieces, hit the ground running and tried to get the best out of players who were in the side at that particular time. He worked his magic, too. Neil Martin, a Scottish international striker who Cloughie had known from his days as a player with Sunderland, scored the winner against Spurs and the following day the papers were full of it.

The team went back to Bisham Abbey after the cup game to prepare for a league game against Fulham in London the following

Saturday and he got another win with a goal from Barry Butlin, a player he had had on his staff during his Derby days.

Like everyone else who he didn't take on the trip, I was keen to find out what it had been like at Bisham Abbey and for one of the lads in particular it turned out to be a few days he would never forget. John Cottam – 'Jack' to everyone on the staff – bore the brunt of the gaffer's opening attempts to stamp his authority on the club. Jack was, shall I say, a sturdy sort of centre-half, and an honest enough player, putting his lot in week after week. But Cloughie must have thought he could do with shedding a few pounds and from what I heard, at any available moment he had Jack out on the Bisham Abbey tennis courts, running here, there and everywhere. Cloughie enjoyed winning so the fact that Jack wasn't quite as good a tennis player as him also suited the situation. It was just as well Jack wasn't picked to start either game – he was substitute against Fulham – because he would have been in no fit state to get through 90 minutes.

I was still an outcast when Clough had his first home game against Leyton Orient, which ended in a 2–2 draw. Then I got my break thanks to a few words from John Lawson, the guy who I asked to help me put together this book. John, who was the journalist covering Forest for the *Nottingham Evening Post*, had gone to Bisham Abbey and spent time talking to the gaffer about the state of the club and what could be done to improve things on and off the field. In one conversation Mr Clough asked John, 'Can you mark my card about anybody? There must be someone on the staff who is good enough to get into this bloody side.' John came up with my name and suggested that I could play but perhaps needed a kick up the backside to get me going.

The gaffer clearly took his advice on board and when Paul Richardson didn't make the next game because of suspension – an FA Cup fourth round tie against Fulham at home – he called me up. I'll never know if I would have come through anyway but I was always grateful to John for tipping him off. I might easily have got through on my own merits at some future date but there was no guarantee and I could just as easily have slipped completely out of Clough's thoughts.

We had four games against Fulham before they went through and eventually went on to reach the FA Cup final that year before losing to West Ham. But I think I took my chance and remember scoring against Fulham in the first replay at Craven Cottage, bending the ball round the wall from a free-kick.

It was all very 'easy as you go' with the gaffer for a long time. As it is with all new managers, I just wanted to impress but sometimes you couldn't do right for doing wrong and the rest of the time I tried my best to keep out of his way around the ground. I remember there was one game against Bolton just a month or so after he arrived – a game we ended up losing 3–2. As time went on I discovered that he always wanted his midfield players to get forward into the box without the ball and that conjures up images of the likes of Archie Gemmill, Ian Bowyer, Roy Keane and Steve Hodge dashing forward to create and score goals. But I was pretty thick then when it came to the nuts and bolts of playing midfield and at half-time in the Bolton game he came across to me in the dressing-room and said, 'When are you going to get forward? Do you think somebody will shoot you if you go into their penalty area?' I thought I would show him and every time the ball was knocked into the opposition half after the break I charged forward and more often than not got caught hopelessly out of position when the ball was returned to our half. It was a bit silly of me really because I was totally out of the game but I soon learned that I had to be selective with my forward runs.

Heading the ball was another issue he had with me. I'll be the first to admit it was not one of my strong points but in an attempt to do something about it, he showed me up in front of the other lads at training one day. His first signing for Forest was a big striker called Bert Bowery, who came from Worksop Town, a non-league side in the north of Nottinghamshire. Bert was a likeable lad and a gentle giant in many ways but you could not hide the fact that he was built like a brick shithouse. One day the gaffer got all the lads in a circle and put me in the middle with Bert and got the players to throw the ball up for me to challenge with him. Not surprisingly, I didn't win the ball once in the air and Bert, who had a smile as wide as the Trent, couldn't stop laughing. Nor could the other lads for that matter. But the point was made. I knew heading the ball was not my forte but I also knew that he wanted me to improve on it – even if it was always going to be in small percentages.

While big Bert was Clough's first recruit, it wasn't long before he went back to Leeds to sign two players who had been key components in Derby's 1972 First Division title win. John McGovern and John O'Hare had gone with him to Leeds and seen at first hand the difficulties that existed for him at Elland Road. In the fall-out of his departure from Leeds, I think McGovern and O'Hare were just delighted to link up with him again at Forest and start afresh.

I knew McGovern more by reputation than anything else. He was obviously a very good player and although not physically robust, he was the type who would go through a brick wall if Cloughie asked him to.

I was more aware of O'Hare, who had played for Scotland during his Derby days. I was a great admirer of the qualities he had as a centre-forward playing with his back to goal. He was not the quickest but he was as brave as they came and had a wonderful touch. I was thrilled that he was coming to Forest because I thought I couldn't help but learn something from him, but when he arrived I was even more delighted to discover that he knew a bit about me. I latched on to him when he first arrived as we trained on occasions at Clifton College but he was just coming back from injury and he lagged way behind the rest of the lads – even me. When we paired off in twos he said to me quietly, 'If you ever want to be a player and you've got any sense, don't train with me!' I reminded him of that story when we won the European Cup in 1979. He acquired the nickname 'Solly' and a lot of people thought that someone had given him it in recognition of his ability because Del Sol was one of the star attractions of the great Real Madrid side of the day. In reality it was because he used to recite passages of the nursery rhyme 'Solomon Grundy' when he was a kid and 'Solly' stuck from a very early stage of his career.

Although they were Cloughie's men, we respected both McGovern and O'Hare as players and people and as time went on they became key figures as we moved forward as a club. There was much I could learn from them but the gaffer continued to hound me at every opportunity.

In one game against York City he singled me out for a bit of stick. As a midfield player I got great pleasure from pinging balls from left-half to outside-right and right-half to outside-left. If I knocked it 40–50 yards to feet I used to get a lot of personal satisfaction but Cloughie summed up passes like that in one dismissive word – 'decoration'.

In my early days I was always taught the value of playing an early ball but on another occasion he gave me the biggest bollocking for turning with the ball and playing a square pass to a team-mate when there was 15 yards of clear grass to move into. He barked at me, 'I don't pay you to be playing little sideways passes when you have got space to go into. Get forward, man!' It was advice that I really took on board and it was of incredible value to me when I started playing out wide.

In my early days with Cloughie I got into a spot of bother that involved Jimmy McCann, who, like Dave Serella, became a really good mate and still is to this day. Jimmy was a fellow Scot, from Dundee, but we seemed to hit it off straight away and we used to go out on the town together quite a bit. One Saturday night we were out in a nightclub in Nottingham called Scamps together with another young Forest player Ian Miller; Jimmy probably saved me from a good hiding.

I was telling this joke about the Lone Ranger and although I'll not bore you with the story, the punchline was, 'Fuck off, Paleface.'

This big lad was standing near us and piped up, 'What did you say?'

'It's all right, I answered, I'm just telling my mates a joke.' Stupid me couldn't let it go at that and I had to say, 'What's it got to do with you anyway?' Before I could say anything else he planted a head butt on me so quickly I didn't know what had happened for a split second.

Being the good mate that he is, Jimmy was at this bloke straight away. He saw it coming and told me afterwards it was the best head butt he had ever seen in his life. But he landed a quick one back at this bloke, who disappeared and the incident was over before it began.

By the following Monday I had two black eyes and a fat nose and didn't look very pretty at all. I knew it would lead to trouble in training but I tried my best to keep out of Clough's way. So Jimmy and I concocted this story that we had been playing cricket and I got hit with the ball and I wasn't happy and we got in a bit of a scrap and Jimmy whacked me one between the eyes. Cloughie could read situations like that all day long and said, 'OK, I hear what you say, but you are both fined. Get out of my sight.'

I couldn't let Jimmy take any rap. After all, he'd come to my rescue in the nightclub and I didn't want him to get fined for an incident that was entirely my fault. I eventually told the gaffer the truth and I copped for the fine and Jimmy got off.

Jimmy was a bit of a snappy dresser and used to wear these skin-tight V-neck jumpers. I used to look at him and think, 'God you look good in them.' I used to borrow them from him and for a time thought I looked the same but in all honesty I just didn't have the figure to pull it off and in the end gave up trying.

He was a centre-forward, who played with his back to goal and took a lot of stick from centre-halves who used to cut through you at will in those days before the tackle from behind was outlawed. Jimmy used to stand his ground and would have loved to have made it properly in the game. He really gave it everything before deciding he wasn't quite going to make it at the top. He was 22 when he was told he wasn't going to be good enough for Forest but he tried to extend his career with Halifax and Stockport before bowing out of full-time football.

But I have immense admiration for the way he went about his life after making that decision. He used to like a pint – still does – and he got to know blokes in the local who were in the roofing trade and spent hours chatting to them. He went on to work for a few people but put his lot in and now he's got his own business – 35 years after he had to accept that football was no longer going to be a big part of his life. Had it been the other way round and I had been the one looking for a new role in life I haven't a clue what I would have done because football was all I knew. I don't think I would have had the balls to do the physical labour that Jimmy has done all his life but, having not quite made the grade at football, he wanted to make sure that he was going to be successful at something completely different.

Jimmy made his debut for Forest at the end of Cloughie's first season with us but in total he only started a couple of games, made four substitute appearances and scored one goal against Charlton the following season.

When we had played our last match that season the gaffer took us all off to Majorca. It was the first time I had been away with a football club on holiday but it was the first of many trips to Cala

Millor, a part of the island that the gaffer loved. He had a place there, was very comfortable in the environment and nobody seemed to bother him when he was trying to unwind. We had many good times in Cala Millor, a lot of drink was consumed and over the years I dare bet that a lot of big decisions in the lives of Clough and Taylor were made.

That summer I went to Spain with a load of the other lads and it was during that fortnight's holiday that I met my first wife Sally in Lloret de Mar. We went on a coach trip to an organised barbecue and Sally, who had gone on holiday with a friend, was also there. On the way back and after a bit of Dutch courage I got chatting to Sally and we decided to meet up the following day in a pub called the OK Corral. Our relationship just went on from there really. We kept in touch when we returned to England, met up on a regular basis – she was living in Nuneaton, which is not too far from Nottingham – and pretty quickly we found ourselves in love.

The 1975–76 season was the first full one under the gaffer and we were all very interested to see how it went. Unfortunately, it didn't get off on the right note for Martin O'Neill, Ian Bowyer and myself. We were all in the throes of agreeing new contracts but we hadn't signed anything before pre-season started and we all got bombed off a trip to Germany, which became a regular pre-season destination for us.

I can't remember what I was asking for but it wasn't a lot. When Dave Mackay was at the club he had given me £65 a week and I had been on that ever since. Before that I had been paid £40 a week and when it came to a new deal Des Anderson asked me what I wanted. I said £60 and he said, 'Go and ask for £70.' In the end we compromised on £65 but as I learned afterwards that was the figure they had settled on all along. I was hoping for a bit better deal from Cloughie but he said, 'You're getting nowt until you have deserved it.'

We were all in limbo but the players came back from Germany and moved on to Northern Ireland to play a couple of games. Bomber and I were back in the squad but Martin was still left out. The gaffer knew that he would want to meet up with his family and friends in Ireland and it was his way of getting one back at Martin over his refusal to agree terms.

I was just pleased to be involved again but it was during those pre-season games against Ballymena and Coleraine that the gaffer first started thinking of me playing wide on the left. To start with he wanted me to tuck in when play was going down our right and then go wide when play went down my side of the field. It meant I was going back to my Scotland schoolboy days. It also meant I was playing in front of Frank Clark for the first time and what a wonderful signing he proved to be.

Frank had had a long and successful career with Newcastle United, where he had figured in their last team to win any significant silverware – the old Inter-Cities Fairs Cup, which Newcastle won in 1969. I think he thought he would finish his playing days at St James' Park and maybe move into coaching with Newcastle but in the summer of 1975 he was stunned when the Geordies gave him a free transfer after he had played getting on for 500 games for them. He was only 31 at the time and must have felt there was a new contract in him in the North-East but Newcastle thought otherwise and amazingly he was on his way out. Stan Anderson, who had played in the Fairs Cup winning team alongside Frank, was manager of Doncaster Rovers at the time and persuaded him to go down to Yorkshire. He was all set to sign when a journalist tipped off Cloughie that Frank was available and he jumped in to bring him to The City Ground.

Frank was a top-class bloke and a brilliant defender and in the years that followed I've got to say it was an immense pleasure to play in front of him. I still see quite a bit of Frank these days – he goes to the same gym where I play tennis – and he told me quite recently that I was the best player he had played with. I can't tell you how much that meant to me.

One of Frank's great strengths was his positional play. He never seemed to get pulled out of position and you very rarely saw him on his backside after a missed tackle. He would stand on his feet and put the onus on the attacking player to figure out a way to get past him. More often than not they failed. Frank was wonderful to play with. With his defensive qualities I hardly ever tracked back and he just gave me the ball and let me go and do my little bits here and there.

When the league season kicked off with a 2–0 win over Plymouth Argyle at The City Ground Martin was still out in the cold. Frank was the only new face in the side because money was still tight and

49

the days of big transfers were still some way off.

But very early in that season the gaffer did persuade the Forest Committee to part with £60,000 to sign Terry Curran from Doncaster at a time when a lot of teams were looking at him. He was quick (very quick), loved taking people on, was daft as a brush but a nice lad all the same. Although he came into his own the following season he didn't get off to the best of starts because on his debut we lost 1–0 at home to our neighbours Notts County with Les Bradd getting the winning goal.

But my football life was still far from rosy and I remember missing two penalties in a match against Hull City at The City Ground on a day when my family were down from Scotland to see me play. It was one of those occasions when you just hoped the ground would open up and swallow you but there is just no place to hide on a football field. Jeff Wealands was the Hull goalkeeper that day. I put the first kick to his right and although he pushed it out, I managed to put the rebound in with my head (thank you, Bert Bowery) but I was gutted when he stopped the second with the score at 1–1 and we ended up losing the game. That was me off penalties – for a year or so at least. My mum and dad were there to witness it and my uncle Eddie, who never travelled far, made a special effort to come down for the weekend and see me play. What a let-down I was.

It also summed up our season in many ways. We showed a fair bit of promise from time to time but never quite delivered. What I would like to say, though, is that you could see the foundations were being laid for something better. And in the 18 months before Peter Taylor joined him, the gaffer made some good signings. No one could fault the quality of McGovern and O'Hare, Clark was a brilliant capture for nothing, Curran was a live wire and towards the end of the season Clough also brought Colin Barrett into the football club from Manchester City.

Colin was a smashing lad who was keen to move on from City because he wanted more regular first team football. He could play anywhere along the back line and was equally at home at full-back or slotting into the middle of the defence. He was still in his early twenties when he joined us so he was the right age with a lot of football ahead of him. Sadly, injury robbed him of having a magnificent career but while he was fit he did a fantastic job for us.

Colin came in before the end of the old March transfer deadline and he entered a side that was beginning to look as though it had promotion potential even if it was clear that considerable work still needed to be done. In the second half of that season we actually had an unbeaten run of eight games and lost only once in thirteen matches and that bred a lot of confidence among the players. We never looked like seriously challenging for a promotion place but we finished eighth, which was a significant improvement on the previous season's sixteenth, and at least we were heading in the right direction.

4

The big bust-up

COME THE START OF THE following season I was still getting used to Cloughie's unique style of management when I was on the receiving end of a bolt from the blue from his mate Peter Taylor.

Playing-wise we had not strengthened during the summer of 1976 apart from the fact that Pete, who had carried on managing at Brighton after Brian left to go to Leeds, was reunited with his partner. The pair of them had been together since their days at Middlesbrough, where Pete was a goalkeeper and the gaffer one of the most prolific strikers the English game has ever known. They struck up a friendship, built around similar football ideals, and they had linked up in management first of all at Hartlepool United, then Derby County and Brighton.

Their coming together again at The City Ground was seen as a natural reunion and for Pete it meant he was returning to his roots, having been born in the Meadows area of Nottingham before making his way in the game. Cloughie described Pete's arrival as 'the best bit of business this club has done in years'. But he didn't get that sign of approval from me following the most one-sided conversation I've had with anyone in my life.

Our pre-season training was again spent in Germany at a place called Augsburg, which was a regular base for us in the build-up to a new campaign. We had played the opening match of the tour against SV Fürth and lost 3–2 but I didn't think too much about it afterwards. It was our first game in pre-season and there was obviously a bit of rustiness flaking off us after the summer lay-off.

On the training ground the following morning the gaffer asked us all to gather round in a circle because Pete wanted to introduce himself properly and say a few words. My only dealings with Pete before that had been a polite 'hello' on the journey over to Germany but he suddenly hit me with a non-stop verbal barrage that took me totally by surprise and genuinely shocked me. As we all sat down, waiting to hear what he had to say, he pointed at me and said simply, 'You, fuck off.' I muttered the word 'Sorry' hoping I'd heard him wrongly.

He raised his voice a few decibels and repeated, 'You, fuck off back to the hotel and I'll see you later.'

To be perfectly honest I was flabbergasted – but who wouldn't be? I looked around, hoping in vain for a bit of support and wondering what the hell I had done wrong. I back-tracked the previous few days in my mind at lightning speed to try and pinpoint where on earth I could have upset him but nothing sprang to mind. I had no option but to troop back to the hotel. It wasn't far but I had a jog back because I wanted to get the hell out of there as quickly as possible. To be honest, I felt like jogging all the way back to Nottingham.

I was sitting waiting for him by the hotel pool and it seemed like an eternity before Pete showed up. It left me with plenty of time to think – no doubt a deliberate ploy on his part – and all kinds of things went through my mind. Had someone been telling lies about me? Was I being blamed for what someone else had done? Was I about to be sold? I wrestled with all those thoughts and more before Pete eventually walked through the hotel entrance and came to where I was waiting.

His first words were, 'What's your problem?' And that in itself didn't give me any clues.

I said, 'I don't know what you mean,' and he just repeated the question.

Then he got down to business. He went on, 'I watched you last night in the warm-up, you shook one leg, shook the other leg and that was that. You're overweight, I'm hearing stories that you don't live right . . .' and he kept on repeating, 'What's your problem?'

If I had had the courage I would have probably said I didn't have one until he came through the door because I was playing games and things were going fairly well for me under the gaffer. Just at that time I felt like saying, 'Why don't you fuck off back to Brighton and leave us to get on with things here?' That was never a serious proposition, of course, and I sensibly took a few deep breaths and came out with my 'The whole world is against me' speech. Pete's no holds barred attack had made me start feeling sorry for myself again and I began to wonder where this was all going to take me.

Looking back on that episode now and considering the experiences I've had with Martin O'Neill in management, it was the last thing I would want to hear from any player. But I was on the defensive, I felt as though I was being kicked to the floor at a time when I was beginning to make a little bit of headway and in the course of our conversation I began to wonder what was left for me as a professional footballer. I tried to tell him my problems and I even brought up the fact that I thought Jimmy Gordon was also against me even though I eventually came to realise that Jimmy was one of the best supporters I had at the club.

Jimmy was a defensive midfield player and one of the 'let's get stuck in' brigade. He went on and on to me about winning the ball and then doing what I could do with it. 'You've got to win it to play it,' he would yell at me. For some time I took it that he was just picking on me but it was all part of the inferiority complex that was going on in my mind. As time went on I appreciated that Jimmy was looking at me and seeing someone who was not making the most of his talent but when you think the whole world's against you, taking criticism, constructive or not, becomes very difficult. In time I was proved so wrong about Jimmy, who liked me as a footballer and, in turn, I had enormous respect for him.

Pete went on about a few more areas in which I was letting myself down before the psychology of football management really kicked in. He ended a long pause in our conversation by saying, 'It's clear that you have got problems but we think you can play.' I don't know whether I allowed myself a wry smile at that stage but those few words counted a lot to me and made me feel a whole lot better about a conversation that had hitherto been nothing short of a character assassination job. 'We think you can play,' he reiterated and there was suddenly a bit of warmth in a voice that had previously been cold and calculated. Tactically, the assault he had made on me worked . . . and very quickly.

I immediately took on board the points that he raised and although it was not an overnight transformation I rapidly came to the conclusion that I had to start doing something with my life otherwise I would end up as another meaningless statistic on football's scrapheap. In the weeks that followed I was very pleased with myself because I took a long hard look in the mirror and decided I had to change my ways. There was a need for me to take more care of myself, eat better food and generally develop better habits. What pleased me most of all was that I was able to absorb the criticism he had dished out without resorting to feeling vulnerable and victimised. It was in my hands, in my control to do something with my life and I congratulated myself on having the intelligence and foresight to do that. The bottom line was that I knew I was a good footballer, I knew I could play but for the first time I fully accepted that I was not getting the best out of myself. The fact that Pete had used the word 'we' meant that Cloughie also thought I had a bit to offer and I was determined from that moment on to try and get the best out of myself.

To this day I don't know why Cloughie hadn't pulled me earlier and given me the same grilling that Pete delivered in Augsburg. After all, he was never the slowest at coming forward when something harsh had to be said – far from it. In the 18 months before Pete came, the gaffer had occasionally come out and said 'well done' after matches without getting too carried away but he was always a bit reserved with his praise without ever giving me the dressing-down that I probably deserved. But Pete's broadside was certainly the turning point in my career – a pivotal moment in my life.

The following day we were playing a team called Jahn Regensburg and I was named as a substitute. Amazingly for me I had developed an 'I'll show you pair' attitude overnight and I was champing at the bit to get on. Eventually I did and from that moment on I was a regular in their first team apart from the odd occasions when I was out injured.

And Pete's opinion of me changed quite drastically as time went on. On one occasion some time afterwards he went into print to compare me with other wingers who had made their mark on the game. He said he wouldn't have swapped me for any of them – even greats like Gento of Real Madrid. I was a bit embarrassed by all that sort of talk but I've got to admit that it makes you feel ten feet tall when someone is talking of you in those kinds of terms.

I genuinely felt there was a purpose about what I was trying to achieve and when we got back from tour, I couldn't wait for the season to start.

Before then we were entered in the Anglo-Scottish Cup and we went unbeaten through our qualifying games against Notts County, West Brom and Bristol City to reach the competition proper, which meant a two-legged affair against Kilmarnock in the first round. While we were beating them 2–1 at home in the first leg, Clough and Taylor were nowhere to be seen but three days later the reason for their absence became obvious when they agreed terms for the transfer of Birmingham City striker Peter Withe.

He was a big, strong, old-school centre-forward who would run all day, create openings for others and get his share of goals himself. 'Googie' – we nicknamed him after the famous actress Googie Withers – came into a side that had started the season pretty well, apart from losing 3–1 at home to Wolves.

I was installed as an orthodox outside-left at this stage and with Terry Curran playing wide on the right, we were a side very much built on attacking ideology. Curran hugged the right touchline and, in fact, couldn't have played any wider if he tried. He could fly and older Forest fans will remember him knocking the ball past his full-back, running round the outside of the pitch, skating down the running track and then coming back into play. He carried immense threat and although his final ball sometimes left a bit to be desired there was no disguising the danger he posed every time he got the ball. He had the qualities that got people out of their seats and he thrived on the adulation he got from the manager as well as supporters.

I was content to carry on doing my bit down the left and I was getting more and more comfortable in the role. It was at that time that we made another signing that proved to be another superb piece of judgement by Pete. Larry Lloyd, who had won silverware at Liverpool and played for England before a back injury knocked his career a bit off course, had moved to Coventry City but was struggling to get himself back on track at Highfield Road. The gaffer and Pete persuaded him to join us on loan and he made his debut on a day when we lost 1–0 at Hull.

Lloydy didn't get the best of welcomes from our fans because he was taking the place of Sammy Chapman, who had been a big favourite at The City Ground. When we trooped onto the field at the start and the public address announcer read out the teams with Lloydy replacing Sammy, it was met by a chorus of boos. Lloydy originally thought it was coming from the Hull fans and wondered what the hell he had done to upset them but he looked over to where the noise was coming from and it was fans in red shirts who were making it. Afterwards I remember Lloydy saying, 'OK, I'm here for a month but then I'm out of this place.'

But that experience was soon forgotten and the defeat did nothing to dampen Larry's confidence. I remember chatting to him about Liverpool and other things. I was hungry for stories of what it was like to play at Anfield, work under Bill Shankly and so on. I went on to ask him what he thought about his move to Forest and Larry, who became one of my big mates, lit up a cigar, sat back, took a big puff, blew out a cloud of never-ending smoke and said, 'Nice little club you've got here.' That was Lloydy to a tee. I remember Martin, Tony Woodcock, Viv Anderson and me being in his company at the time and we could have burst out laughing. But we didn't say too much because Lloydy was a big item . . . the sort you didn't want to upset. But underneath our breaths I'm sure we all thought to a man, 'What a big-time fucking Charlie we've got here.'

Lloydy stories are endless and after a loan spell with us, he eventually got down to negotiating the possibility of a permanent transfer. The gaffer initiated the talks because Larry did really well for us and you could tell he was going to be a real asset. But long afterwards the gaffer revealed that when he started talking to Lloydy about joining us permanently, the big man uttered the words, 'I've not seen anything that's turned me on yet.' But Lloydy did sign and what a magnificent buy he proved to be – as well as a source of continuous entertainment with a banter that was as big as his huge frame.

We've been big mates from the time he arrived at the club – and we still are to this day – even though one or two of our conversations have developed into debates, which in turn have ended up as full-blooded arguments. One of them came just as we were getting out of the bath after training one day and we were discussing the merits of Brian Kilcline, a big centre-half who was making his way with our neighbours Notts County. The argument got more and more heated because at that time I thought Brian wasn't a particularly good player and Larry did. 'What the hell do you know about centre-halves?' was just one of the things he threw at me. Brian was only a young kid and Larry thought he could go on to be a really good player and, as usual with us, the words got louder and stronger. Larry got out of the bath and was drying himself down and I'd got a bit wound up by this stage and threw the soap into the bath and the water splashed up all over Lloydy. That was it, he lost his rag with me, came storming across to the bath and threw a punch at my stomach. Fortunately for me he held it back a bit just at the last second and I thought, 'Thank God for that,' because Lloydy has always been a big powerful bloke. I've got to admit that Larry was proved right because Brian went on to have a very good career in the game.

When Lloydy came into our side most of the action was at the other end of the field to him. Opposition teams were having all kinds of problems coping with our attacking threat and a glance back at our results at the time will tell you that The City Ground was the place to be for entertainment. We beat Hereford 4–3, Carlisle 5–1, Sheffield United 6–1 and then Burnley 5–2 but the Burnley game had a lot of significance attached to it.

Curran, who was irrepressible at the time, limped out of the match with a nasty knee injury and that night everyone began to fear what consequences it would have on our chances of going up to the First Division. We were also given a penalty in the Burnley match when we were losing 2–1 so it was very important. But Curran was off by that stage and, with me not taking a penalty for over a year, there was no obvious candidate to step up. Then Ian Bowyer said to me, 'Go on Robbo, it's yours.' I grabbed the ball, stuck it away and carried on taking them for years. And there were plenty of them.

Curran's injury was a real sickener, however. Even the gaffer was reported as saying, 'You've just seen promotion limp out of the door,' when Curran left his office on crutches after the game.

But as a door temporarily closed for one player, it certainly opened for another. Tony Woodcock, who was a quick young striker from Eastwood in Nottingham, had hardly had a look in since Cloughie arrived at the club. So much so that he was loaned out to Doncaster Rovers in his first full season; at the end of the 1975–76 season he joined Graham Taylor, who was managing

Lincoln City at the time. Taylor, who became one of the most respected managers in the game with Watford, spotted something in Tony and was keen to sign him in a permanent deal but there was obviously a doubt in Cloughie's mind and he resisted all attempts to part with Tony. That was about to prove one of the most astute decisions he made.

We had reached the semi-final of the Anglo-Scottish Cup and after a 2–1 home win over Ayr United headed for Scotland in the hope of winning through to the final. I can't remember why but Barry Butlin, who had been in the team for the most part, was not included and Tony was called in to partner Peter Withe up front. It was a horrible, rainy, miserable Scottish night but it was the first time that Withe and Woodcock had played together. They both scored, struck up an instant understanding and a top goalscoring partnership was born.

It was also the night that I met Jock Stein for the first time. He was a legendary figure in Scottish football for his days managing Celtic and the gaffer made a point of introducing me, as a Scotsman, to him. Playing for Scotland seemed a million miles away for me at the time but little did I know at that stage that I would go on to get most of my caps under Mr Stein.

Withe and Woodcock continued to prosper and Tony was like a breath of fresh air on the scene; in no time at all Forest fans had overcome the disappointment of losing Curran to injury. The two lads up front were a dream for me. Without wanting to be too technical, they were both very left-footed and whenever they got possession, their natural tendency was to look to play the ball in my direction and that suited me down to the ground.

Peter was brilliant at showing for you. No matter how well or poorly he was playing he would always make sure he provided a target and was there to be picked out. Like Garry Birtles in later years, he would never hide. Tony, for his part, was as sharp as a tack, twisting this way and that and he had the pace that took him past defenders almost at will. All he needed was that bit of self-belief. They gave me options and the really great thing for me playing with them was that, in their different ways, they made up my mind for me. Whether it was playing the ball into Googie's feet or putting the ball over the top for Tony to run onto, I had choices and it was a joy to play with them.

They were flying as a partnership by the time we met Leyton Orient in the final of the Anglo-Scottish Cup and although it might not have been much of a competition to win for a lot of people, the gaffer was never slow at building it up. I scored a penalty in the first leg to give us a 1–1 draw at Brisbane Road and we romped to a 4–0 win in the return just two days later.

Cloughie's argument was, 'If you think it doesn't mean much, ask the players in my dressing-room. Most of them haven't been to a final and won anything before so they might get a taste for wanting other prizes.' Not for the first time or the last he was spot on with his judgement and for the rest of that season we seemed to go from strength to strength. The Anglo-Scottish was a trophy we could put in the cabinet and little did we know that it was the first of a few coming our way in subsequent years.

We had defeated West Brom, who were a First Division side, in the qualifying rounds and Kilmarnock, who we beat in the first round proper, were a top side north of the border. They had Davy Provan, Gordon Smith and Iain McCulloch, who later played for Notts County, in their side and we had some difficult games along the way.

Winning games was a good habit to get into and we went on a run of fourteen league and cup games without defeat to move up the table; I also remember us smashing six past Bristol Rovers in an FA Cup replay at Villa Park.

We were beginning to think we could go on and win promotion but we got a few kicks in the teeth around February time. Southampton knocked us out of the FA Cup, we lost at Wolves and at home to Luton in the league and were in danger of losing a third successive match in the Second Division when Southampton came to The City Ground. They were leading 1–0 and we were having a poor night but two minutes after half-time the fog came rolling in from the Trent and the referee had no alternative but to call it off. You could hardly see a handful of yards in front of you. When the game was played again the following month we won 2–1 and those two points made all the difference at the season's end. There was a bit of banter going around our dressing-room at the time to the effect that while we knew the gaffer could walk on water – as he frequently boasted – we didn't know that he had that much control over the elements as well!

It was also around that time that the alarm bells were ringing among Forest fans when Derby made an attempt to get Clough and Taylor back at The Baseball Ground. New Derby chairman George Hardy led what was almost a crusade to get them to return and when Brian Appleby, his opposite number at Forest, gave permission for the approach, we all feared the worst. The press were camped out at The City Ground and across at Derby and as players we realised there was a good chance the gaffer and Pete, who had made no secret of their love for Derby, would return. But at the end of a cliff-hanging sort of day it was announced they were staying and would get on with the job of trying to get us into the First Division. As if that wasn't enough for Derby, the gaffer then made a cheeky attempt to sign Archie Gemmill from them before the deadline but it fell through.

It would have been a massive loss for Forest if Clough had gone and there's no doubt in my mind that there would have been none of the success that was to come in the thrilling years that followed. But I would like to think that the gaffer felt he had started something at Forest that he didn't want to leave when the job was only half-finished.

We won five matches on the bounce to reinforce our promotion claims but back-to-back defeats by Chelsea and Cardiff threw up fresh doubts towards the end of the season.

It was getting very nervy on the field and away from the football action I had a different kind of confrontation with a well-known actor. We played Bristol Rovers and Plymouth Argyle in successive away games and I scored when we came back to draw 1–1 with Rovers. That night we stayed in a hotel in Plymouth and David Soul, of *Starsky and Hutch* fame, was also there. My mother-in-law at the time was a big fan of his and I went up to him in the hotel, saying, 'Excuse me, would you mind signing this for my mother-in-law?' His quote back to me was, 'I've signed 500 of these today,' and it was said in such a manner that suggested he could do without it. He signed it, gave it me back but I ripped it up and said, 'Thanks very much but I don't want it now.' Later on, to his credit, he came over and apologised and sent over a drink for the boys.

We beat Plymouth but in the final two weeks the promotion issue was taken out of our hands. In our final game we defeated

Millwall 1–0 thanks to an own goal but then we had to wait to discover our fate. Bolton needed just three points from their last two games to join Wolves and Chelsea in winning promotion but, as coincidence would have it, their penultimate game was against champions Wolves at Burnden Park.

At the time that game was kicking off, we were Majorca-bound for our usual end of season trip with the gaffer arguing, 'We've done everything we can now, it's out of our hands, what will be, will be.' We were in mid-air when the pilot came across on the radio to tell us that Wolves had scored but there were no celebrations at that time. They were only about 20 minutes into the game so there was a long way to go. Then, as we prepared to land, the pilot told us that he thought he had heard that Wolves had won 1–0 which would have meant, of course, that Bolton could not overtake us and we had gone up. No one – least of all the gaffer – was taking that as final and only when he rang Mary Dryden, the wife of Stuart Dryden, who was on the trip, did he accept that Wolves had won and we were on our way into the First Division.

It was a case of let the party begin. I was probably not on my own in admitting that I was drunk for most of the week but we had a great time. John McGovern had a tape of Fleetwood Mac's new album *Rumours* and we sat around the pool drinking and listening to it non-stop.

I know I had a reputation for being a bit of a boozer but I was never the huge drinker that a lot of people would have you believe. Yes, I went out after games and had a few but I can remember occasions in Uriah Heep's wine bar in Nottingham when people were staring at me to see what I was going to down. There were times when I would order a glass of milk just to throw them because you couldn't really disguise what was going down! I think I stood up on one occasion, pointed to my glass and said, 'Yes, it's milk.'

But, hands up, I had my share of drink that week in Majorca. And why not? We were back in the First Division and I knew what that meant to a lot of people – not least myself.

5

That champion feeling

REGAINING FIRST DIVISION FOOTBALL AND getting the opportunity to test ourselves against the best sides in the country was uppermost in the players' minds as we sat back during the summer of 1977 to reflect on promotion. Once the elation had subsided, there was an element of apprehension and doubt as we looked forward to heading to Old Trafford, Anfield and Highbury, wondering whether we could cope with what the so-called 'big boys' would throw at us.

But Brian Clough and Peter Taylor would never allow their minds to stray into areas of negativity. As far as they were concerned winning promotion was the platform for better things, but I doubt whether even those two could predict the kind of events that were about to unfold over the next twelve months as we unbelievably swept to the First Division title – more or less leading from start to finish – and captured the League Cup for the first time.

They only bought one player during the summer but it turned out to be one hell of a signing, Kenny Burns joining us in a £140,000 transfer from Birmingham City. The day he signed for us the gaffer took him to a sweet pea competition that he was judging somewhere in Nottingham and although Burnsy was so far removed from the image of sweet peas, he had no option but to go along with it. But it wasn't long before we got to know all about Burnsy's qualities and I can tell you they were more akin to muck and nettles than sweet peas.

Burnsy had a reputation as a bit of a firebrand but outside of that I didn't know too much about him apart from when he captured the headlines for scoring the perfect hat-trick against

Peter Shilton in a match between Birmingham and Leicester. One goal with his left, one with his right and one with his head. Although he had played the odd game at the back, I always knew him as a centre-forward but when he arrived at The City Ground it was made clear that he was being signed as a centre-half to play alongside Lloydy.

He immediately looked the part. He wasn't the quickest but he could head the ball all day long, read the game superbly, had two good feet and would go through brick walls if it meant getting a win bonus. When he took his two false teeth out at the front, which had been knocked out during some aerial battle in his past, he looked a formidable sight . . . the kind that not many strikers wanted to mix it with.

But he was prone to the odd indiscretion on and off the field and when he first joined us he got into a bit of immediate bother on our pre-season stay in West Germany. The gaffer had his wife Barbara and children on the trip and we were invited into a beer tent where Burnsy took full advantage of the hospitality and got himself absolutely pie-eyed – so much so that he was rolling around drunk and eventually spewed up in full gaze of Mrs Clough and others.

Burnsy was told to get to his room and the following day he was full of remorse. He was walking towards Brian and Barbara and asked if he could have a word. Barbara said she would go back to the hotel and see Cloughie in a little while but Burnsy asked her to stay because he wanted to apologise to them both together. Afterwards Cloughie said to him, 'It's just as well you did that, son, because otherwise you would have been on the next plane out of here.'

Burnsy didn't really bother too much about anything. He used to moan about everybody – even the best players in the world. I used to joke with him that, 'You must be the only bloke in the game who thinks that Pelé is only "not bad".'

He wasn't the best at remembering people's names either. For years and years he used to call John Wark, who played for Ipswich and Scotland, 'George'. John was mystified with it for years but didn't want to ask Burnsy why he couldn't get his name right.

To this day nothing bothers Burnsy too much and he still gets things wrong. Long after we had all finished playing I was watching Coventry Reserves one night and Burnsy was there doing a bit of scouting for Peter Shilton, who was managing Plymouth at the time. Martin O'Neill, Burnsy and myself were having a cup of tea at half-time when Jim Blyth, the former Coventry goalkeeper walked in. Burnsy turned to me and said, 'Have you seen that Jim Blyth? He's bald!' I turned round and looked at Kenny with his two hairs on his head and wondered where the hell he was coming from. Burnsy must have looked in the mirror at night and seen Robert Redford staring at him!

Anyway, Burnsy got over the episode with Mrs Clough as we headed into the rest of our pre-season programme. It took us to Switzerland, Austria and West Germany but I distinctly remember the management making a major decision when we got back home and we played in a friendly against non-league Skegness a week before we were set to kick off the season against Everton at Goodison Park. There were a couple of thousand people in the ground and it turned out to be the last game that Terry Curran played for the club.

The gaffer and Pete had what the players believed were long discussions about how they could tackle the First Division – what they could get away with and what they couldn't. One of the big decisions they made was to say that they would not go with two wingers. It was thought that Curran and myself would both play and we would tackle matches in the manner that won us promotion. But they believed otherwise.

Curran could be a bit of a sparky character and didn't enjoy the fact that he hadn't always been a regular in the side in the promotion season after regaining his fitness after knee surgery. Cloughie liked him but he had a few run-ins with Pete and after one of them Curran stormed into his office one day, threw down a piece of paper on his desk and shot out. Curran thought it was the transfer request that he had painstakingly written but Pete unfurled the piece of paper, went chasing after him and inquired, 'Do you want me to pay this for you?' It turned out to be Terry's gas bill! When Curran realised he wasn't going to figure as a first choice he understandably got the hump and soon afterwards was loaned out to Bury. A little while later he joined Derby for £50,000 and in some ways he was a loss because there was no doubt he was an exciting player and opponents were frightened of his pace.

His bad fortune, however, was good news for Martin O'Neill,

who came into the team and never looked back. Martin had come from Distillery in Northern Ireland to join Forest in 1971 and we had hit it off very soon after he joined the club. I got the impression he suffered in his early days at the club because he didn't have an out and out position. Some people thought of him as a forward player and that was backed up by the fact that he had scored a couple of goals to help Distillery win the Irish Cup just before he moved to The City Ground. But Martin always had strong views on the subject and, given a choice, he was focused on playing in the centre of midfield. He was strong, very difficult to knock off the ball and you always felt there was a lot of untapped potential in his game at that stage of his career.

You didn't really get a choice of where to play in Cloughie's sides and I think Martin was just delighted to be on the teamsheet when we headed for Merseyside for that first game. It was a feeling of excitement at going to play in the First Division again but as individuals there was also an air of trepidation in terms of whether we would be good enough to match up to the demands of top flight football.

The curtain raiser at Goodison Park was always going to be a massive test for us because at that time Everton were one of the strongest sides in the country and one capable of challenging for the title. I distinctly remember Martin and me sitting together on the team bus approaching Liverpool and watching the crowds starting to wend their way towards the ground. It was as if everyone was heading to the match. It was a mixture of nerves and excitement as we trooped off the bus and made our way into the ground but you could tell by the numbers outside the stadium that this was something we had not been used to. There was a crowd of 38,000 in the ground and when we went out to have a look at the pitch, there was a different feeling of anticipation to the one we had experienced in the Second Division.

When the game got underway I could hardly get my breath – such was the pace and intensity of it. It was quick, there seemed little time to dwell on the ball and I was just wondering when it would all settle down. Everton seemed to have a lot of possession but I was more concerned with my lung capacity than making an impact on the game! As luck would have it Peter Withe put us ahead and I got a second, pulling a cross down from the right with my left foot, shooting and it went away into the far corner of the net. I couldn't believe it . . . back in the First Division and scoring a goal at Goodison Park. Dave Jones, who went on to manage Southampton, Wolves and Cardiff City, was in opposition to me at right-back that day and we just seemed to grow in strength and confidence as the match went on. As a team you could sense the belief that was rising in us by the passing of every minute. Martin got a third goal for us and we finished up winning 3–1 which, bearing in mind Everton's quality, was a fantastic result for us as new boys on the block.

Mind you, it wasn't all sweetness and light for me on the day. In a break in play while one of our players got treatment, there was a quietness settled over the ground until I heard someone shout from the crowd, 'Hey, Robertson.' I turned around and nodded and then came the request, 'Get out of the way, I can't see the game!' I took that as a reflection on my weight because I wasn't exactly your natural slim-line winger but I accepted the comment in good faith, had a little laugh and got on with the game.

The important thing for us was that we had got off to a good start but we were brought a little bit down to earth in our first home game when we struggled a wee bit to find our rhythm against Bristol City. However, Googie scored another goal with a header and we managed to win 1–0. Four points from two games and we were flying.

It got better. We beat Derby 3–0 at home in the next game, Googie scored twice to make it four in three games for him and I scored the third – when the ball came to me in the box, I controlled it and side-footed it into the corner. I was chuffed to bits that we had beaten our biggest rivals 3–0 and there was just no holding us.

In the next game we played West Ham in the second round of the League Cup – we got a bye in the first round – and whacked them 5–0. It was one of those nights when everything went right for me and although I had some great times after that I've got to say that it was one of my best performances in a Forest shirt. I was up against Frank Lampard senior and he was a good player but everything went for me. I couldn't do any wrong, confidence was oozing out of me and whatever I tried turned to gold. People have talked to me since about the game and my performance but, to his credit, Frank never made any attempt to kick me off the park as

I'm sure he felt like doing. I think Billy Bonds, who wasn't renowned for hanging back when there was a need to deliver a bit of a threat, did try and kick me into Row Z but I saw him coming and managed to jump out of the way.

We were in such a rich vein of form that we wondered where it would end and the answer, unfortunately, was in the next match. We were facing Arsenal at Highbury and we went down 3–0 . . . a rude awakening if you like. But the repercussions were aplenty and the 'Red Trees' were flying around afterwards. The Red Trees meant only one thing to us players – we were picking up a fine, delivered in an envelope bearing a Forest red tree – and on that day in North London both Burnsy and Lloydy were in bother.

During the game there had been a suspicion that Burnsy had butted the Arsenal player Ritchie Powling on the back of the head and when Cloughie asked him about it afterwards Burnsy answered, 'I didn't touch him, gaffer.' Sadly for Burnsy, the clips of the game on *Star Soccer* the following day showed that it was plain to see that he had and he suffered the consequences. Lloydy was also fined for something he did on the day and in the team meeting the following Monday, the Big Man was also accused by Pete of 'losing his heart' during the game. I know they weren't very happy about the way Frank Stapleton had won the ball in the air for their third goal. Lloydy, being Lloydy, answered back, 'Excuse me, have I heard you properly?' It got a bit scary before Pete backed down and the gaffer stepped in to make sure it didn't go any further. It was amusing afterwards but Lloydy was not far away from exploding.

I had my share of Red Trees but they were more for being late and things like that, but as soon as any of us saw one of those envelopes you knew it wasn't exactly an invitation round to the gaffer's house. Some time afterwards I got a Red Tree for asking to go to the toilet when we were on the training ground. I said I needed to go and was told in no uncertain terms that I should have gone before we left the ground. Whatever happened to the call of mother nature?

We bounced back from the Highbury episode by beating Wolves 3–2 at Molineux and then came the moment that confirmed to us that the gaffer and Pete were intent on taking the club onto a new level. There had been much speculation in the press about them going after Peter Shilton, who was playing for Stoke City at the time after they had been relegated into the Second Division. In fact, the story goes that the gaffer and Pete went to watch him play just up the road at Mansfield.

Shilts had won his first cap with England during his Leicester days and he and Liverpool's Ray Clemence had a great rivalry for a time for the No. 1 shirt at international level. He was top quality and although we had started the season well, it was generally thought within the game that if Shilts was going to go anywhere he would go to one of the glamour clubs of the day like Manchester United. But the gaffer and Pete were very persuasive men once they had got their teeth into something and they had the added bonus of knowing that Shilts quite fancied the idea of playing under them. Negotiations seemed to go on for weeks but, as they usually did, they got their man and Shilts signed for us for what was then a record fee for a goalkeeper. The press weren't convinced and I think there were a few murmurings among Forest officials about the merits of paying so much money for a goalkeeper.

The gaffer answered that kind of scepticism in his own inimitable way and once you had seen Shilts in action at close quarters you knew that he was something special and worth every penny . . . and more. Big money went on goalscorers but goodness knows how many points he was worth to us over the course of a season.

Everything about his work on the training ground was perfection. He would stay behind long after we had left and if there was something he wanted to work on he wouldn't leave until he was happy about it. It was in the days before goalkeeper coaches but even without having someone to drive him on in training, he used to work harder than anyone I've seen. He used to love getting involved as an outfield player in the games we played at the end of training and while he might have been the best goalkeeper in the world, as a centre-forward he was enthusiastic but basically useless. In my eyes he was as good as if not better than any goalkeeper there has ever been.

When he wasn't playing football he used to enjoy the social life and when we went out as a group, you would always find Shilts in the corner with his ice bucket, quietly sipping champagne. But that was fine by us. It was his drink and he was a champagne goalkeeper in our eyes. From a very early stage us outfield players got a massive boost from knowing that he was our last line of defence. On the rare days when teams got the better of Lloydy, Burnsy and Co. then they had to find a way past Shilts, whose frame and presence was enough to put off any striker.

Soon after signing Shilts we made another superb signing when Archie Gemmill joined us from Derby, where he had won Championship medals under the gaffer and then Dave Mackay. Archie came to us in a deal that saw John Middleton, a young goalkeeper who had been our No. 1 for about 12 months, go to The Baseball Ground in part exchange. I think there was about £20,000 that changed hands and it must rank as one of the best bits of business that we did because Archie was brilliant – what a steal! There wasn't much of him but he jumped like a 6 ft plus striker, tackled like Burnsy, had the pace of Tony Woodcock and could play the ball as well as anyone in the team. For years the gaffer used to wind him up about his ability. 'When will you learn to play the ball, Gemmill?' he used to say. But Archie was nobody's mug and knew all along that the gaffer rated him highly and it was just a means of getting the very best out of him. Archie, who was a strong character in his own right, thrived on the banter. He knew the game inside out and in addition to bringing his energy and talents into our midfield he was always willing to offer advice and help.

I don't know whether it was because we were both Scottish but I always got on well with Archie even though down the years I've heard that a few people didn't take to him. But you speak as you find and he was superb with me, he had great knowledge of the game and I always thought he would make it as a manager in his own right.

To add Burnsy, Shilts and Archie to the team that had come out of the Second Division really gave us an all-round strength and we grew in stature as the matches went by.

We smashed Ipswich 4–0 at The City Ground on a day when Peter Withe scored all four goals and I got credited with all four assists. It sticks in my mind that we went into the game after Mick Mills, the England full-back who played for Ipswich, had said something about us – whether it be the way we played or not being good enough . . . I can't recall. But the upshot of it was his comments took the place of the gaffer's team talk. Mills wound us up and we went out and played superbly. I liked Mick but I think he must have regretted what he said on that occasion.

It was around that time that there was more speculation about the gaffer's future – but this time it revolved around the possibility of him succeeding Don Revie as England manager. I don't know whether we took our eyes off the ball for a bit but while the England business was boiling up, we were not at our best. We lost 1–0 at Chelsea on the day that Forest gave permission for him to be interviewed by the FA and a fortnight later we lost again at Leeds to a goal by Ray Hankin while Shilts was in a daze after being slightly concussed in a challenge with the Leeds striker.

Immediately after that game we went to Israel to play against Maccabi Tel Aviv and during the trip the gaffer and Stuart Dryden went to the Wailing Wall to put a note in it. I don't know what he wrote but I very much doubt he was predicting what we were about to achieve over the following 12 months.

We were still top at that stage, however, and soon got our act together again and that 1–0 defeat at Elland Road turned out to be the last before we embarked on our marathon 42-match unbeaten run.

Off the pitch, the England affair would not go away and there was a strong feeling in our dressing-room that if the gaffer was offered the job he would take it. Let's face it, there was no better or more well-qualified candidate, having won the First Division title with Derby as well as taking them to the semi-final of the European Cup and he was on the verge of great things at Forest. He had a huge media profile to go with his achievements but there was always the thought that the powers that be at Lancaster Gate would be in fear of him wanting to tear the place apart and do it all his own way. The gaffer went for an interview at which he evidently made it clear that any appointment would have to include Pete as his No. 2.

I think most people at Forest were resigned to the fact that he would go but there was a huge sigh of relief by the Trent when it was announced that Ron Greenwood had got the job. Over the years I've often wondered deep down whether he really wanted it. He was nobody's fool – far from it – and he knew what the FA officials were like. I thought that if he wanted the job that badly he would have swallowed a bit of pride and kept some of his more caustic thoughts to himself in a bid to curry favour with the people who were going to make the decision.

I might be way off beam in thinking that but one thing I am convinced about is that had he been given the opportunity he would have been an unbelievable success. I don't think it would have mattered to him that he wasn't involved on a day-to-day basis and come what may his genius would have shone through. I'm sure players would have loved to have played for him and he would have commanded their greatest respect.

The gaffer shrugged off the disappointment – if that's what it was – of the England job and got back to his normal business by signing another player. Lloydy had broken a small bone in his foot and we badly needed someone to step in and partner Burnsy in the middle of the back four. The gaffer turned immediately to David Needham, who had made his name across the river at Notts County before leaving for Queens Park Rangers the previous summer. I think we had tried to sign him then but there was no chance that Notts would let their star man come to us, but Rangers got a handsome return on their investment and Needham arrived to play his part in the success that followed.

Mind you, he had a bit of a rude awakening when he took his first steps into our dressing-room. Dave was a very polite person and went round introducing himself to all the lads and when he got to Lloydy, he inquired, 'Are you all right?' knowing that he had been injured. Lloydy's reply went something like, 'I'm not that fucking well, otherwise you wouldn't be here!'

Dave went straight into our team for a game against Manchester United at Old Trafford that ranks as the best team performance I've ever been involved with. We were so good on the day we could have scored seven or eight . . . and this was Manchester United we were taking on in their own back yard. They just couldn't live with us, we sprang forward with a pace and penetration that they just couldn't handle and it was no exaggeration to say we looked like scoring every time we got into their half of the field. United might not have been the power they were in later years but they were still United – and we were something else. It was one of those days when we were all on our game from 1–11, passed the ball brilliantly and it was a sheer joy to be part of the 4–0 win.

We were full of ourselves afterwards, particularly as we were off for a few days' break in Benidorm the following day. Our wives had gone up to Manchester to watch the game and meet up with us afterwards. I think we all went out to a Playboy Club in Manchester after the game but when our wives came back to Nottingham we jetted off to Spain to let our hair down.

We were pretty good at that, too, and after a result like that we had a great time. Around then 'Mull of Kintyre', which ironically is a song that Forest fans have adopted over the years, was No. 1 in the charts. We used to go in this pub in Benidorm called the Robin Hood and whenever Paul McCartney and Wings came over the speakers in the bar, John O'Hare used to grab a snorkel that was positioned behind the bar and pretend it was bagpipes. It was so funny when he did it for the first time that we encouraged him to get up time and time again and Solly was always good for a laugh.

Breaks to Torremolinos, Benidorm and Cala Millor were fairly commonplace for us during that era and the gaffer used to say we would get the benefit of them for weeks afterwards. He was big on rest, particularly when we were playing so many games, and I don't think anyone could argue that the get-away breaks were not good for us.

When we came back from Benidorm our next game was a massive one against Liverpool at The City Ground and although Archie Gemmill gave us the lead, we ended up having to settle for a point.

But the wins continued to flow in the league, the League Cup and the FA Cup and for a time we began to look a good bet for all three competitions. We beat Swindon, Manchester City and saw off Queens Park Rangers after three games to reach the quarter-finals of the FA Cup but injuries hit us hard when we met West Brom at The Hawthorns and we were so stretched that Archie and John McGovern figured in the game despite being well short of fitness. Ian Bowyer, who put his lot in whenever he played, had to fill in for Viv Anderson at right-back and had the unenviable task of keeping tabs on Scottish international winger Willie Johnston. Bomber did quite well in the circumstances but goals by Mick Martin and Cyrille Regis put us off one Wembley trail.

There was no stopping us in the League Cup and we put in a fantastic performance against Aston Villa in the fourth round at home. We conceded two goals late on to take some of the gloss away from the performance but we were superb on the night, winning 4–2. It was one of my best games for Forest. I was up against John Gidman, who was one of the top right-backs around, and without wishing to brag about it, I gave him a hard time. I was in the best form of my life but I don't mind admitting that I didn't always have my own way.

I regularly got asked which full-backs were the most difficult opponents I encountered – and my answer will surprise a lot of people. The one I had most problems getting the better of was David Langan in his Derby days and he was closely followed by Brendan Batson, of West Brom, and Notts County's Pedro Richards, who died at the terribly sad early age of 45 in 2001.

Langan, who had a good run in the Republic of Ireland side, used to stick to me like a limpet and if I'm honest I always had most problems with full-backs who wouldn't give me an inch never mind a yard. The minute I stepped onto a pitch against Langan, we may as well have been in the same strip – he was that close. He was a good player too, very quick, and I always regarded him as one of the best attacking full-backs of his time. Unfortunately for me, he was concentrated totally on defensive aspects of his game whenever I was up against him.

Brendan was regarded as a cultured type of defender but he never gave me any space in which to work and the same applied to Pedro who always relished the chance to get stuck in to me quickly in Forest–Notts games.

I don't think any winger enjoyed playing against defenders who were dogged and were prepared to latch on to you for 90 minutes no matter what was going on elsewhere on the pitch. I was talking to Ian Storey-Moore about it and he felt the same way and cited Leeds United's Paul Reaney as his most difficult opponent simply because he could never shake him off. I suppose it was a compliment in some ways.

We had some of our best days when I was tightly marked for the simple reason that it created a lot more space for other players in the team. In games like that the gaffer used to scream at me from the dugout, 'Robbo – come and stand by me and bring the nugget with you.' In turn it left space for the likes of Withe, Woodcock, and later Birtles and Francis and the rest to run into and cause mayhem.

Throughout that League Cup campaign I enjoyed a lot of freedom, probably because we were new to the top flight, and we went on to reach a two-legged semi-final showdown with Leeds United. The first leg was played in Yorkshire and the gaffer sprang a late surprise when he called up Solly in place of Frank Clark and switched Colin Barrett to full-back. Solly was brilliant that night and deservedly got a third goal to add to the two scored by Peter Withe; we had a 3–1 lead to take back to The City Ground for the second leg.

Despite that Leeds made it difficult for us on our pitch, led 2–1 on the night and Tony Currie smacked a shot against our crossbar that would have completely wiped out our lead. But we came to life and Bomber, Martin and Tony Woodcock added goals to one that Peter Withe had scored earlier in the game and we were in a final for the first time in nineteen years. Only a small matter of Liverpool stood between us and major silverware.

It was my first appearance at Wembley and when I was kicking the ball round the back streets of Uddingston as a kid, I could only dream that one day I would be walking down that famous tunnel to play in a match. The gaffer was a master at easing the pressure on us so he tried to turn it into just another game but I don't mind admitting that walking out there made the hairs stand up on the back of your neck. The one thing I remember more than anything about Wembley was the turf. It was so soft and lush that I told myself if I ever got back there to make sure I wore the longest possible studs. My feet sank into the ground and I was slipping and sliding all over the place.

Our journey to the Wembley final had been quite remarkable because all along the way we had had to go in without Shilts, Archie and David Needham, who were all cup-tied. Being without Shilts was a huge loss but his stand-in Chris Woods, who had only celebrated his 18th birthday in the November of that season, had been magnificent. But Wembley was Wembley and there had to be big question marks about the kid's ability to handle the pressure of the occasion – never mind what Liverpool would throw at us. He had played for England at youth level but he was in our first team for the League Cup games without having made his league debut and it was a big ask for someone so young and inexperienced.

But he went out and answered every question asked of him on

the day. We put in a poor performance by our standards and Liverpool battered us, particularly in the second half, but couldn't find a way past Woodsy. The kid was magnificent.

We nearly nicked it near the end but Ray Clemence made a great save from Tony Woodcock and extra-time came and went without a winner. It would have been tough on Liverpool had we won it late in the game . . . but needless to say we would have taken it.

The replay was scheduled for Old Trafford the following Wednesday and a league match at Middlesbrough in midweek had to be postponed. With the Middlesbrough game in mind the gaffer and Pete had planned on taking us to Scarborough for a couple of days and even though we were in the replay of the final in Manchester they still went ahead with the trip to the North Yorkshire coast.

We used to go to Scarborough quite a bit – not least because Pete had a place up there that he used to scarper off to from time to time. Our trips up there normally coincided with Pete wanting to take some bits of furniture and things up to his place and it was the coach driver Albert Kershaw's job to make sure there was enough room for the skips, which contained the players' kit, once Pete had got his stuff on board.

Football-wise we made a small but nevertheless highly significant change to our line-up for the Liverpool replay because the gaffer was concerned about us being over-run by Liverpool in the way that we had been for much of the game at Wembley. Just as he had decided when we were to dispense with two wingers, we were to adopt a tighter policy in midfield with me being tucked into a midfield four with not so much licence to attack the full-back at will. It was a master stroke. It made us more compact as a team and it was a system we deployed for many of our difficult away games in the years that followed, particularly the big European matches that were around the corner.

We were less vulnerable in the replay and early in the second half got the goal that won us the League Cup. Solly, who had replaced the injured John McGovern in midfield, got through to the edge of the box and was brought crashing to the ground by Phil Thompson, who would have been sent off under modern-day rules. To a man Liverpool appealed that the tackle was made outside of the box – and I think they had a point – but referee Pat

Partridge awarded us a penalty and, thankfully, I tucked it away to Clemence's right to give us victory.

It might have been a close affair with Liverpool but I don't think anyone could say we didn't deserve to win the competition. We had scored twenty-four goals in the League Cup that season and only conceded three – and that was an amazing statistic. Victory in the final also guaranteed us a place in European football the next season but we were all after the big prize. We wanted to win the League and with it entry into the European Cup.

But we were visibly tiring. It had been an unbelievable season and there was no doubt we were beginning to feel the strain of playing so many games with virtually the same side operating week in, week out. There was tremendous character and resilience about us, however, and we dug out some great results to keep us ahead of Liverpool and Everton, the two sides most likely to catch us.

We just wanted to get over the line as quickly as possible and we were virtually there when I scored the only goal of the game with a penalty against Queens Park Rangers at The City Ground. Only Liverpool could catch us but even though our goal difference was far superior to theirs, there were no celebrations. We needed a point in our next game against Coventry City at Highfield Road to make it mathematically certain that we would be champions and when Shilts pulled off a great instinctive save to keep out a header from big Mick Ferguson, we knew our name was on the trophy.

We had won it from the front, produced some fantastic football, defied all the critics who kept saying our bubble would burst and in the end won it with plenty to spare.

We still had four games remaining and even then the management made sure there would be no free-wheeling. After the title had been won we went to Ipswich in midweek for what turned out to be a memorable match for Frank Clark, who started the game as substitute. The gaffer had one of his nights when he wasn't happy about Peter Withe – they happened every now and again – and he dragged him off to put Frank on. Always the polite one, Frank asked where he wanted him to play and he was told, 'The centre-forward is coming off, so get yourself up there.' Frank had made a career out of hardly crossing the halfway line so it was a completely new experience for him but he was in the right place at the right time to score from a rebound and put the seal on our 2–0 win. It was his first league goal in 16 years with Newcastle and Forest and we mobbed him like excited schoolboys because we were so pleased for his sake. Such were the celebrations you would have thought we had won the European Cup and I am sure Ipswich fans were a bit perplexed by our somewhat over the top actions.

We drew our next games at home against Birmingham and away at West Brom and we went into our last match against Liverpool at Anfield wanting to put on a performance worthy of champions. For their part Liverpool were out for a bit of revenge. We had beaten them in the League Cup final of course, and they were still sore about the winning goal – and we had also taken the league title away from them. We went to Anfield under-strength, too, with Kenny Burns away receiving his Footballer of the Year award and Tony Woodcock injured. But, showing all the guts that had gone with the glamour throughout a magnificent season, we withstood everything Liverpool had to offer on the night to finish the season with a goalless draw and an unbeaten run stretching to 26 games.

From a personal point of view, I was desperately keen to play against Liverpool – the last thing I wanted was a rest. I had played in all 41 league games and wanted to go through the entire season with a 100 per cent record and I'm delighted I was able to do that.

I am sure I speak for all the lads involved when I say I find it difficult to fully describe how much satisfaction we all got from defying the odds in squeezing into a promotion place and then powering on to win the First Division title, having led from the front. It was also a smack in the eye for the critics, some of whom were from inside the game, who regarded us as a bit of a 'ragtag and bobtail' outfit that was a mixture of has-beens and nobodies.

I'm not sure what category I dropped into – probably a ragtag – but the popular perception, quite often put around by the gaffer, was that I was this scruffy, overweight little Scotsman, who shuffled around in the same pair of loafers that I had had for years. It was an identity that stuck with me, too, when at the end of the season I came out on top in the merit marks that everybody in football used to look at in *The People* newspaper every weekend. All the numbers added up in my favour but the heading that was splashed right across the sports pages was 'The tramp is king.' It was something I got used to over the years but when my mum saw it she was livid. 'How can they write that about my son?' was her take on things but I put it down to gaining a bit more respect as a player.

The fact was that we had some truly talented players in the squad and they were eventually getting some of the credit they deserved. There were gifted players already at the club when Cloughie arrived and it took the gaffer to get the best out of us. He and Pete made some wonderful signings to mould a side that was shortly capable of taking on the best that Europe had to offer.

What we also had was a great camaraderie. We socialised a lot, had regular nights out with our wives and girlfriends, and even after training there was never a real rush to get away from the group. We had a bolt-hole called Mackay's café, which was little more than a stone's throw away from The City Ground and most days after training we would pile in there as a group for a coffee, a bite to eat and to chew over what had gone on that day. It was run by a bloke called Bill, who knew everything that the lads liked and on Fridays he knew it was chip butty day and had extra supplies of bread and potatoes. Mackay's was so popular it became a little institution in its own right and if you ever needed to speak to one of the other lads after training, it was always the first port of call. We had other places where we would congregate from time to time – sometimes we'd meet at the Pepper Mill in Nottingham city centre and then go on to a wine bar – but Fridays meant only one thing: chip butties at Mackay's.

But considering the heights we were about to achieve, a diet of caviar and champagne would not have been out of place in the two years that followed.

6
Marvellous Munich

I TAKE GREAT PRIDE FROM the fact that there are two photographs hanging side by side at The City Ground that put the history of the club in a pictorial nutshell. The first is captioned 'One second from glory' and the second says 'Another moment of glory'. They are the moments that captured the goal that won the European Cup for Nottingham Forest in 1979 and then the goal that made sure the magnificent trophy returned to Nottingham in 1980.

On top of the unbelievable European Cup journeys to Munich and then Madrid we continued to enjoy great success on the domestic front and it was just a sensational time for anyone to be connected with the club. I will return to our experiences on the 'home' front in a later chapter but I would like to dwell for the time being on the unforgettable European glories.

It was Roy of the Rovers stuff for a club the size of Forest to take Europe by storm for one year – let alone two. And I still pinch myself to this day when I think that I supplied the cross for the goal that beat Malmö in Munich and then went on to score the vital goal when we repeated the remarkable feat by beating Hamburg in Madrid 12 months later. European Cup glory was for the likes of Puskás and Di Stéfano – not for a tubby little lad from Uddingston who would have needed the wildest and most vivid of imaginations to have dreamt up such stories as a kid.

To score the only goal in a European Cup final is in the land of sheer fantasy but as I stood in the Bernabéu Stadium in Madrid on the evening of 28 May 1980, it was as if I had been transported into another world where only dreams were made.

As personal performances go, I wasn't particularly proud of my contributions in either final – neither game was the spectacle a world audience had wanted to see. But the early summer's night in Spain turned out to be a magical one.

We were 20 minutes into the final when Frank Gray ended a typical forward run by finding Gary Mills, who had a hand in forcing the ball into my path. I thought about heading for the line but decided to cut inside, gave Garry Birtles a pass that let's say wasn't one of the most precise in my career and went for the return. Garry stretched every sinew in his body – as he did on countless occasions that night – to get the ball back into my path and as Kevin Keegan came in to challenge I managed to side-step him and create the space I yearned. I was a little bit off balance but despite that managed to get a good enough strike on the ball to know that it would cause the Hamburg goalkeeper Rudi Kargus a bit of a problem. I looked on, knowing I couldn't do any more, as the ball curled towards the far post.

'It's got a chance,' I remember saying to myself, and as the ball eluded Kargus and squeezed inside the framework of the goal, it was a moment of unbridled joy that I appreciate few of us experience. 'I've scored!' I shrieked. 'I've scored in a European Cup final!' And the next thing I knew I was mobbed by ecstatic team-mates who I dare say all shared the incredulity of it all. I've seen the film of the goal time and time again and it amuses me to see my outstretched arms pointing into a balmy Spanish night and then to see them slowly disappear as I was engulfed by my mates.

It was the pinnacle of my career but little did I realise when we were soaking up the joys of winning the First Division title that the European journey on which we were about to embark would yield many more magnificent memories.

The summer of 1978 was one of great satisfaction and high anticipation as we reflected on our League Cup and First Division championship double success and looked forward to what we all expected would be a bit of a flirtation with European football.

My wife Sally and I had been married a year earlier and 12 months later we had gone on holiday to Barbados with Tony Woodcock and his wife Carole. I remember the holiday well because everyone used to take the mickey out of me because of my paler than pale skin. I was always the same and Bill Anderson used to rib me at Forest by asking, 'Where have you been on your holidays? The Isle of White?' Nobody had seen me with a suntan but I was determined to do something about it. 'I'll show them what a tan looks like,' I told myself as I headed for the beach at 11 o'clock, all set for a day under the sun. By that time I had taken to reading books and was reading *The Boys from Brazil* and got quite engrossed in it as the hours passed by. There was a lovely breeze coming off the sea so I didn't feel the heat too much and to be honest it was quite idyllic as I lay there hour after hour. I wasn't one for eating much during the day so carried on with the reading and sun-bathing until late into the afternoon.

I eventually decided I'd had enough and ventured back to the hotel to shower and the four of us went off to a pub called the Coach and Horses. Being a man of simple tastes I ordered chicken in the basket and quite enjoyed it, but 20 minutes later I started feeling really sick and suddenly started shaking all over. For a time I hadn't a clue what the hell was happening to me but Sally was a nurse and she reasoned that I had got sunstroke from laying my body open to the sun for most of the day. It was horrible, I continued to be sick and the shaking didn't calm down for ages. I felt really guilty afterwards because I spoiled the holiday for the other three and I seemed to spend the rest of our break getting myself back to normal.

I tell the story because I felt so poorly that I felt things couldn't get any worse – but they did when we rang home to discover who we had drawn in the first round of the European Cup. 'Liverpool – you must be joking. Come on, pull the other leg.' That was the reaction of both Tony and myself when we heard that we had been drawn out of the hat against Bob Paisley's reigning European champions. We were looking forward to a trip to France, Spain or maybe Italy. But after all our efforts to win the First Division and get Forest into Europe, we were heading to Anfield. As the disappointment sank in with both of us we took the view that it was the worst possible draw we could get. We were playing the champions, we were being denied a nice little trip to the Continent and, above everything else, our chances of getting through to the second round had just taken one hell of a jolt.

I've got to say that I never really enjoyed playing at Liverpool despite the fact that we had so much success against them in that period. The reason was that Liverpool were such a good side you knew that they were going to have something like 60–70 per cent possession during any game at Anfield and you always had your work cut out to get a result. It was always more a case of going there, putting in a shift for the team and trying to contain them. If you got the chance to hit them on the break then all well and good but survival was very much the name of the game. We had played Liverpool four times in the previous season – twice in the First Division and twice in the League Cup – and they couldn't beat us. I always felt that if you didn't concede against them, they would start to play longer and, as we had a brilliant defence, they played into our hands. They could come up with goals from all areas but we usually had an answer to it.

Kenny Dalglish, who was a wonderful player and probably the best I ever played with during my times with Scotland, never really stood out in our games against Liverpool. Larry Lloyd had a theory that you should never get tight on Kenny, who liked to feel where the defender was at his back. That gave him the opportunity to turn you but Lloydy believed that if you gave him a yard you were in a better position to deal with him. Lloydy used to look into his top pocket and joke, 'You can come out now, Kenny,' but as well as the Big Man used to play him, it was never quite as easy as that.

Liverpool were always capable of sneaking match-winning goals and around that time Ray Kennedy was a master at arriving late at the far post, but we were lucky to have Viv Anderson. I lost count of the number of times Viv would get a flick header to clear the ball or stretch out one of those telescopic legs of his to clear the danger.

But as Tony and me and my red skin came to terms with the fact that we were meeting up with Liverpool again, we took some comfort from the fact that we could boast that good recent record against them. And slowly but surely we convinced ourselves that it wasn't quite the daunting prospect we initially feared. Yes, it was going to be mighty difficult but it wasn't an insurmountable challenge.

The two-legged affair came round pretty quickly, in the September in fact. By that time we had a major change to our side with Peter Withe being sold to Newcastle, Stephen Elliott being given a chance and then Garry Birtles being thrown in at the deep end.

Birtles had made his debut two years earlier after joining us in a £2,000 deal from local non-league side Long Eaton United and he was quietly learning his trade and wondering when he would get another chance. It came the Saturday before we met Liverpool at home in the first leg on a day when Gary Mills made his first team debut as a 16-year-old and became our youngest ever league player at that time. Birtles did really well and stayed in the side four days later when a crowd of 38,000 crammed into The City Ground for the visit of Liverpool. And what a night it turned out to be for him. In what was only his third appearance for us he scored our first goal, steering the ball home after Tony Woodcock had penetrated Liverpool's defence.

Liverpool would probably have settled for 1–0 as they attempted to slow down the game but we kept bombing forward and the enthusiasm of our play was epitomised by the second goal we scored through Colin Barrett. He won two tackles inside his own half to send Birtles free and he tricked his way past Phil Thompson to cross for Woodcock to nod right into the danger area. Could anyone get on the end of it? The answer was supplied by Colin, who had sprinted forward into the box and produced a stunning volley that flew past Ray Clemence in the Liverpool goal to give us a two-goal advantage to take to Merseyside. It was such a massive goal in our history and without it I often wondered if we would have gone on to achieve the success we did.

Having said that I did hear afterwards that when Colin started to make his surging run from the back into their box, the gaffer and Pete were heard to say something like, 'Where the fuck is he going?' They were clearly thinking of what we had, we hold, but Colin had other ideas and his goal summed up all the qualities that he had as a player. He might not have been the most naturally gifted member of our squad but he had boundless enthusiasm and there was always a freshness about the way he played the game. It was as if he was determined to maximise every bit of ability that he was blessed with.

With that second goal we had the insurance policy we needed as we headed for Anfield. At 1–0 we had a chance of going through, at 2–0 we fancied our chances of getting the right result anywhere on the planet.

Unfortunately, Colin suffered a serious knee injury against

Middlesbrough before the second leg and although he made a comeback he was never the same again and sadly had to finish playing at an early age. It was a tragedy for him and us because there was no doubt he would have been an integral part of our side for years to come. He was playing out of his skin at the time and the gaffer loved him.

But I've got to stress the immense value of his goal that night – not just for the immediate future but all that was to follow. It was one of the most important goals in Forest's history because one goal might not have proved to be enough and we could have gone out of Europe at the first hurdle instead of taking the Continent by storm for two years. The goal and 2–0 victory gave us the belief to push on and ever since that day I've always maintained that the value of Colin's strike is absolutely inestimable.

In the stories that abounded after our home win over Liverpool much of the after-match talk surrounded Birtles, who had come from nowhere to play such a crucial part in our win. I don't know whether or not it is true but Bill Shankly, who had given way as Liverpool manager to Bob Paisley a few years earlier, was asked about Birtles on the radio and answered, 'They say that nobody knows anything about him but they certainly fucking do now.'

We knew it would still be hard, very hard at Anfield but we couldn't see them scoring three times to beat us as they had to do – not with our back four and Peter Shilton behind them. Frank Clark came in for Colin and played his part on a night when Liverpool worked themselves up into a frenzy in front of the Kop to try and turn the tie around and hold onto the trophy for a third successive year. But we withstood everything they could throw at us and in the end Liverpool had to concede there was no way through and the game ended in a goalless draw. Paisley went on record as saying we could go on and win the trophy . . . and that was nice for us to hear.

Victory over Liverpool opened up the European flavour of it all and we were paired with AEK Athens, a side we had drawn 1–1 with in a pre-season game in Greece. They were managed by one of the all time greats, Ferenc Puskás, the Real Madrid and Hungarian legend, who I had tried to imitate as a kid when I was trying to improve my left foot by bashing a ball against a wall. We knew it would be a hostile atmosphere in the first leg in Athens –

and the Greeks didn't disappoint us with a tremendous noise building up and flares going off in the stadium.

A goal by John McGovern removed much of the hostility but it didn't stop one of their players, a Uruguayan, planting a left hander on Burnsy's jaw. Fortunately for us, the referee saw it and produced a red card and, fortunately for the boy, he was banned from the second leg and didn't have to face Burnsy again. He was one who had clearly not heard about Burnsy's fearsome reputation.

Just before half-time I set Frank Clark off on one of his rare forward runs and he in turn found Birtles to beat the AEK keeper. Although the Greeks pulled a goal back we were still in pole position for the second leg.

Before I move on from Athens, it was in the Greek capital that my mate Larry Lloyd had his infamous 'blazer' row with the gaffer. We were preparing for the journey back to East Midlands Airport and all the lads were in the hotel foyer in grey slacks and blue club blazers – apart from Lloydy, who was in jeans. Lloydy asked John McGovern the skipper, 'Were we told to be in blazers?' McGovern said 'no' but he preferred wearing his to stop it getting creased in his bag. The gaffer was in his green sweater and tracksuit bottoms but was listening in. Then he went missing for a while and returned in his blazer.

Nothing was said until we got back to Nottingham but at the next team meeting Lloyd got a Red Tree with a £100 fine. Lloydy said something like, 'I'm not paying that, you can shove it up your arse.' It wasn't the done thing with the gaffer, who told Lloydy to shut up and if he didn't he would fine him an extra £50 for every word he said. Lloydy said 'you had better make it £1,000' but his maths wasn't that good because that represented only another 20 words and Lloydy was always a man of many.

Back on the field, Birtles' rapid emergence continued when he scored two more goals in the return leg as we ran up a 5–1 win and a 7–2 aggregate victory over AEK. It was a memorable night for Gary Mills, who got a taste of European football at a tender age. Millsy was one of the most talked about young footballers in the country as a schoolboy. He went on to have a long career in the game and was a great professional and I was always envious of his looks . . . a handsome boy he was.

Although we had only got through two rounds, Peter Taylor

was making noises that 'We could go on and win this.' And there was no doubt we were very comfortable and were more than happy with the system we were playing that went back to the League Cup final replay against Liverpool the previous season. Away from home we were compact with Woodcock and Birtles retreating to the halfway line and it left the opposition with the conundrum of whether to play high up the pitch and risk being done for pace, which those two certainly had.

In the next round we faced Grasshoppers of Zürich, who had won acclaim for knocking out Real Madrid in the previous round, and when Swiss international Claudio Sulser gave them the lead in the first leg at The City Ground, it wasn't really in the script. But after half an hour Woodcock set up Birtles for another goal and then I put us ahead from the penalty spot. Time was running out for us to build up a sizeable lead but it all came right in the last three minutes when Archie Gemmill hammered in a cross by Lloydy, who headed home the fourth from my corner.

The 4–1 lead meant the odds were stacked in our favour but Sulser, who scored eleven European Cup goals in three rounds, gave the Swiss the lead on the night of the second leg and there were some hairy moments until Martin O'Neill grabbed an equaliser.

That took us to the semi-final and a meeting with a Cologne side that had emerged as favourites after we had seen off Liverpool.

I went into the game four days after my brother Hughie had been killed in a car accident in Scotland and although my head was obviously spinning, I looked at the game as something of an escape from my personal trauma. I'll deal with the travesty of Hughie's death in detail later, but in a football context the gaffer left the decision whether or not to play with me and I felt I would be better off going ahead. I figured – and the rest of the family convinced me – that it was what Hughie would have wanted me to do. All the same I went into the match with all kinds of different emotions but I tried my best to focus for 90 minutes on the football. Because of that I had a strange carefree attitude to it all. It was as if football wasn't that important any more and it took all the pressure of the occasion away from me.

I remember Peter Taylor saying on the eve of the match at The City Ground that he felt we would be too good for the Germans.

'They can't head it, they can't pass it and they can't run, so go home and have a good steak, a good night's sleep and you'll walk it tomorrow.'

I'm not sure what he thought when we were two goals down as Cologne surprisingly attacked us from the start and gave us a mountain to climb. But the twists and turns of the game had not really started. Before half-time Birtles headed into the top corner to give us a foothold . . . and in the second half we pummelled them. Ian Bowyer shot through a crowded box to make it 2–2 and I must have got a nosebleed because I scored a third with a header!

That was a real collector's item. The ball was played into Birtles, who did what he did superbly with his back to goal. He crossed with his right foot and to this day I don't know why but I just decided to get across the full-back and the ball came to exactly where I was going. I just flung myself at the ball, more in hope than expectation, but I managed to make contact and it was a marvellous feeling to see it hit the back of the net. The City Ground erupted and the noise was deafening, and as I made my way back to the halfway line I remember looking to the sky, thinking of Hughie and saying to myself, 'That's for you, my boy.' For a split second I felt isolated with my thoughts and in some weird way the goal gave me a bit of comfort and strength.

The game still wasn't over though and Cologne came back at us to lock the game up at 3–3 when, in the final few minutes, Yasuhiko Okudera, the only Japanese footballer playing in Europe, tried a speculative shot that dipped under Shilts' body. Shilts was such a perfectionist that he was beside himself at conceding a goal so late on . . . a goal that led to inevitable headlines the following day of 'Japanese sub sinks Forest.'

We were a bit flat after the game and with Hughie's death banging on in my head, I certainly wasn't at my best that night. But I distinctly remember going home and seeing the gaffer's post-match interview on television in which he spelt out very forcibly that we were more than capable of going to Germany and beating them on their own ground. I don't think the interviewer thought Clough was giving an honest appraisal of his thoughts but I could tell in the way he delivered his words that there was an inner belief in what he was saying. It came across to me that it was not just bravado – he and Peter genuinely thought we had the qualities in our side to turn the tie back in our favour and reach the final.

He took the same tack when we arrived in Cologne for the second leg and faced the press on the day before the game. Normally the gaffer and Pete used to build up the opposition before a game to lull them into thinking we were the underdogs but for some reason they adopted a different stance with this game and could not be more positive about us beating the Germans in their own back yard. I think it really appealed to them.

Not for the first time in their managerial careers, they upset the odds and we picked up a 1–0 win in Cologne thanks to Bomber's goal.

Cologne had looked comfortable at the start, playing on their nice flat, grassy pitch that was nothing like the quagmire they had experienced in Nottingham a fortnight earlier. They had plenty of the ball, as you would expect, but we dug in – as we had learned to do away from home in Europe – and grew in confidence ourselves. Then in the 65th minute the moment we had been waiting for came along. Birtles flicked on my corner at the near post and Bomber, who was a master goal poacher in situations like that, was perfectly positioned to stoop and conquer.

Predictably, it was like the Alamo after that as Cologne bombarded us in search of an equaliser but we had something to defend and with our back four and Shilts, we were not going to let it go. We also had midfield players and strikers who were willing to throw everything into the line of fire and get the result we wanted.

It was an amazing feeling but it didn't sink in straight away that this little boy from Uddingston was going to play in a European Cup final – just like Jimmy Johnstone had done for Celtic years before. We just wanted to celebrate but, as was often the case after those European games, we had a flight straight back to East Midlands Airport. A few of us couldn't wait to get into a nightclub in town and celebrate. I don't know what time it was when I went to bed . . . but it was a great night.

Before the final we had seven or eight games left to play in a matter of five weeks as we attempted to home in on consecutive league titles. We figured in so many matches around that time they were almost joined up!

But playing in a European Cup final was something special.

JOHN ROBERTSON – SUPER TRAMP

Some of the world's greatest players have never figured in one but there we were – little Nottingham Forest – in the final against even smaller Malmö. They were the Swedish champions and were managed by an Englishman in Bobby Houghton, who went on to have a spell as No. 2 at The City Ground to Dave Bassett in the late 1990s.

The gaffer and Pete went out to see them play a couple of weeks before the big day and their levels of kidology had to be at their finest when they came back to Nottingham. We discovered after the final that they had been anything but impressed by Malmö, whose journey to the final had been even more surprising than our own. The gaffer played everything low-key and actually took his family off for a holiday in Crete, which had been booked for some time – no doubt thinking that our season would have been well and truly over by that stage.

Most of the pre-match talk revolved around our injury problems to Frank Clark, Archie Gemmill and Martin O'Neill, who were all, understandably, desperate to play. The gaffer joined up with us in Germany and when he asked the three lads if they were fit, all three naturally said, 'Yes.' But he wasn't prepared to take risks. Frank got the nod at left-back but he left the other two on the bench and their disappointment was plain for all to see. I could have cried for them myself because I knew that chances like that didn't come along very often – if at all. They were my mates and they were distraught and I couldn't describe how I felt for them.

Their misfortune guaranteed that Trevor Francis, about whom I'll write much more later, would parade his £1m skills for us in Europe for the first time – he had been cup-tied until the final – but he and the rest of us struggled to raise the levels of what was a poor game. Malmö had been quite badly hit by injuries themselves and were content to sit back and soak up what pressure we could exert which, on the night, wasn't very much. They just got people behind the ball and I'm not knocking them for that because 12 months later we did exactly the same to Hamburg.

Let's be honest, the Malmö game was a totally drab affair but in injury time at the end of the first half we produced the match-winning moment. I picked up a pass from Bomber wide on the left and managed to do a little bit on the ball to create space for a cross to the far post. I could see from where I was standing that it was going to cause problems and Trevor came hurtling in at pace to plant a lunging header into the net.

What joy that created not just for us players but the 20,000 Forest fans in the stadium and many more thousands watching on television back home in Nottingham. It should have been happiness all the way but afterwards I got a bit upset with the opinionated words of Barry Davies, who was commentating on the match for the BBC. After the goal had gone in, he bellowed out, 'That's what I wanted to see Robertson do,' and when I watched the recording of the match later I couldn't help but think what right has he got to say what he expected of me?

What he failed to realise is that sometimes the opposition don't allow you to do what you want to do and that was the case that night in Munich. As much as I would have liked to turn on a brilliant display and for us to win in style, football doesn't work out that way and an experienced broadcaster like Davies should have seen enough games to know that. Malmö had a little guy called Robert Pritz, who played on the right side of their midfield and he doubled up on me with the full-back throughout the game. He went on to have a great career with Glasgow Rangers but that night his only intention for 90 minutes was to stop me.

The goal came about because I got a pass quickly from Bomber. It was a great ball, although initially I struggled to keep it in play, but once I had done that I knew this was my chance. I was left with the full-back to beat and decided it was an opportunity for a foot race. As I went to go past him my right arm came out instinctively and held him off and I managed to get the cross over. That was just the start of it though because Trevor had to make up an awful lot of ground and it was a great header because he had to throw himself at it.

The goal didn't raise the standards of the game and the second half wasn't much better than the first but I should have scored to make sure the trophy was heading back to Nottingham. Trevor did well with his pace to get to the by-line and cut the ball back. The goal was opening up ahead of me and as one of their defenders came out to try and get in a block I managed to make good contact and round him but looked on in anguish as the ball hit the foot of the post and bounced out. I think you would have to say that I should have scored and had I done so we might well have relaxed and gone on to win more comfortably. But in all honesty Malmö didn't have too much to offer as an attacking threat and we were quite comfortable with our 1–0 lead.

No, it was never going to go down as a great final but did we care? Did we hell. We felt we had had our final when we knocked out Liverpool in the first round because that was a wonderful achievement at that time. And then we went on to eliminate Cologne, the team who had replaced Liverpool as favourites.

After the Munich final we stayed the night in the city and met up with Herman Hoppe, who was a road manager for Deep Purple. He organised for us to go to a disco called Sugar Shake in the German city. We used to call him 'Ozzie' and he was pally with Graeme Souness. He was introduced to us and we kept in touch for a while and he arranged for us to go to concerts by David Coverdale and Whitesnake. Ian Paice, the Deep Purple drummer, was a Nottingham lad and we also met up with him from time to time.

It was a top night in Sugar Shake even though I can't remember too much about it now. What I do recall was sitting in a beer garden in Munich at seven o'clock the following morning. It sounds a long time but when you think of what time we got back to the hotel after the game, we weren't really going out until the early hours of the morning.

The one big regret I have of the final was not looking after my mum and dad, who had come out to see the game with the official Forest party. They came to the final less than two months after they had lost their son in tragic circumstances and I should have been with them after the game. I didn't pay as much attention to them afterwards but they should have had my time that night. My dad, in particular, was still suffering quite badly at the loss of Hughie and I should have been there for them, by their side. Instead I was celebrating with the other lads and I don't feel very proud of myself for that. It's something that has bugged me down the years but when you do things in life you have to live with them and it's one of those times that I would like to have relived because I would certainly have done things differently.

7
Magical Madrid

WHEN WE PROUDLY STOOD ON the balcony of the Council House in Nottingham's Old Market Square you sensed how much our European Cup final win meant to so many people. They estimated that more than 200,000 fans crammed into the city centre when we attended a civic reception and paraded the trophy in Nottingham. Until then the city had been synonymous with Robin Hood but it was almost a case of move over Robin Hood, Brian Clough has arrived – he had that much influence on the city and the people.

It's a great feeling, being in that situation and knowing that you had helped to put a smile on so many faces. When you set off to try and make a name for yourself in football, it's moments like that you want to experience. Having thousands of people cheering your name is something very special, I can tell you.

The enormity of the achievement is perhaps gauged by the clubs that had won the trophy before us. They read like a 'Who's Who' of football. Real Madrid, of course, but there was Benfica, AC Milan and their great city rivals Inter, Ajax, Bayern Munich, our own Manchester United and Liverpool – and who could forget Celtic's marvellous success in Lisbon in 1967? No city the size of Nottingham and its 300,000 population had ever won the greatest prize in European football and it was something of which we were unbelievably proud.

It annoys me these days to hear some pundits claim that the Champions League, as it is now, is much harder to win than the European Cup in the days that we won it. I just don't understand the argument. Nowadays you can finish 20 or more points behind the domestic champions and still stand a chance of lifting the European prize. In our day you couldn't get into the competition unless you were champions. Now you see Manchester United, Arsenal and Chelsea in it every year with the likes of Liverpool, Tottenham and Manchester City also competing for a place. I know, because in the interests of making as much money as possible, teams nowadays have to go through qualifying and group stages, there are more games to be played but it was all cut and thrust in our day.

In my opinion the name Champions League is so misleading because you can get a club finishing fourth in, say, England, Italy or Spain going on to win the trophy. It's not about champions any more and I do think there is now a lot more familiarity and less romance attached to it. How many times have Real Madrid played Lyon in recent years or Bayern Munich met Inter Milan? I do feel a certain mystique has gone out of the competition. But back then European football was a magical experience. We had had a taste of it and we wanted more.

We had finished as runners-up to Liverpool in the First Division championship of 1978–79 but qualified for the European Cup as holders – and we couldn't wait to defend the handsome trophy we had captured in Munich. Unlike the previous year when we knew all there was to know about our first round opponents Liverpool, the Swedish side Östers Växjö were, with due respect to them, not a household name in football. When we first heard the draw we didn't even know which country they represented.

We battered them in the first leg at The City Ground but with an hour gone and the scoreline still goalless, it was beginning to look as if it might be one of those nights. But Ian Bowyer fired in a cross from Tony Woodcock and then Bomber got a second by way of a deflection to give us the 2–0 lead that we were always happy to take away and defend.

The second leg was far from easy, though, as Östers put absolutely everything into a performance that brought them a goal that cut our lead in half and created some anxious moments. My memory tells me that I had a night to forget but Tony Woodcock came up with a header from Gary Mills' cross and in the end we went through with a degree of comfort.

The second round took us to Dracula country in Rumania to

face another side we knew precious little about in Arges Pitesti. Tony certainly knew more about one of their defenders who kicked him all over The City Ground in the first leg and eventually paid for his troubles by being sent off. By that time Tony and Garry Birtles had given us a two-goal lead and although we might have been expected to go on and win more convincingly against ten men, we were once again happy with the lead we had before the second leg.

I'd never previously been to Rumania – and haven't been since – but my abiding memory of the trip was arriving at the airport and travelling along a long road to our hotel. It was lined by row after row of chimneys and the entire landscape looked like one big chemical plant. I always remember the locals looking so depressed and downtrodden and I genuinely felt so sorry for them. I asked myself, 'How can people live in this kind of environment?' The food we had was probably the worst I've ever had anywhere in the world and I've thought many times since that anyone who feels they are having a bad time of it should go and take a fortnight's holiday in Pitesti and they might be much happier with their lot.

We played the game in the afternoon in front of a huge crowd and the atmosphere was very hostile. They were obviously up for dumping the European champions on their backsides but we started like we had done in the first leg and after Bomber scored his third goal of the campaign to put us ahead, Birtles slid in the second after good work by Woodcock. They got a goal back from a penalty that followed one of the most innocuous challenges Kenny Burns has ever made but on an afternoon when the Rumanians put themselves about, we were just thankful to head home with no serious injuries.

By the time the third round came around in March we had lost Tony, who was sadly sold to Cologne, and perhaps we could have done with his sharpness and goalscoring ability when we took on Dynamo Berlin. The East Germans were an emerging force in Europe at the time and showed their resilience in the first leg in Nottingham when they absorbed everything we had to offer. And when we did look like scoring they had a giant 6 ft 7 in. goalkeeper called Bodo Rudwaleit, who made some important saves. His work was put into perspective when Berlin broke away after the hour mark to score the winner on the night through Hans-Jürgen

Riediger, who had the ability to match his growing reputation.

The second leg was played just four days after we had lost the League Cup final to Wolves at Wembley and with a couple of league defeats around that period, we were not having the best of times. We were conscious of the fact that if we didn't defy the odds and beat Berlin our season might be over in terms of winning trophies, so there was a lot riding on the game.

Although we obviously stayed in the city, it was the days before the Berlin Wall came down so the east part of the city had nothing like the comforts of the west. What I remember more than anything else about the trip was how unbelievably cold it was. It's probably the coldest I have ever been in my life. When we went out to warm up before the game all their players came out in tights and I'm sure if we had brought some with us we would have risked any questions about our masculinity by wearing them. But the temperature was so freezing that we had to do something and somebody came up with the idea of wearing two strips, one on top of the other, to give us some protection.

It was a game that we were not expected to win but the gaffer again rammed out a positive message, telling us that as well as Berlin had done he had seen nothing in terms of pure skill to frighten us in the first leg. He knew there was pressure on us to get a goal after losing the first leg and I think he made Trevor, in particular, aware of that because he had not had the best of games in the League Cup final.

Trevor's response was magnificent. Although he had scored the winner in the Munich final, he had probably his finest hour in a Forest shirt that night. He was amazing and if there had been any doubts about his £1m price tag, he certainly answered his critics in what was a superb individual display. The East Germans couldn't get near him but, more importantly, he came up with two goals in the first half that turned the tie on its head. Then before half-time Frank Gray went on a great run that led to me being brought down and I knocked in the penalty to make our comeback complete.

Berlin did pull a goal back early in the second half after I had conceded a penalty – not sure what I was doing back there – but I will go to my grave knowing that I didn't touch the boy. I saw replays of the incident on television and it looked as though there might have been contact but I swear there wasn't. But that was where their hope started and finished and we eased through.

We were thrilled but we couldn't wait to get back on the plane and into a bit of warmth.

The games did not come any easier and in the semi-final we were paired with one of the real powers of European football – Ajax. The Dutch masters were in the era after the great Johan Cruyff and Co. but they still had so many top-class players like Soren Lerby, Frank Arnesen and Rudi Krol, who was a highly influential player not only for Ajax but in the Dutch national side. Ajax had put their name in European folklore, there was magic in the name and we knew we would have to be at our very best to go through.

But Trevor, having shown Dynamo Berlin what he was all about, put on a show for our fans when we met Ajax in the first leg at home. He put us ahead after I landed a corner at the near post, where Larry Lloyd and Garry Birtles had made a nuisance of themselves. The ball eventually dropped for Trevor to drive the ball home. Then a superb piece of skill by Trevor led to them conceding a penalty from a handball offence and when I managed to send their keeper Pete Schrijvers the wrong way, we were back to the old 2–0 scoreline that we used as a yardstick for defending away from home. But just as Trevor had shown, once again Peter Shilton revealed his world-class talents by keeping out an effort by Lerby that prevented us taking just a slender lead to Amsterdam a fortnight on.

In between the two games, we took off for the Persian Gulf to play a couple of matches and although the wisdom of the trip was questioned at such a crucial time, the gaffer and Pete had all the answers. When we got back, our league match against Arsenal was postponed because they were in an FA Cup semi-final so the trip to the Middle East not only gave us the chance to get a bit of sun on our backs, it also provided us with a bit of match practice.

Such was the clamour to see the second leg that it was switched to the Olympic Stadium, which had a 65,000 capacity, and the atmosphere that the Dutch generated that night rivalled anything we had experienced on our European travels.

In the build-up to the game we heard that Ajax had suffered only one defeat at home in forty-six European ties but we didn't need to be fed that statistic to know how difficult it was going to be.

Krol was magnificent as he prompted, cajoled and urged Ajax forward and we needed all the resolve we had shown the previous season at Anfield to withstand the onslaught that built up in front of us. But while Krol was their inspiration, it was a game in which Kenny Burns showed once more what a brilliant player he had become. He was masterful in the air and on the deck, breaking down wave after wave of Ajax attacks. Shilts also made a couple of top-drawer saves but there was nothing he could do about the headed goal by Lerby that gave Ajax the belief that they could loosen our grip on the tie. But with Burnsy in one of those 'thou shalt not pass' moods we held on to go through on a 2–1 aggregate.

Remarkably, it was the first time in that era that we had lost away in Europe but that meant nothing against the fact that we were in the final for the second successive year. Our opponents were a much-fancied Hamburg side but we didn't have time to think about them because we had problems of our own to consider.

The biggest revolved around Trevor, who had snapped his Achilles tendon in a match against Crystal Palace at The City Ground. He was on fire at the time, had scored two goals in the Palace match that we won 4–0 but the sight of him limping out of the game was the worst one imaginable for us. With Tony Woodcock having left in mid-season, we were going to be stretched to the limits, particularly when it came to attacking options. We had problems elsewhere and Larry Lloyd was a big doubt after spraining his ankle playing his first match for England in eight years against Wales at Wrexham.

On top of the injury problems Stan Bowles, who had joined us from Queens Park Rangers, walked out on the squad just before we went off to Majorca to relax and prepare for the final. Stan was a fabulous character and he and the gaffer had a bit of a love–hate relationship going. But although he had shown the skills that made him such a huge favourite at Loftus Road, Stan wasn't always certain of his place in our side – and he didn't like that. He didn't like flying either but I don't think that was the reason he failed to turn up at the airport before our trip to Majorca. The irony was that had he come along with the rest of the lads, we were getting so short of numbers he would have been virtually certain of a place in what would have been the most important game of his career. But Stan had made his stance and once he had failed to turn up, there was no way in this world that the gaffer would pick him for any game – let alone the European Cup final.

So off we went to Majorca for what turned out to be nothing more than a holiday. I don't think we even trained throughout the trip. That wasn't good enough for Shilts, who was so wrapped up in his job that his autobiography was named *The Magnificent Obsession*. There was no way in this world that he was going to go without training and he found a bit of grass on a nearby roundabout in Cala Millor to go through his routines . . . ever the perfectionist.

There were no curfews and the gaffer's only request was to report at 11 a.m. every day to make sure we were not over-indulging. I've got to own up to the fact that I didn't stick to that particular instruction. The day we were due to come home Scotland were playing England at Hampden Park and Frank Gray and I, being particularly keen to see us put one over the auld enemy, found a bar where we could watch the match on television. We were sitting in the Manchester Arms, having a bit of lunch and maybe a cup of tea – well, that was the plan. The barman asked us if we wanted a liqueur and to start with I just said, 'No thanks – we're going home today.' But the barman was very persuasive and kept on going on and on so in an effort to shut him up I said, 'Go on then, just the one.'

I looked up at the array of different drinks on the shelf and saw this bottle of Tia Maria, which I had never tried before.

'I'll have a Tia Maria,' and Frank had something else. I sipped away at this Tia Maria and thought it was very nice so I had another, and another and another. They just kept on coming.

By the time we left to pick up our bags at the hotel I was pretty well gone and in that state I didn't usually do the most intelligent of things. On the way back there was an off-licence and I couldn't resist going in and coming out with a bottle of Tia Maria wrapped in a brown paper bag. We got our bags and got on the bus, which was not a full-size coach but a medium to large minibus and we were crammed in a little bit.

The gaffer was sitting at the front and, unfortunately for me, my tongue had become loosened by the booze I had consumed in the bar. The conversation got round to England and I think Garry Birtles got talking about them going to the European Championships in Italy and possibly winning it. My mouth was well and truly open for business by this stage and not in a very quiet voice I piped up, 'Win it, you won't even get to the semi-final.' Once I said that the gaffer was all ears and asked what I had said. Unwisely, I repeated it and he instantly came back with, 'You don't want to put any money on that do you?' I was very surprised by this stage that my loudness had not got me a bollocking but he kept going along with me and suggested we had a £100 bet. I thought I had seen a bit of sense and backed off but Kenny Burns and Frank Gray were up for it at that stage and whispered, 'Take it – we'll go three ways with you.'

We won the bet but we didn't get paid for about six months!

I was still very much under the influence when we got to Palma Airport. Things were a lot more relaxed in those days and as we were going through Customs I put the bottle of Tia Maria, which was still in its wrapper, on the ground at which point a load of change spilled out of my top pocket. Coin by coin I picked them all up and put them back in the pocket only to see them all spill out again when I went to pick up the Tia Maria. Much to the amusement of the other lads this happened two or three times and I was staggered that the gaffer let me get off scot-free. Deep down I think he knew exactly what state I was in but he had clearly decided that he wanted us all to be as relaxed as possible and he didn't want to do anything to upset the mood among the players.

We came back from Majorca and I had a testimonial 'do' in Nottingham the following day.

Within another 24 hours we were back on a plane heading for Madrid and our hotel 20 miles outside of the Spanish capital. We hardly did any training but I suppose Pete and the gaffer were concerned about us picking up any more injuries that we just couldn't afford. It was almost a case of anyone who was fit would figure and there were certainly one or two of the players carrying knocks that would probably have kept them out of a normal league game. Shilts and Frank Gray were two of the bigger doubts.

On the day before the game we had a team talk in which Pete outlined plans that we would concentrate our attacks down the left, my side, because he and the gaffer felt that Hamburg's right-back Manny Kaltz, while brilliant at going forward, had defensive weaknesses. We were going 4-4-2 with young Gary Mills going up front alongside Garry Birtles. But all that went out of the window around teatime. They had a change of heart and decided they would bring Millsy back into midfield and go 4-5-1 and try and deny Hamburg space in midfield.

Millsy was named in the side and so too was Lloydy after he had passed his rather unusual fitness test. The gaffer deliberately stood on his ankle the day before to see what pain he was under. He had been left behind in Nottingham when we went off to Majorca in order to try and get fit. Knowing Lloydy, missing out on the trip to Majorca would have hurt him so there was no way he was going to miss the final.

One way or another our preparations for such an important game had been far from ideal. We hadn't practised anything on the training ground, we had hardly done any work at all in the build-up to the game but here we were with a patched-up side being thrown out against one of the best teams in Europe and told to play in a way that was foreign to us. But it just shows that the game is all about players and not necessarily tactics boards and dossiers. The gaffer and Pete obviously had faith in us being able to adapt to the system and go out and do a job. And Burnsy set the tone for what was ahead of us when we left the dressing-room. He said, 'Don't worry, gaffer – we know what we have to do.'

We knew we were up against a very talented set of players. They had Wolfgang Magath, Kevin Keegan, Kaltz and many others. They also had a big boy who started the match on the bench called Horst Hrubesch who was nicknamed 'The Heading Monster'.

We found it very difficult at the start to get a foothold in the game because they were very good in possession but we were disciplined, very disciplined. We tagged runners all over the place. Burnsy and Lloydy were superb, Birtles ran until he could hardly walk, Martin O'Neill was great and we extracted every bit of energy we could out of ourselves for 90 minutes. And, of course, we got the goal after 20 minutes that Hamburg, try as they did, could not cancel out.

To be brutally honest I might have got the goal but it was about the only kick I had in the game. I used to be at my best when I had plenty of possession and wanted the ball all night long but we seemed to spend the night chasing Hamburg shadows – even though it was to such great effect.

But after the goal one little incident sticks in my mind to this day and it's odd how you get inspiration from seemingly minor incidents. I can remember Lloydy being in a half right-back position and flicking the ball over one of their players with his right foot, which was not his strongest, and coming out the other side and striding confidently away with it. I remember thinking, 'Not bad, Lloydy, we've got a chance here.'

I'm not pretending it was anything but difficult to hold out but we did even though we lost Frank Gray, who was struggling with a hamstring. His departure gave Bryn Gunn the opportunity to play in a European Cup final and there's a lovely little story that Bryn happily tells against himself. When it was clear that Frank had to come off, our substitutes were nervously warming up on the touchline and Pete anxiously inquired, 'Who have we got to go on? Who've we got?' Somebody said, 'Gunny is getting ready,' and Pete's immediate response was, 'Christ, we're really in the shit now.' To be fair Bryn has told that story himself a million times but the fact of the matter is that he went on in a European Cup final and helped us keep a clean sheet.

Another tale from the final involved John O'Hare, who went on earlier for Millsy with instructions to try and 'calm it down'. His first touch was a mistimed tackle and a booking but Solly also played his part – as he always did.

It was a big game for Keegan, playing against another English side, and the press tried to make out that he had been intimidated in some way. I think Lloydy, who had played at Liverpool with Kevin, might have had a quiet word with him in the tunnel to the effect that, 'You might be a pal but you're in for a rough ride tonight.' I wasn't aware that Burnsy said anything but he might have looked at him in, shall we say, a less than convivial manner. But Keegan got more and more frustrated as the match wore on and ended up going deep into his own half to try and ignite something from his team-mates. We were delighted to see him going backwards because he could not do us much damage playing deep. I think Kevin, who was clearly very upset, was critical of our negative tactics but I'm sure in the fullness of time he will have realised that we had no option but to play that way.

It was a case of needs must and I was a bit disappointed to hear comments that Jack Charlton had made during the game. Evidently, he said I had played too deep and should have been attacking Kaltz more often. I would love to have been in that position but Jack failed to realise that we didn't have the ball for much of the night. We couldn't build up play and get the ball to me and in reality part of my job was to stop Kaltz getting forward and doing the damage that we knew he was capable of inflicting. I thought Jack, being such an experienced football figure, might have been more understanding of the situation and what was required of us in those circumstances.

At the end of the game we were so blitzed from a physical point of view that we could hardly raise our arms in salute and I think several of our lads just dropped to the ground out of sheer exhaustion and relief that it was all over.

But we soon came round and our thoughts turned to how we would celebrate that night. Our wives were waiting for us in Madrid city centre, we had no other game to play that season but the gaffer and Pete decided that we would all be going back to the hotel, which was, as I say, some 20 miles up into the hills.

We were not very happy to say the least. Lloydy was our spokesman and he asked the gaffer in the dressing-room and again on the bus if we could go and see our wives but the response he got was, 'We came as a team and we go back as a team.'

That's when I muttered, 'That's ridiculous.'

Clough told me to shut up but I didn't. I said, 'It's still ridiculous,' and he told me to shut it again. Then he added, 'You were on the outside looking in all night so be quiet.'

I was getting a bit wound up by this stage, getting a bit braver and said, 'That might be so but I made the goal last year and I've scored the winner this time.'

At that point he boomed out, 'If you say another word I'll knock your fucking head off.' And at that point I didn't reply!

So it was a very quiet bus ride to the hotel and when we got back I seem to remember there being a cake in this room where we congregated for a bit of a reception. Some bleeding celebration . . . thanks a lot!

But there were a few of us who were determined we were going back to Madrid to have a few drinks and see our wives. Fortunately for us, the son of the hotel owner was on his way back into Madrid city centre but the only trouble was he had a little Seat with me,

Lloydy, Burnsy, Martin, Frank and Viv all wanting to get in. Don't ask me how we did it but we all somehow squeezed into the car and if we had been stopped by the police we would probably have spent the rest of the night behind bars – and not the kind we had in mind.

When we got to the wives' hotel unfortunately my wife Sally wasn't too well and she just wanted to go to bed and try and get some sleep. So the rest of us piled into the room of Sue Lloyd, Larry's wife at the time, ordered some champagne on the club and passed a few happy hours.

We had to get back to our hotel at some stage because all our gear was there and we were flying back early that morning. We also knew that Pete was an early riser and didn't want to run the risk of him catching us out. I think we got taxis back and turned up at about seven o'clock as the cleaners were vacuuming and dusting. We went to the bar and asked if there was any chance of a drink. There was a game of Connect Four in the hotel which we had been playing before the game so we got that out and pretended we had been playing all night. Sure enough Pete came down, saw what we were doing and said, 'I can't believe you lot have been up all bloody night playing that game.'

Neither Pete nor the gaffer revealed that they knew what we had really been up to but they were masters at digging out information and it would have surprised me greatly if by the time we got on the flight home they weren't aware of what had happened.

I could have got into more trouble at the airport with the press but, fortunately for me, the gaffer was supportive. The reporters wanted to speak to me because I'd scored the goal and I had a bit of a pop at people not giving us the full credit we deserved as players. We were all aware of the genius of Clough and the contribution of Taylor but behind them there were some very good players who didn't always get the recognition we deserved. In some of the newspapers the following day it was turned round as if I had had a go at the gaffer and Pete and I think one headline read, 'J.R. fires the bullets', indicating I was having a go at our management. But, fortunately for me, the gaffer was at the press conference with me and heard every word I said.

I was never that keen to get too involved with journalists because their job was to dig out the nasty stories and they were not always true. I preferred to keep a low profile and, to use a well-worn cliché, do my talking on the pitch, but I also realised that reporters had to get stories.

But as far as I was concerned, the real story was that we had won the European Cup for the second successive year – and it made pretty good reading to me.

8

Staying at the top

WE WERE IN NO MOOD to let ourselves become one season wonders when we approached the 1978–79 season. Returning for pre-season training as First Division Champions and League Cup winners meant there was an immense self-belief among the players and, as that was a quality never lacking in our management team, we felt there was no reason why our success should not continue.

We spent our pre-season in Yugoslavia, Greece – where we drew 1–1 with an AEK Athens team that we were to meet in the European Cup – and Spain, where we took part in a four-team tournament. We had six matches on foreign soil and didn't win any of them but we did have an emphatic victory over Bobby Robson's Ipswich Town in the Charity Shield curtain raiser at Wembley.

On the way to the title the previous season we had beaten Ipswich 4–0 at home and 2–0 at Portman Road and although they had some very good players, we felt we had the measure of them. Despite our indifferent form in other build-up games we paralysed Ipswich 5–0 on a day when the scoreline could have been even more convincing. They were stacked with international players but it was one of those days when we couldn't do anything wrong and did a lot right.

Martin O'Neill enjoyed himself by scoring a couple of the goals but got the 'hook' – he was pulled off before the end. I think the gaffer joked that he was bringing him off to stop him scoring a hat-trick. Why he did that I'll never know but if it had happened to me I would have been less than happy. Peter Withe and Larry Lloyd also scored and I got the fifth after cutting inside and hitting a shot really sweetly past Paul Cooper.

After that we went out to Vigo to take part in the four-team tournament. Our second match was against Porto on the Wednesday before we opened the season with a home match against Tottenham, who had just signed Argentinian World Cup stars Ossie Ardiles and Ricky Villa. We lost 1–0 to Porto but it wasn't ideal preparation to be playing abroad three days before such a big opening game, particularly as we wanted to try and make a statement as defending champions. We didn't go home to our families after returning from Spain and stayed in a hotel at Burton-on-Trent before reporting at The City Ground for the Spurs game. In all honesty Spurs, who had just been promoted, were the better team on the day and we were quite happy to come away with a 1–1 draw.

The signing of the Argentinians meant there was a lot of focus on them and the arrival of Ardiles and Villa signalled the start of what has been an ever-increasing supply line of foreign talent coming to Britain over the last three decades. I've no qualms about the very best players coming to play in our game and the two boys from Argentina, particularly Ardiles, who had just played a massive part in their World Cup success, were very much in that category. I think the British public wants to see world-class players coming into our game but, over the years, it has inevitably led to a lot less talented foreigners getting a chance to come to England and Scotland and make it increasingly difficult for home-grown footballers. But EC rules make it very much open season nowadays and it is something we just have to accept.

That game against Spurs turned out to be the last that Peter Withe played for us before being surprisingly sold to Newcastle United for £200,000. Googie was having a bit of a dispute about a new contract. The gaffer dug in, Googie did the same and when Newcastle came in with what was a big offer, he was on his bike up the A1.

I was really sorry to see him go. He had been great for me to play with and whenever I had the ball I knew that Googie or Tony Woodcock would always make my job easier. He was a great leader of the line, scored goals, wouldn't shirk anything and, to be honest, I thought we were making a mistake in letting him go. In fact, he is the one example I can think of regarding a player who the gaffer and Pete let go and who went on to have a more successful time elsewhere. He didn't get it at Newcastle but after a couple of seasons in the North-East he was transferred to Aston Villa for £500,000 and went on to play a big part in them winning the European Cup in 1982. In fact, it was his goal that gave Villa their 1–0 victory when they defeated German side Bayern Munich in the Rotterdam final.

I'm sure he would have carried on scoring goals and helping us to more success but the gaffer wasn't one for changing his mind and although I believe Googie said he was willing to back down at the eleventh hour, it was all too late.

We were finding it tough to score goals without him and it got tougher in the early weeks of the season as we lacked the cutting edge of the previous 12 months. In fact, we drew our first four games with three goalless matches against Coventry, Queens Park Rangers and West Brom following the match against Spurs.

During that time a young striker called Stephen Elliott, who was a smashing lad from the North-East, was given the opportunity of filling Googie's place in the side but try as he did nothing came off for him. He was such a genuine kid that you really wanted it to work out for him but he just couldn't get that bit of luck we all need from time to time. Had he got a break when he needed it most in his career he could easily have flourished, being surrounded by top-class players. It might have been all so different for him had he managed to get a goal in his first game against Coventry when a shot looked destined for the net but came back off the post. That was typical of how his fortunes went and eventually the gaffer and Pete pulled him out of the side. He was later transferred to Preston, where he had a productive career, scoring 70 goals in 208 league appearances.

When he was taken out of the firing line it presented Garry Birtles with the chance to make a name for himself. It was a chance that he took with amazing success. I think Forest supporters viewed Birtles' call-up as a stab in the dark to find a replacement for Withe. He didn't score on his debut against Arsenal at The City Ground – I got the first from a penalty and Ian Bowyer added a second as we ran out 2–1 winners – but Birtles more than played his part in the win and it was easy to see the quality and unbelievable work rate that were to become trademarks of his game for years to come.

For a time in the game it looked as though Arsenal would give us a lot of problems. Liam Brady, who was always a top player in my eyes, was tormenting the life out of us for a spell. So much so that I shouted across to Frank Clark, who was our left-back, to go and kick him and knock him out of his stride.

I'm not sure what response I got from Frank but Liam looked at me out of the corner of his eye and said, 'Hey, you. I'm not going around telling our lot to kick hell out of you – or would you like me to?'

I thought about it for a split second and said, 'You're right – I'm sorry. I'll keep my mouth shut.'

In some ways I felt a bit embarrassed about it because I always thought of Liam as being one of the game's shining lights. He had a wonderful left foot and as well as having the ability to spray passes all around the ground he also had the close control and trickery to go and take defenders on and, more often than not, go past them. Here was me telling one of our players to go and kick a world-class player up in the air. It was something I wasn't very proud of but at least I apologised and Liam thankfully didn't encourage anyone to put me in row Z.

Having got our first win of the season we started putting more wins than draws on the board as our unbeaten run, stretching back to the Championship-winning campaign, just kept on getting longer and longer. When people discuss the achievements we had at Forest, it's inevitable that the subject goes straight to our two European Cup successes, the First Division title and our League Cup triumphs. But in my eyes there is something we can look back on with equal satisfaction – and that is our 42-match unbeaten run in the First Division. It overlapped two seasons – 1977–78 and 1978–79 – and it's always been a sense of great pride to me on a personal level. I played in every one of those games – Peter Shilton was the only other player to do that – and to this day I get a kick out of having been a part of that record. To go 42 games unbeaten, home and away in the toughest league in the world, was an incredible achievement and the enormity of it should not be underestimated.

Brian Clough always regarded the league as being his bread and butter. It was what he insisted we took care of before anything else and I think he was spot on. It is something I have always believed in myself during my days assisting Martin O'Neill. The league is what you are judged on over an extended period but if you are lucky enough to get favourable draws in cup competitions you can win trophies in six games.

The unbeaten record was previously held by Leeds, who went 34 games unbeaten, so that gives another insight into what it all meant. So much so that when it was broken by Arsenal in 2004 I felt like something had been taken away from us. Arsenal's Premier League record of 49 games unbeaten under Arsène Wenger was highly acclaimed, and understandably so. They were given the tag of 'The Invincibles' and it's an identity that has stuck to this day.

I know there is a great deal more media exposure these days but I still don't think our class of 1978 and 1979 got the credit they deserved. Another thing that rankles with me is that nowadays it is almost as if football before the Premier League didn't count! We are always hit these days with statistics 'Since the Premier League began' and I think that is a bit of an insult to the great teams like Liverpool, Leeds and ourselves from yesteryear. After all, it's only the title of the league that has changed – not the quality of it.

In fact, during the period we achieved the 42-match unbeaten run we played no fewer than 76 matches in league, cups and friendlies. That is a staggering number of matches and for the most part the group of players who figured in all those games was no more than 15 or 16. These were the days before resting and rotation . . . believe me.

Our run eventually came to an end against Liverpool at Anfield on 9 December 1978 when Terry McDermott scored both goals in a 2–0 win. We were certainly not pleased about it but we took some consolation from the fact that it took a side of Liverpool's pedigree to beat us. There were no complaints from us. We were beaten fair and square by Liverpool and it was a big win for them because we had not lost to them in the six matches we had played since we won promotion – two in the league, two in the League Cup final and two in the first round of the European Cup.

Once again that season we had hopes of doing well in the FA Cup and after beating Aston Villa 2–0 in the third round and York City 3–1 in the snow at The City Ground, we reached the fifth round and a home tie with Arsenal.

Steve Walford, who worked with Martin O'Neill and me for

many years as a coach, played for Arsenal that night and we absolutely battered them on a mud-heap of a pitch. We just could not find a breakthrough and Pat Jennings, who was in their goal, was magnificent. He certainly kept them in it and Frank Stapleton came up with a late winner to send Arsenal through. After he had scored I had a last-ditch chance to get us an equaliser from a free-kick just outside the box. I hit it perfectly and I must admit was guilty of waiting for the net to ripple until the big hand of Jennings stretched out and touched the ball onto the post.

Jennings was a top-notch keeper and Martin, who played with him on many occasions for Northern Ireland, put him in the top-drawer category. I could understand why. But because I had seen at close quarters how consistently brilliant Peter Shilton was I always looked upon him as being the undisputed No. 1.

In February 1979 the gaffer and Pete, who were never far away from the next move in the transfer market, stunned football by paying £1m to sign Trevor Francis from Birmingham City. If you believed the publicity at the time, the gaffer insisted on paying just £999,999 to 'avoid Trevor getting big-headed by the deal'. I'm led to believe with taxes and things the fee went well beyond a cool £1m – but that's fairly irrelevant. They had signed one of the best strikers in the game, but I must admit I had mixed emotions about it at the time.

Trevor's arrival raised inevitable questions about who he would replace and most people looked in the direction of Tony Woodcock, who had been a fantastic player for us since he got into the side two years earlier. I'm not sure whether the seed of doubt actually got into Tony's brain or not but it's more than coincidence that the following season he was on his way to Germany for a new career with Cologne. Perhaps I wanted to be protective of the group that we had got together at The City Ground because we were such a tight unit. We won things with Peter Withe and Tony and I just wondered why there was a need to tinker with a team that had proved it could win trophies.

Don't get me wrong, there was no resentment of Trevor or anything like that, even though we knew he would probably arrive as our highest earner in a team in which all the players were basically on very similar money. The only exception was probably Peter Shilton but we didn't mind that because he was an established international player and proved himself one of the best goalkeepers in the world.

In some ways Trevor, who hadn't achieved anything at that time, still had to show that he possessed what was needed to rise to a higher level. We knew he was an outstanding individual who had made a huge impact at Birmingham, where he had made his debut as a 16-year-old. He once scored four goals in a match against Bolton when he was only a boy and he went on to emerge as one of the most exciting talents in the game.

The signing did bring a lot of publicity to 'unfashionable' Forest but the gaffer made sure Trevor's feet were kept on the ground. He played him in an A team match – that was the equivalent of our third team – against Notts County and he was certainly not given any special treatment.

As a player in his early days we never got to know Trevor very well because he lived further out than the rest of us – somewhere near Newark – and we didn't get to socialise very much.

On the pitch it wasn't long before he started to show what he had to offer. He made his debut at Ipswich and scored his first goal in the last minute of a home match against Bolton to earn us a valuable point when we looked like losing the match. Playing with him you couldn't fail to recognise his quality. Trevor was lightning quick but, unlike a lot of players who rely on speed, he also had great control and awareness. He had a keen football brain and could score goals out of nothing.

We only had Trevor for league games, of course, because he was cup tied and he couldn't play any part in us retaining the League Cup by beating Southampton 3–2 at Wembley in a real Jekyll and Hyde performance from us.

Our route to the final had not started very convincingly and we needed a replay to overcome Oldham before thrashing Oxford 5–0 at The Manor Ground. We had our most difficult hurdle to overcome when we met Everton in the fourth round at Goodison Park on a night when Kenny Burns limped through the match after suffering a cartilage injury. But we were inspired against a top-class Everton side and Burnsy soldiered on to help us to a 3–2 win. Viv Anderson scored a wonderful goal that night with a spectacular long-range effort. It was a big win for us because Everton had not lost to an English club until that point of the season. We went on to beat Brighton 3–1 in the quarters and then Watford by the same scoreline in the two-legged semi-final to book a date with Lawrie McMenemy's Southampton.

We were terrible in the first half at Wembley with England World Cup winner Alan Ball dictating much of the play as Southampton took the lead through David Peach. And they could easily have had more goals. But we were a different team after half-time and in addition to scoring twice Garry Birtles had two other 'goals' disallowed as we piled forward in wave after wave of attacks. Garry was sensational and at least one of the disallowed efforts, if not both, should have stood. He was denied his hat-trick but Tony Woodcock scored our third before Southampton got a late second through Nick Holmes.

Why were we so poor in the first half? We will never know whether it was a contributory factor but the night before the game the gaffer insisted that we all had a few drinks together in the hotel. I don't want to sound blasé but the gaffer never treated Wembley as anything special in terms of our preparations. He would never have us going down to London for two or three days beforehand and sitting around hotels waiting for the hours to pass.

We just landed on the day before the match and on the eve of the Southampton game we were staying at West Lodge Park and he got us all to report in the hotel lounge as soon as we arrived. He had got a load of drinks set out, champagne, wine and anything you fancied. He said, 'Come on lads, let's have a drink,' and although nobody enjoyed socialising more than me I was never that comfortable about boozing before a game, never mind a cup final. But it was his way of getting us in a relaxed state of mind and it was a ploy he used on other occasions.

It turned out to be a really nice evening because the boss and Pete regaled us with stories from their past, particularly their days at Hartlepool and their 'tussles' with the chairman Ernie Ord. When they were in that kind of mood they were a very funny pair and Morecambe and Wise in their heyday couldn't have had entertained us better.

At least a couple of the lads were, shall we say, a little bit worse for wear before the night was out but even amid the laughter one or two weren't happy, particularly Archie Gemmill, who was very keen on getting to his bed on the night before a game. But we didn't have a choice in staying up and we were all expected to have a drink. I had a couple of dry martinis and tonic but I certainly didn't have too much.

It might have been the drinking and merry-making that affected our first-half display but who will ever know if that was the reason? I don't think you can blame it entirely because as a team you can't just switch on the way we did at half-time on the day in question. In my eyes it was more about the fact that we knew we had not done ourselves justice in the first half and wanted to do something about it. We did go out in the second half with the words from the gaffer of, 'Right, you lot, don't go blaming this on last night.' But in the end we were superb and there was no blame attached to anything.

Because of our cup commitments and bad weather that saw a lot of games postponed, we ended up playing catch-up in the league that season . . . in more ways than one. Liverpool were determined to regain the title we had prised from their grasp and were front runners all the way, breaking the record for winning the league with most points. But we came with a late flourish that produced four wins and a draw in our last five games to take second place. Those five games were played over a period of seventeen days – great preparation for a European Cup final.

In some ways it was probably our best ever season because although we had to be satisfied with second place in the league to Liverpool, we won the European Cup and had also retained the League Cup.

At that time we could have been forgiven for thinking that our success would just run and run. During that summer, however, the gaffer made what he readily admitted was one of his biggest mistakes in football management by allowing Archie Gemmill to leave for Birmingham City. Archie had been livid about being left out of the European Cup final side when he said he was fit. That unsettled Archie a bit and although he and the gaffer were big friends in later years, there was a bit of friction between the two after the Munich final. Archie, who had known the gaffer longer than most of us because of his time with him at Derby, was a strong character in his own right and once he got something fixed in his brain, it wouldn't go away. It seemed like it was a battle of wills and something had to give and, unfortunately for us, Archie went down the road to St Andrew's. Archie had been a big player for us and, like Withe and Woodcock, I was very sorry to see him go. With another European Cup campaign around the corner I thought we would need all the quality and experience we could muster going forward and Archie had plenty of those characteristics.

The gaffer was made to regret his decision a lot sooner than he thought because he brought in Asa Hartford that summer – Frank Gray also joined us from Leeds United – in a move that backfired on him. I'm not sure why Asa's transfer to The City Ground from Manchester City didn't turn out to be successful but it was one of those instances when the gaffer felt he had made a mistake and didn't hang around to rectify it. Asa had been bought to take over from Archie but the fact of the matter was they were different types of players. I don't know whether or not the gaffer and Pete thought they were similar because they were of the same height and stature but that's where the likeness ended. Asa was a 'give and go' type of player, while Archie's game revolved around his ability to drive forward down channels. In time Asa might well have settled down and fitted into the side but he wasn't given that chance.

The season was only four matches old and we were on our way to a League Cup tie at Blackburn and had stopped off en route for a meal and afternoon sleep at Oldham. The gaffer and Pete pulled Asa and asked him how he felt things were going since his move and Asa said something like, 'I'm fine but it will probably take a bit of time.' They had clearly decided otherwise and said that Gordon Lee, who was manager of Everton at the time, was due in half an hour to speak to him about a move to Goodison Park. To say that Asa was taken aback by it all was a huge understatement but he was philosophical enough to realise that his days at The City Ground were over and he may as well look at the possibilities open to him.

Frank Gray was given the opportunity to show what he could do and was a regular in the side from the off. He slotted into the left-back spot that had been largely occupied by Frank Clark, until he retired, and Colin Barrett, until he had his career sadly cut short by injury.

Frank Gray will not mind me saying that he wasn't quite as good a player as his brother Eddie, who I had the utmost respect for, but he was a top-class player in his own right and made a big contribution in the time he was at The City Ground. He had a lovely left foot – his right was, quite literally, to help him stand up – and he had the experience of playing in the Leeds side that had lost to Bayern Munich in the 1975 European Cup final.

While I am on the subject I can't help but expand on my admiration for Eddie, who, in my opinion, would have been the nearest thing to the next George Best if he had been able to steer clear of injuries. He had a wonderful footballing brain, could go past people for fun, was quick and a great dribbler in tight situations.

Our league form at the beginning of that season was good but in the latter stages of 1979 we experienced the kind of results we were not used to. We were beaten at Norwich, Manchester City and Tottenham and then suffered a heavy 4–1 loss at Southampton and that wasn't like us. Three games later we suffered a defeat that came as a bit of a jolt to the system when we lost 1–0 at home to Brighton – a defeat that marked the end of an unbeaten home record in the league stretching back a remarkable fifty-seven matches. That was another staggering achievement to go on the CV but the Brighton defeat, inflicted by an early goal by Gerry Ryan, was difficult to take.

It wasn't the best of games for Tony Woodcock to bow out on as he looked forward to a new career in Germany. His departure was a sickener because with Woodcock, Birtles and Francis I felt we had a strike force that was as good as any around. It was hard for me to take that I would never get the ball again and look up to see him make one of those darting runs that were his trademark.

His transfer to Cologne was a bit of a surprise really because Tony had been brought up in Eastwood just outside of Nottingham and was one of those local lads made good figures. He was a very quiet, unassuming type and I thought he would be like a fish out of water in a new country. To be fair to him, within six months he had settled down so well he was speaking English with a German accent! He took to the foreign experience as if it was second nature and he went on to have a marvellous career with Cologne and then, of course, Arsenal on his return to English soil.

People have often asked me whether I ever fancied playing abroad and there was a time when I thought I might be faced with a decision to make. In 1981 I was sitting at home one night when I got a phone call from an agent called Dennis Roach, asking if I would be interested in a move to Spain. He wouldn't tell me which club it was but it turned out to be Real Madrid, who were also eyeing another English player at the time. We had played them in May 1981 in a friendly before they met Liverpool in the European Cup final and I had done quite well on the night. I played in a roving role in the game and the boy Camacho was marking me, but although we lost 2–0 I was pretty pleased with my performance in the Bernabéu. Nothing came of it but I found out afterwards that the other player, incidentally, was Tony Woodcock, who was making waves in Germany by that time.

Would I have fancied the idea? I'm not sure that I would have been really comfortable living abroad and I'm not sure the little lad from Uddingston would have settled into the Spanish way of life. In some ways the football would have suited me because it would have meant more time on the ball because in the midfield areas the continentals seem to let you have plenty of possession. You only have to look at the great career that Liam Brady had with Juventus to realise that it could have worked for me. I'm left thinking now that I will never know whether I would have been up to that particular challenge or not but I was happy with my lot, playing for the European champions and earning what was at the time a very good wage.

The personnel in our side was constantly changing and halfway through the 1979–80 season Charlie George joined us on loan from Southampton. He was a fantastic player with unbelievable flair. He had so much going for him – and who will ever forget the goal he scored against Liverpool to win the FA Cup for Arsenal in 1971? And what about the goal he scored for Derby against Real Madrid in the European Cup? I was delighted to have someone of his calibre coming to play with us because lining up alongside players of that ilk could only improve your own game.

By then Stan Bowles had joined us from Queens Park Rangers in a permanent deal and he was another who on his day could make the ball talk. Stan had a reputation as a 'Jack the lad' and there's no doubt he liked a drink, loved being with the women and, in the absence of any other wager, would bet on two flies crawling up the wall! But he was a character and deep down had a heart of gold.

117

I remember going out with my dad to celebrate a birthday on one of his visits to Nottingham and we bumped into Stan, who was out on the town enjoying himself. We lost him for a minute or two and he came back with a bottle of the best Moët & Chandon he could find and presented it to my dad as a birthday present. I thought it was a lovely gesture on Stan's part and, for all his reputation, it was the kind of thoughtfulness he had.

My dad didn't live any kind of champagne lifestyle but he was thrilled to bits that Stan had bought him the bottle and clung onto it for the remainder of the night. He took it back to Scotland with him and it had pride of place in the home. He didn't open it until the night I scored the winning goal in the 1980 European Cup final against Hamburg. He clearly wanted to save it for a big occasion and although he couldn't be in Madrid, it was great to think of him back home sipping that champagne from Stan.

That was a very poignant moment in my life because sadly, less than two months after the final, my dad died while I was away with Forest on a pre-season tour of Canada and America.

Stan was another player with tremendous individual skill and to have him and Charlie playing in the same side was certainly a recipe for entertainment. Charlie made his debut for us in a 2–1 win at Leeds and the game always sticks in my mind for the last 20 minutes. We kept the ball for fun and it was a privilege for me to be involved with them that day.

I think it was their arrivals at the club that got me into yet another debate with Lloydy. I referred to them both as being very skilful and when he asked what I meant by that I said, 'You know, clever with a ball, a good passer . . . that sort of thing.'

Lloyd's immediate retort was, 'Don't you think that I'm skilful then?'

I said, 'Well you head it and that,' and he came back with, 'Don't you think that heading is a skill then?'

Initially I said 'No' but I got to thinking about it and he was right. It's just that the definition of a skilful player to me was someone like Stan, Charlie, Rodney Marsh and Charlie Cooke. After the conversation had gone backwards and forwards several times I had to admit that footballing skill could manifest itself in so many ways. I had to accept that you had to be brave, technically good enough and have good timing to head a ball and that in its own way required talent. I think that was 1–0 to Lloydy . . . and we never got round to talking about tackling!

Charlie George, who was striving to overcome injuries at that time, only played four games for us but he stayed long enough to help us win the European Super Cup against Barcelona and scored the goal that gave us a 1–0 lead from the first leg at home. We drew 1–1 in the Nou Camp so Charlie at least left us with a permanent reminder of his days at The City Ground.

Stan could easily have done even better than that had he not walked out on us before the 1980 European Cup final. Stan wanted to be loved and I know he took it hard being left out of the European Cup semi-final second leg against Ajax after he had played in the first game at The City Ground. I think my testimonial match against Leicester before the final might have also played a part. The gaffer picked the team and left Stan out and he was disappointed about that because it was our final match before the game in Madrid.

The European Cup was our last remaining hope of a trophy that season because we had finished fifth in the league and lost to Wolves in the final of the League Cup, missing out on holding the trophy for three successive years.

We didn't perform against Wolves that day and it was a blow because it would have been a passport to Europe at a time when it looked as though we were not going to figure in the title race. The League Cup final was also four days before we headed off to Berlin to play in the European Cup quarter-final with a one-goal deficit from the first leg.

So there was huge disappointment losing to Wolves in a game that will always be remembered for the major cock-up involving Peter Shilton and David Needham that led to Andy Gray running the ball into an empty net. It was one of those things and, although you could count Shilts' mistakes on one hand, that had to go down as one of them because Needham was dealing with the long ball into our defence and Shilts could have stayed at home.

Losing to Wolves was all the more heart-breaking because, not for the first time, we had seen off the challenge of Liverpool in the semi-final. It was over two legs and boiled down to a normal time shoot-out between me and Ray Clemence from the penalty spot. We won the first leg at The City Ground 1–0 after I scored with a penalty two minutes from the end of a game in which Liverpool had acquitted themselves very well. I struck it to Clemence's right so that was the second penalty I had scored in the same direction – the first having been in the League Cup final replay win at Old Trafford – and when Martin O'Neill got brought down at Anfield in the second leg after about 20 minutes it became a real battle of wits between me and the Liverpool keeper. I just thought I would continue going the same way but I changed it and went to his left. Fortunately for me, I got a good contact on it because Clemence did guess right and got a good stretch across but it crept just inside the post. David Fairclough pulled one back near the end but we went through on a 2–1 aggregate and we had seen off Liverpool again.

They did knock us out of the FA Cup at the fourth round stage when they won 2–0 at The City Ground and later in the season they also beat us 2–0 at Anfield in the league. Their victory that night gave the Kop the last laugh for something I decided to do before the game. We had had a lot of joy against Liverpool with me having some good moments, particularly from the penalty spot. So when we strolled out to have a look at the pitch before the game I went up to the Kop end, pulled a tennis ball out of my pocket, placed it on the penalty spot and rolled it into an empty net. I got some fearful stick for that as chants of 'Fatty Robbo' rang out around Anfield but it was good, harmless fun and it was meant and taken in the best possible spirit.

But there is no doubt that the edge we held over Liverpool in that three-year period was very much key to our success. We knew that if we finished ahead of Liverpool or knocked them out of cup competitions there was a good chance we would win silverware . . . and it proved to be the case on several occasions.

9
The football genius

BRIAN CLOUGH COULD CALL ME all the names under the sun but none of his mischievous words got under my skin. To be perfectly frank most of what he said referred to my appearance, my weight, my eating habits and so forth. He slagged me off mercilessly at times but I knew it was mostly done with his tongue firmly in cheek. And more often than not his comments were followed by recognition of my football ability – and that's all that mattered to me.

One of his earlier pops at me was, 'Robbo didn't look like a professional athlete when I first clapped eyes on him. In fact, there were times when he didn't resemble a member of the human race.' He called me a tramp, he said I was scruffy, unfit and 'an uninterested waste of time'. But then he said things like, 'Give him a ball and a yard of grass and he was an artist . . . the Picasso of our time.'

I'm not sure I deserved that kind of accolade or the ones when he said I was comparable to the Brazilians and the Italians but I tell you something, when I heard that kind of thing from him I felt as though I could take on the world.

Too much was made of the quips he made about the gear I used to wear or my unshaven appearance. What was important to me was what he thought about me on a football field – nothing else mattered in my eyes.

Perhaps I wasn't exactly a snappy dresser but I liked to wear what I wanted and also enjoyed the desert boots that became part of my life. I've been the butt of so many jokes because of those boots and Peter Taylor once said to me when we were walking

121

near the Berlin Wall before our European Cup tie, 'Robbo, I've seen your boots walking on the other side . . . on their own!' Even now when I bump into former players who used to be my team-mates with Forest and Scotland, almost inevitably they ask about the desert boots. They want to know whether I still wear them now but the answer is 'No'. Since I moved into the management side of the game I tried to smarten myself up a bit so the boots just had to go.

My scruffy appearance was never helped by the fact that I didn't like shaving – and still don't to this day. I've always regarded it as a bit of a chore and the longer I can avoid getting out the razor, the better I like it. These days I'm probably down to once a week but when I was working with Martin I had to set a better example where the players were concerned and tried to shave every day.

But I must confess there were times when I could have passed for the sitcom character Rab C. Nesbitt and the gaffer never tired of ribbing me about it. He regularly marched into the Forest dressing-room on a morning and took one look at me and said, 'Robbo, I felt so rough this morning I didn't want to get out of bed. Then I come in here and see you and I feel like a million dollars.' I had a little snigger and just went about my own business but the reason why I never got upset or reacted to his barbed comments was simple – I knew he respected me as a player.

I know people have heard the stories of how he took me to task about my personal welfare and the way I dressed but when it came to footballing matters he never left me in any doubt about what he thought about my ability. There was one little action that meant so much to me and if I got that magical sign, I was ready to take on the world. When he shouted, 'Robbo,' and then proceeded to make a circle with his thumb and forefinger I knew he was happy with me. It's a gesture that he used hundreds and hundreds of times – with other players as well as me – but when I was the recipient I could have done cartwheels. I had so much respect for him I wanted to please him and that was his way of showing that he was delighted with what I was doing. I often felt it was like a dog producing some trick that pleased its master and in return receiving a reward. That was my pay-off and it gave me the incentive to go on and produce more of the same that pleased him so much. It might have come after scoring a crucial penalty, putting a full-back on his backside, riding a tackle, tracking an opponent (that wasn't too often) or just a simple pass that he admired. But I never got fed up of seeing that sign and even now when I think about it I still have a wry smile to myself because of how much it inspired me. It was the best example I can think of for his man-management with me but there were many others over the years.

I know Cloughie could be one of the most abrasive characters you could ever meet but his man-management and subtle ways of currying favour were second to none. In the glory days at Forest he used to take us off on trips abroad to play friendlies or just to have a break in the Majorcan sun. We didn't mind too much, particularly the times we spent relaxing in Cala Millor, but our wives and girlfriends were less than happy about seeing their partners being whisked off on another jaunt. Quietly, he got a lot of stick for that but usually the day after we had departed, a bunch of flowers and box of chocolates arrived at the door for our better halves and with it a note saying, 'Love Brian'.

Suddenly he was the bee's knees – he was good at that sort of thing.

He was big on the family unit and when he used to give us our many days off, he would send us away from training with the message, 'Go and spend time with your wife and bairns.' When any of us were in settled relationships he never missed an opportunity to encourage us to get married because he reckoned it brought more stability to our lives. And he reasoned that a more contented footballer was a better footballer.

He could have been a politician, a psychologist . . . virtually anything he wanted because he was a very clever man. In terms of academic qualifications he had virtually nothing but he used to tell people that his medals were his A levels and O levels. Cloughie's intelligence came from being unbelievably aware of what was going on around him and the term 'streetwise' could have been invented especially for him.

What he also had was an amazing way with words and I used to marvel at the speed he would think up a one liner to fit a certain situation when most people would spend half an hour trying to do the same and come up with nothing as sharp or original. One of his most famous lines about having disagreements with players was that 'We would sit down and talk for 20 minutes and at the end of it we would both decide I was right.' I've heard that line thousands of times over the years and it's still funny now, but the originality of that – and the host of other comments he made – left individuals like me marvelling at his special talent. He originally came up with that comment in a television interview but what amazed me was that he didn't even know what question he was about to be asked but, quick as a flash, he not only came up with an answer but one that people still talk about now.

He was as bright as a button. One day he asked Tony Woodcock why he was growing a beard. Tony replied, 'Because I want to be different.'

The gaffer hardly drew breath and came out with, 'Be different then – go out and score a hat-trick!'

On another occasion he fined me £50 for being late for training. I apologised and said, 'I've got to be honest gaffer, I slept in.'

'Young man, it would have been cheaper for you to get yourself a decent alarm clock,' came the instant reply.

He had such mastery of anything he was talking about he could well have been a politician. I know nothing about the subject really but if politics is about putting up arguments for and against and outwitting opponents verbally then I don't think he would have had any problems.

Without doubt he was the most charismatic man I have ever met. You knew when he arrived in a room because the place would go silent – he had that kind of effect on people.

Stories of Brian Clough are legion. At his peak he was a journalist's dream and it's a fair bet that he used to have more column inches written about him than any other person in the country. When he was leading us to so much success in the late 1970s and early 1980s, you never picked up a newspaper without seeing his name splashed all over it and, as he would say, a picture of his 'Big Head' to go with it. I used to think to myself, 'Not even the Prime Minister is getting as much coverage as the gaffer.' He was utopia for the newspaper industry and journalists used to flock to The City Ground to hang on his every word. I think he sometimes led them a merry dance but more often than not they would leave the place after a long day with a good story in the notebook and a big headline coming up the following day.

The gaffer was so funny at times he could have been on the

stage. So too was Peter Taylor and between them they often reduced team talks to a comedy half hour. They had great individual wit and built up a great chemistry. They played off each other's humour and the banter they initiated used to kill the bursting tension that exists from time to time in a football club.

I remember one day the lads were all together sitting in the Guest Room, where we used to meet, talking about bonuses and Pete more or less took over the meeting. After a bit of arguing Pete, making sweeping motions with his arms, said, 'Listen, lads, if you do the business for us we will absolutely shovel the money at you.' He carried on pushing this pretend money across this huge table towards us but then realised he was giving us too much so he started sweeping some of it back to himself. We could have all cracked up but we waited until we had all left the meeting and had a good laugh about it all.

But when it was time for the laughing to stop and the business to begin, nobody was more serious or focused on the job in hand than Cloughie. There have been many myths peddled about the gaffer down the years and I've always thought that the one that was so grossly untrue was the theory that he ruled by fear. It was usually put about by rivals who struggled to find ways to undermine the genius that was Brian Clough.

As I have mentioned previously, I wasn't exactly the strongest character in the world, particularly in my younger days when I was sensitive to any kind of criticism. Although I toughened up a little bit by the time I was in my twenties and playing under him I didn't exactly have a ring of steel around me. But I can honestly say I was never afraid of him. I had the utmost respect for the man and, yes, I was in awe of his very presence. But fear never came into it. When you cross that white line and the game starts there is no way in this world that you can function properly as a footballer if you are racked with fear of the bloke who is bawling and shouting at you from the touchline.

Can you imagine Larry Lloyd or Kenny Burns living in fear of him? Not a prayer. But that went for all the players who were fortunate to have the privilege of working under him over the years.

I've lost count of the number of times people have asked me – before and after he sadly passed away – what made him so special.

And if I had to come up with one word that summed up his qualities, it was that he made everything sound very 'simple'. Whether it was coaching on the training ground or confronting a problem off the field, he used to take everything down to its most simplistic form so that people could understand.

He hated centre-forwards just flicking balls on for the sake of it; he loathed full-backs who wouldn't stop crosses getting into the box; he loved midfield players who bombed forward into the penalty area; he demanded that centre-halves headed it; and he preached the gospel of passing to a player 'with the same colour shirt on as you'. I know it sounds simple but you would be amazed how many managers and coaches didn't employ the basic philosophies that oozed out of him.

One of the most regular instructions he used to bark out from the dugout was 'stop the cross'. In his eyes if you stopped potential trouble at source – i.e. preventing someone delivering the ball into our box – you were doing your job. It was basic stuff for us in our playing days but it's amazing how many managers and coaches never even thought about it. Steve Walford, who worked with Martin O'Neill and me for many years and was a top-class coach, admitted to me in one of our many conversations that he had never heard the phrase 'stop the cross' in all his time in the game.

The gaffer's coaching manual would probably have fitted on a couple of sides of A4 paper. I know the game has moved on at a pace and while there is certainly room for improved diet, fitness techniques and such like, I'm very much from the old school when it comes to the philosophy of coaching. I had around fifteen years assisting Martin and I've not had one coaching badge to my name throughout that time. These days there are too many managers and coaches trying to make the game something that it's not.

It's not rocket science but the fact of the matter is that teams who make the fewest mistakes win the most football matches. Almost every goal scored will either come from a mistake or an incident where someone in the defending side could have done better. You can work all week on the theories and the dossiers but come Saturday afternoon it is a totally different ball game. I've seen players who were world-beaters in training but come matchdays were shrinking violets – and the opposite can also apply.

No, the gaffer had his own ideas about the game and it was all so very straightforward. He hated the ball being hoofed upfield for the sake of it but I'll tell you this, he had no qualms about any of us kicking the ball over the stands if it meant not conceding a goal. There was a time and a place for everything in his eyes and he used to implore centre-halves like Lloydy and Burnsy, 'You just make bloody certain that ball doesn't get in my net.'

He certainly wasn't the archetypal football coach – ask Liam O'Kane. During his playing days at The City Ground, the gaffer took him to task at half-time in one match about not getting in a tackle. 'When are you going to get in a tackle?' he roared at Liam. Raising his voice and getting nearer to Liam, he repeated, 'When are you going to get in a tackle?' Again he repeated, 'When are you going to get in a bloody tackle?' And finally he screamed out, 'If you don't get in a tackle soon and back off any more, you will end up in the fucking Trent.' Pointed yes, precise yes but the message was clear and in the second half Liam knew full well what was expected of him.

The easy-to-understand methods, laced with a bit of Anglo-Saxon emphasis that he regularly employed, meant Cloughie had no peers in the communications business. When we went onto the field our brains were not full of information force-fed into us. He had no time for dossiers, never dwelt on the strengths and weaknesses in the opposition and so forth. He was far more concerned with us imposing ourselves on the team in the other dressing-room. 'Let them worry about us' was one of his favourite sayings.

Another indication of how he always kept things simple was at half-time in matches when we were not doing particularly well. He never filled our heads with unnecessary stuff. He made two or three salient points and left it at that. He was a great believer that if you went on chattering to players, by the time you had got to your last point, the first had been well and truly forgotten. Time was always precious to him and he would rather spend half an hour telling an individual about the benefits of having a good, solid family life because he felt that contributed as much to what went on during a Saturday afternoon as any amount of tactics or brainstorming sessions before a game.

Yes, we had certain jobs to do but he never went overboard

about that kind of thing and at the end of the day he never asked us to do anything that we were not capable of.

He preached good habits and used to come down like a ton of bricks on players who argued with referees. I think it's fair to say that during Cloughie's 18 years at Forest there was not a more popular side in the country among referees because they got an easy ride from us. We knew that if we had a pop at officials a Red Tree would be heading in our direction, and hitting players in their pockets is one sure-fire way to get them to do what you want. I'm certain we lost some big decisions because we never hounded referees but the gaffer always worked on the theory that our good behaviour would win more friends in the long run.

Another quality he had was his decisiveness. He had no time at all for fence-sitters – couldn't abide people who dithered over making up their minds. If something isn't working then fix it and if it costs you, so be it. That was certainly his way of dealing with things. We saw that so many times after he had brought players into Forest only for them to struggle, for whatever reason, to produce the kind of form that persuaded him to buy them in the first place. Asa Hartford was a classic example. A good player in his own right but he didn't hit it off at Forest and he was out the door and on his way to pastures new within a blink of his eye. It's a rare quality to own up to the fact that you are wrong and be decisive in doing something about it.

I thought it was a real shame because I had a lot of time for Asa as a player and a person but he had his mind made up for him and we never saw him again. But the way the gaffer and Pete went about rectifying what they believed to be a mistake on their part was so instant.

The same happened to other midfield players like Gary Megson and John Sheridan, who were bought and sold in no time at all. And there was no finer example than Justin Fashanu, who was bought from Norwich for £1m in the early 1980s. But when the gaffer got to working with big 'Fash' he realised he had dropped a clanger, and at the earliest opportunity he was on his way.

He also had this uncanny knack of being able to give a player the biggest bollocking imaginable and then somehow spring it round to his advantage by giving the same individual an unexpected lift at the end of the conversation.

He was fearless, too. He could walk into any situation and confront it head on – there was no such thing as walking away from a problem and hoping it would sort itself out. If he didn't have a ready solution to something he would find one. Occasionally, it meant bending the rules or bending somebody's ear but he would let nothing beat him. There was always an answer and, more often than not, he provided it.

One of the gaffer's other qualities was his elephant's brain and I've lost count of the number of times he came up with something we had been talking about months, if not years, before. I remember one night I was doing a question and answer session with him and Larry Lloyd in the Manor Club in West Bridgford. At the start of the night someone, who we could hardly see, stood up at the back of the darkened room, mentioned that he was from Coventry, asked his question, got an answer and we all moved on. Later in the evening we were sitting having a cup of tea when this bloke, who we had hardly been able to identify, walked past us and the gaffer instantly said, 'Now then, Coventry, have you got anything else to ask?' He never missed a trick.

I had my moments, usually over minor issues like being late for training, but generally speaking Cloughie was nothing but fair and straightforward in all his dealings and there were times when he showed the tenderness that most people would never associate with him.

He was always pretty straight when it came to contract negotiations – even though it was some time after he arrived at Forest that he eventually got round to thinking I was worth a pay rise. In our promotion season from the Second Division he pulled me into his office one day after we had lost to Charlton to talk about a new contract. I'd been on the same money for about four years and we lost the game 2–1 and Cloughie must have thought I had played well because he told me to come in and talk terms. I was still on £65 a week at the time and when he asked what I wanted I said £100. Immediately he said 'Done' – no discussions, no haggling. He just said he would sort it all out to come into effect at the start of the following season and I went on my way from his office.

Neither he nor I knew at the time that we would go on and win promotion and I was going to be a First Division player by the time the new deal kicked in. When we got promotion I was debating whether to go in and ask him about upping the figure because we had done so well. In the end I thought, why not? Nothing ventured, nothing gained. I said to him, 'I know I've signed a contract, gaffer, but that was before we won promotion and I was wondering if there was any chance I could have a bit more, please.'

He said, 'What do you think, son?' and I replied, '£120.'

He came back and said, 'Because you have been so polite and nice about it, have £125.' It took me aback a little bit because I had almost doubled my money and didn't really have to argue much of a case. I should have asked for more.

So I was on £125 a week the season we won the First Division and it was increased to £225 in the year that we won the European Cup for the first time. Before we played in the final Pete badgered me about signing a new deal and he really went for it when we went down to Southampton to play in a testimonial match for their manager Lawrie McMenemy. He followed me everywhere that day – even into the dressing-room toilets – and kept asking, 'What do you want?'

I said I would see him out on the pitch before the game. I was prepared to see my contract out but Pete was insistent and wanted to get something sorted. I said I would like a testimonial and Pete said, 'No problem – what about wages?'

'I want £500,' at which point Pete nearly choked and muttered, 'I'll have to have a word with Brian.'

When we got back to Nottingham the gaffer called me and said, 'So tell me, what do you want?'

We went through the conversation about the testimonial and the £500 and he came back at me with, 'Nice round figure, young man. It rolls off the tongue – done!'

At that point I was a bit annoyed with myself for not asking enough but this is where Cloughie got one back at me.

He said, 'Why don't you scale it over three years? Take £400 next year, £500 the year after and £600 the year after that.'

Sounded reasonable enough to me but it dawned on me some time afterwards that he knew I would be back in 12 months' time anyway and in the meantime he had saved himself and the club £100 a week!

He was very cute where money was concerned and, looking back, he was a brilliant negotiator when it came to sorting our players' bonuses. After we had won the First Division in 1978, we sent a delegation, I think of skipper John McGovern, Kenny Burns and Larry Lloyd, in to see him to discuss our team bonuses for the following season. We were talking about wanting £100 a point, £200 if we were in the top six and so on.

He turned to them and said, 'Is that it, boys? Well, fuck off, I'm not paying you a load of money when you could get it near the bottom of the table.'

Cloughie was great on incentives and he offered us £25 a point and when we got to 54 points he would pay us £1,000 a point from 54 onwards. He knew that if we got to that level we would be somewhere near to winning the league because there were only two points for a win in those days. At the end of the season we finished as runners-up to Liverpool with 60 points so we earned more than we had done when we won the League 12 months earlier. But from his point of view, his incentives had got us close to the top of the table.

That was Cloughie the bright spark but there were so many different sides to his make-up. And one of them involved an incredibly caring nature.

When my brother was killed in a car accident a few days before the 1979 European Cup semi-final against Cologne he could not have been more understanding. Here he was, on the verge of taking a team to a European Cup final again, having felt he was cheated out of achieving that during his Derby County days. They had reached the last four in 1973 but went out in controversial circumstances against Juventus and when Forest got through to the same stage he probably thought it was his last chance.

Football-wise I'm sure it meant everything to him at the time but when I got word about my brother's death, the gaffer pulled me to one side and said, 'I'm so sorry, son . . . you just take as long as you like. Forget about what's going on here and let me know when you want to come back.' People might say that he couldn't have said anything other in the circumstances but you have to remember what the European Cup opportunity was for him as a manager and he was willing to jeopardise that.

There were times, very rare I must admit, when I didn't see his point of view. And one of them involved Johnny Giles, who was a brilliant player for Leeds United and the Republic of Ireland. Cloughie disliked Leeds intensely, anything to do with them and, of course, Giles was part of that great Elland Road side. He was a player I admired very much. I was injured one day in a tackle with him during a league game against West Brom. It wasn't anything particularly nasty but the gaffer thought it could have been avoided and never forgot the incident.

Some time afterwards Giles was playing against Forest in Sammy Chapman's testimonial match and Cloughie said, 'If you get the opportunity, get your own back.' Anybody who knows me will tell you that I wasn't exactly a Kenny Burns or a Norman Hunter when it came to tackling but sure enough during the game there was an opportunity for me to exact a bit of retribution. The ball was going towards Giles and I was going in the same direction but as the ball approached him I ducked out and he stuck the ball through my legs. I just said to myself, 'Well played.' It was a superb piece of skill and after that all the heart went out of me. But I honestly don't think I was equipped to go and physically sort anybody out on a football field.

That was a one-off instance when I didn't necessarily agree with Cloughie's normally persuasive views but overall he was quite simply football genius. People often ask me now whether the gaffer could have been as effective in today's game as he was in my time as a player. I don't know the honest answer to that because the power in modern football has fallen much more on the players' side. There is so much money in the game and following the Bosman ruling, the benefits and influence are stacked so high in favour of players. But it would have been a lot of fun finding out how the gaffer would have approached the challenge. I would like to think that he would adapt himself and find a way to deal with the very different demands and power base that there is in the game now.

He was, without doubt in my mind, the greatest manager the game has known. And the day I stopped playing for the gaffer, it seemed like there was a huge void in my life. It's a matter of some regret that for many years after that our paths never crossed. We did meet up on one occasion at Stoke, where his son Nigel was playing for Liverpool Reserves. I went up into the directors' box and saw Archie Gemmill so I went to sit beside him and then realised that the gaffer was the other side of Archie.

When he saw me he got up and gave me a big hug. When he pulled away he said, 'You're still smoking, son, aren't you?'

'Aye, gaffer, I am – it's difficult to stop,' I muttered.

'I've given up drinking,' he announced, moving back to his place to sit down again. Then he stopped sharply and concluded, 'But if you believe that, you'll fucking believe anything.'

Unfortunately, his health deteriorated and it was an unbelievably sad day when I heard he had died in September 2004. It was a great loss because of what he had to offer not just football but the game in general. On a personal level it was the passing of someone who had played such a huge part in my own life and what I had achieved. A lot of people who claim to have been his friends went into print to pour out the problems he had with drinking but don't expect me to join them. The only thing I will say was that Martin and I met up with him when we were at Leicester and he looked in a bad, bad way. Pat Murphy, the radio sports journalist, arranged for us to meet and we were shocked by how much the gaffer had gone downhill. And I remember Martin saying to him something like, 'How can you let yourself get like this? We are only here today because of you.' I honestly believe he picked up a little bit after that but he deteriorated again.

I had so much respect for him that I just wanted to remember him for what he was at his peak when he was a brilliant manager and a hugely inspirational man. During my time at Forest, he was in his pomp. He was clear-headed, focused on his football and had no equals as far as I was concerned.

His funeral was a very private family affair but there was a memorial service held at Derby County's Pride Park stadium soon afterwards where Martin was asked to speak. We were at Celtic at the time, had been playing in the Ukraine against Shakhtar Donetsk and the Celtic owner Dermot Desmond gave us the use of his private jet so that we could fly to East Midlands Airport and get back in time to attend the event. Martin spoke superbly that night – from the heart and with the kind of humour the gaffer would have appreciated – but it needed something special to be said about a very special person.

10
Parting of the ways

I SUPPOSE I HAVE ALREADY gone down in history as the man responsible for the much-publicised split between Brian Clough and Peter Taylor. It's obviously something that I'm not particularly proud to be labelled with but my view is that the episode involving me was the straw that finally broke the camel's back. I'm convinced there were other factors in the break-up of what was arguably football's most celebrated managerial partnership but it was my move to Derby that was put forward as the popular reason.

In my opinion the relationship between the two of them had been on a downward spiral for several months – if not years – before I made the decision to leave Forest at the end of the 1982–83 season. The partnership had been built, for many years before they arrived at Forest, on the contrasting qualities of the two men, which dovetailed superbly.

Pete was the ace talent spotter who spent hours trawling the football grounds of the country in search of bargains and players who had a point to prove and needed a stage on which to do it. Once he had identified the targets, the gaffer went to work on clinching the transfer and then bringing into play his own unique brand of man-management that got the best out of most of the players who passed through his control. But by the time the early '80s had come around and we were no longer winning trophies, there was a falling away of the standards that made the partnership so special. It was common knowledge to us all that Pete was spending less and less time at what he did best. We hardly saw him at the ground on a day-by-day basis and the signings that were being made were simply nowhere near the quality of players like

Lloyd, Withe, Burns, Shilton, Gemmill, Francis and the rest. I don't mean this in any disrespectful way to the players who were coming into the club but the likes of Ian Wallace, Peter Ward and Justin Fashanu were simply not in the same league as Tony Woodcock, Garry Birtles and Trevor Francis and that was one of the main reasons why we fell away so quickly.

We started the 1980–81 season with Wallace having arrived from Coventry in a £1.2m deal and Raimondo Ponte, a Swiss international midfielder being signed from Grasshoppers of Zürich after the gaffer and Pete had taken a bit of a shine to him when we played them in the European Cup. Wallace was a decent player, who had scored a lot of goals in a partnership with big Mick Ferguson at Coventry, but he wasn't a Woodcock and there was a lot of pressure on him to deliver. It was at a time when Francis was recovering from the Achilles injury he had suffered the previous season and then in October the decision was made to sell Garry Birtles to Manchester United.

It wasn't the happiest of times because we lost our two-year hold on the European Cup when Bulgarian side C.S.K.A. Sofia, who wouldn't have lived with us over the previous two seasons, dumped us out in the first round after winning both legs 1–0.

As the season went on we lost more key players who had been the backbone of the side during our European days with Ian Bowyer going to Sunderland and Martin O'Neill leaving for Norwich. In his last game for us Martin scored twice in a 3–1 home win over Arsenal, so it was very strange to see him leaving when he was still making a big contribution. But, even though they got on famously in later years, he and the gaffer had something of a love–hate relationship in those days. I was very sad to see Martin go – not least because he was my mate.

But as a wide right player he had become one of the best in his position in the country. The likes of Steve Coppell was starring for Manchester United and Jimmy Case was playing for Liverpool but Martin was certainly their equal in my eyes. Martin was a much underrated player. He had pace, could go past people, got his share of goals and, as he often reminded me, was always willing to do his stint when it came to defensive work.

The younger Martin O'Neill always had an answer to the gaffer and perhaps there was a bit of that in his reasoning to allow him to go. I'm sure that he regretted it – along with many other decisions to let other top players leave. It wasn't as if the players we are talking about had passed their sell-by date. In most cases they were still in their late 20s and ought to have been in the peak years of their careers. But the key thing was, we weren't replacing them with players of a similar standing.

Forest were still regarded as one of the top sides in the country and in February 1981 we represented Europe in the World Club Championship in a match that I – and I dare say the other players – would like us to have taken a bit more seriously than we did. The game was played in Tokyo in midweek; we had a First Division game against Manchester City on the weekend before we left for Japan and an FA Cup tie against Bristol City on the following Saturday. I don't think any team would be expected to go all that way now in midweek without the cancellation of at least one of the weekend fixtures.

The flight took us via a stop in Anchorage but even before we had got to the stopping off spot in Alaska, there had been a fair bit of 'refuelling' done *inside* the plane. We were just into the flight when I spotted an airhostess coming down the aisle with a load of bottles in a plastic bag. They turned out to be champagne and we polished them off long before Anchorage was in sight. Which was just as well, because when we got back on the plane after the stop we were told to expect thunderstorms in the second half of the trip. I was delighted to say that the drink helped me get off to sleep and I conveniently woke up as we were beginning the descent into Tokyo.

The group Queen were on the same plane – they were heading to a gig in Tokyo – and although they were flying first class and we were very much in second, Trevor Francis got talking to Freddie Mercury and Brian May.

On arriving in Tokyo we went out to sample the nightlife and went to a series of bars that were seemingly charging 20, 30 or even 40 dollars just for entry alone. It was a tidy sum in those days but we didn't fancy paying that kind of money just to get in so we went back to the first place we looked at, which had 12 dollars written above the door. I went to the bar and remember ordering a Campari and soda for myself and whatever the other lads wanted. I got some money out of my pocket ready to pay but was told that the drinks were included in the entrance price. And we had walked halfway round Tokyo trying to find the best deal – not to mention wasting valuable drinking time!

On a second night out in the Japanese capital we approached this other club with a monster of a doorman barring our path. I thought I could use my Scottish charm on him and strode purposefully forward with the other lads lining up behind me. I launched into something like . . . 'We football players from Nottingham and last night played Nacional of Uruguay in big World final. We well-behave footballers and would like to come in for a small drink.' This brute of a bloke took one look that suggested he thought I was the thickest of the thick and promptly replied in the broadest Scouse accent, 'It's all right lads – get yourselves in.'

During most of the trip we hadn't a clue what time of day it was because a decision had been taken, on medical advice, to keep us on Greenwich Mean Time while we were in Japan. That was designed to prevent us being jet-lagged, particularly when we got back home.

We lost the game 1–0 in front of a crowd of 70,000 and a guy called Victorino scored Nacional's goal. I missed a sitter in the last minute to equalise. A ball dropped between Larry Lloyd and me and I shouted for Larry to leave it and I hit it really well from a central position in the six-yard box but somehow the Nacional keeper got his body in the way without knowing too much about it. Although we lost the game, we battered the Uruguayans for most of the 90 minutes and had we given the game the importance we felt it deserved, we could easily have been calling ourselves World Club Champions, which would have had a nice ring about it.

Three days after playing in Tokyo we were back in England lining up against Bristol City in the fifth round of the FA Cup. Understandably, we were very jaded and for a long time in the game looked to be going out. We were 1–0 down but thankfully I scored a penalty and Ian Wallace got the winner to get us off the hook. But what we were doing having to fly back from Japan and then playing an important game so soon afterwards, I will never know.

That victory over Bristol gave us hope of ending our hoodoo in the competition but we lost to Ipswich 1–0 in a replay at Portman Road after drawing 3–3 at home. Earlier in the season Watford had whipped us 4–1 in the League Cup – another result that you didn't associate with the Forest side of that era. So that was the end of our cup runs for another season.

All the time it seemed that the gaffer and Pete were getting further apart. We saw them less and less together and Pete certainly seemed to be losing the hunger that he had in his early years at the club. They just survived a major falling-out in 1980 when Pete wrote a book, *With Clough by Taylor*. Pete went ahead with it without telling the gaffer and when he found out about it, the air was, shall we say, a little bit on the blue side. There was a further deterioration in their relationship when Pete decided he wanted to retire in the summer of 1982 even though we could understand that he had probably had enough. But what upset the gaffer was that Pete was adamant about quitting, yet did a complete U-turn in coming back as manager of Derby County that November. There was no doubt in my mind that the rift between the two of them had widened considerably by the time that I joined Derby in June 1983.

The player drain at Forest naturally coincided with us falling away in the league and we finished seventh in the 1980–81 season. That summer Frank Gray was sold back to Leeds and very early in the following season Kenny Burns had also gone to Elland Road. Trevor Francis, who joined Manchester City in a deal that made sure Forest got back their £1m outlay on him, followed them out of the door.

Why did they let him leave? Maybe, it was thought that Trevor wouldn't quite be the same player after his injury problems and they couldn't afford to lose money on such a big investment. But Trevor went on to prove that he had lost none of his sharpness by producing the goods at Maine Road, leaving us to search in vain for the potency that he had given us.

A couple of months before Trevor's departure we had signed Justin Fashanu from Norwich in a £1m-plus deal but it turned out to be one of the worst buys the gaffer and Pete made. Justin had won a lot of acclaim at Carrow Road the previous season, particularly after scoring a spectacular goal against Liverpool that won the BBC goal of the season competition. I suppose he was signed to take over from Trevor but the two were poles apart in their respective strengths and weaknesses. Justin had a great physique – I think he had done a bit of boxing in his time – but he had none of the pace and flair that Trevor possessed. As it turned out, he didn't have any of Trevor's goalscoring skills either and from day one he struggled to make any kind of impact. The only impression he made on his arrival was being sent off in the second match he ever played in a Forest shirt. I know because I was red-carded myself for the only time in my professional career.

We were playing in the four-team La Línea tournament in southern Spain and had won our first game 3–0 against a Malaysian Select XI. Our next game was against Athletic Bilbao and let's just say that Spanish referees seemed to favour their club sides. 'Fash' went after just 17 minutes and although all the decisions seemed to be going against us, we had to be careful what we were doing and keep our mouths shut because it seemed that the referee was just waiting for an excuse to punish us further. At half-time I eye-balled the referee but knew I couldn't say anything so trooped off to the dressing-room as quickly as I could. Soon afterwards Liam O'Kane, who was our coach, came in and said to me, 'You've been sent off.' I was flabbergasted but had no option but to sit out the second half as we played on with nine men. Not surprisingly we lost 3–1 but on a personal level it was obviously the only major blot on my disciplinary record. I suppose you could say I was sent off for foul and abusive staring!

Meanwhile Justin's career never really took off at Forest. In his first season with us he only scored three goals in thirty-one matches and I got the impression that his arrival drove another wedge between our managerial partners. Peter believed in Justin's potential and from what I could gather was largely responsible for pushing the transfer through. The gaffer was a little bit more reserved in his judgement but went along with the deal. It didn't take him long, however, to realise that they had dropped an almighty clanger.

In later years Justin 'came out' as being gay – I think he was the first footballer to do so – and sadly his troubled life came to an end when he committed suicide in Shoreditch, London, in May 1998. No one will ever know what torment he suffered in his last few years but none of that was evident during his playing days, and for long periods he seemed a likeable enough lad. In fact, he always seemed to have a smile on his face. It's easy to think of things in hindsight but there was one incident that might have given us an insight into what was going on inside his vexed mind.

Soon after the La Línea episode we returned to Spain before the season started to take part in another tournament in Huelva. During the trip all the players were woken from their sleep by the sound of someone seemingly trying to break into one of the rooms but if it was a potential intruder he wasn't going about it in a very discreet manner. It turned out that Justin, who was seemingly still half asleep and in a bit of a trance, had got out of bed and was experiencing something akin to a wild nightmare. He had started thumping hell out of the bedroom door and the mess he made of it would have done justice to Muhammad Ali in his pomp. The door, which was splintered to bits, had a massive hole in it and as one of the lads said, 'Why didn't he just turn on the air conditioning?' Justin had been sharing a room with Viv Anderson and poor Viv had witnessed all this at close hand. From what I heard afterwards he was perched on the windowsill ready to take a jump if things had got any more frightening.

The gaffer wasn't on the trip – he had stayed at home to do some scouting for new players – but Ron Fenton was in charge and he managed to keep the incident out of the papers. It was surprising really because Justin's hands were cut to bits and he started the season with bandages covering the wounds.

While Justin was with us there were a lot of rumours around the ground about him being gay, particularly when he was linked with going to a Nottingham club called Part Two that was renowned as a gay bar. One day I must have had a drink or two, plucked up a bit of courage and accepted a bet with one of the other lads that I would ask him about his private life. I just came out with it, 'Are you gay, Justin?' To which he replied, 'If you give me a kiss I'll tell you.' Fair play to him, I thought. Needless to say I didn't take up his offer and thankfully he didn't take exception to my question because he was a formidable specimen.

Justin also had a penchant for collecting car-parking fines after leaving his range of vehicles in all parts of the city without tickets but I won't hold that against him because I was just as guilty as him on that score. In fact, I had a sponsored car taken off me for that very reason. Gregory's, of Worksop, very kindly let me have use of a car but because they were the owners, any notices of fines went directly to them. I'm afraid that they eventually received one too many and said enough was enough and took the car from me.

It was clear that Justin's days were numbered and after being loaned out to Southampton, he was eventually sold to Notts County for a mere £150,000 in October 1982. I don't know whether it was a case of him being in the wrong place at the wrong time but I just couldn't see Justin fitting into our way of playing possession football.

On one occasion before he left I said to him in the dressing-room after a match, 'When are you going to make a move for me?' With that I meant him moving into space and a good position and making up my mind for me in the way that Withe, Woodcock, Birtles and Francis had done before him.

Justin's answer was, 'Just put it in there and I'll get it.' But that was an anathema to me because there was no way I was going to play a ball into space, hoping that someone would get on the end of it. As the gaffer always used to say, 'You've got to treat the ball as a friend.' And in Justin's world that was the easiest way I could think of for losing your friends!

It's not often that I lost my temper but I said to Justin, 'You can fuck off if you think I'm just going to play a ball in there for the sheer sake of it.'

There were two ways to look at it because in more recent years as a coach I have probably said to wide men to get crosses in and if strikers don't get on the end of it, I'll have a go at them. But as a player, possession was too precious for me and I didn't want to lose the ball on a mere wing and a prayer.

Although Justin struggled individually we were not too clever as a team and I remember us having a horrendous run early in 1982 when we wondered where the next point was coming from. We finished 12th at the end of that season and it was then that Pete, who I am sure had been questioning his own previous high standards for spotting players, decided that he had had enough. There were stories around that Peter felt that he 'had shot it' and was ready for retirement but while he took his leave, the gaffer still had the motivation to try and build another successful side.

But Justin was sold after John McGovern had gone to Bolton

and Peter Shilton to Southampton and the break-up of our European Cup winning side was almost complete with only Viv Anderson and myself remaining. And my days were somewhat numbered.

In the early weeks of the 1982–83 season the gaffer took me to task about my smoking, which he had always seemed to turn a blind eye to as long as I was producing on the pitch. He pulled me after we had lost 4–3 to Liverpool at Anfield – a match in which Steve Hodge scored his first senior goal for the club. The gaffer offered me a wager that he could last longer without a drink than I could without a cigarette and we shook hands on a £100 bet. We had a picture taken for the club programme with me tossing cigarettes in the air and him pouring a bottle of booze on the ground. Of course, I carried on smoking and I'm absolutely certain that he continued drinking.

But he caught me out when we were staying in a London hotel prior to an overseas trip to Kuwait for a couple of friendlies. I had gone up to my room after the evening meal to have a crafty fag and was standing with the bedroom window open as usual to try and keep the smell away and waft the smoke into the outside air. There was a knock on the door and I instantly thought it was the gaffer so I flung open the window as wide as I could for a couple of seconds, swallowed a couple of Polo mints and took as long as I could to answer the door. When I did it was Ronnie Fenton, who had been appointed his No. 2 when Pete left, standing there with my boots in his hand, saying I had left them downstairs in the hotel.

I brushed away the perspiration from my brow and uttered to myself, 'Got away with that one, Robbo,' but a couple of minutes later there was another knock on the door. By that time I had lit up again and answered the door, thinking it was my roommate but to my horror the gaffer was standing there in all his smug glory. 'Fair cop,' I said as he just stood there smirking. But he didn't enforce the wager and instead said something like, 'I tell you what, just for now you have a fag, I fancy a drink, so we'll call the bet off only for tonight.' That was good-natured banter but soon afterwards he said something to me that I foolishly allowed to get under my skin.

It was in January 1983. We lost 2–0 to Manchester United at

Old Trafford and I ended up on crutches and in need of surgery to repair cartilage damage in my knee. The players always sat at the back of the team bus and as I gingerly made my way up the aisle, the gaffer looked at me struggling to get through and said, 'Bad timing young man, bad timing.' He was referring to the fact that my contract was due to expire in the summer and we were about to have talks over a new deal.

Mindful of all the things he said to me down the years I should have taken his comments with a proverbial pinch of salt but I let it fester and cast doubts about my future at the only club I had known throughout my career. The game was two days after my 30th birthday so there was a psychological aspect to it and I must admit I felt a bit vulnerable by his comments. It was the last thing I wanted to hear at that time.

I also wore the No. 7 shirt that day at Old Trafford because Colin Walsh, a talented young Scot who everyone saw as my natural successor in the side, wore the No. 11. I didn't think too much about it at the time but the fact remained that I had always been given the No. 11 when I played and it was yet another small reason for wondering where this was taking me.

I was fit again long before the end of the season and we finished quite well, winning seven and drawing two of our last nine matches to end up fifth in the table and qualify for the following season's UEFA Cup. It was the first time we had qualified for Europe since 1980. By that time Pete had had a few words, quite a few words actually, with me about the possibility of going to Derby and there was a lot of uncertainty swilling around in my brain.

I had been at Forest for 13 years and there were bits of speculation in the press about me leaving; Manchester City, where Trevor Francis and Martin O'Neill had become reunited, were mentioned as having an interest in me. But Pete wouldn't let go and was nothing if not persistent.

My last game was on a Wednesday night at The City Ground against Notts County in the final of the Nottinghamshire County Cup. We won 4–3 and I scored the last goal. I had played quite well on the night in a free role but whatever I thought it was tinged with sadness because deep down I thought it would be my last game for the club.

After the match the gaffer told me to come in the following day to talk about a new deal but unbeknown to him I had already shaken hands with Pete about going to The Baseball Ground. The gaffer said, 'If I look after you, will you take a two-year contract?' He knew I was after the security of a three-year deal but in his own way wanted to do what was right with me as well as the club. I told him I would think about it and give him my answer the following week when we were going out for an end of season trip to Canada.

On the Saturday of that week I had arranged to go to The Baseball Ground to finalise things with Pete and I set off for Derby with my wife Sally telling me, 'Whatever you do, don't agree anything today. Have a think about it.' I went over, ignored what Sally had said – wished I hadn't – and told Pete I would join Derby on a three-year deal.

Looking back it was the worst thing I could have done. I don't generally look back on my football career with too many regrets and I am proud of what I achieved but I do chastise myself when I think back to that day. I can also recall the telling-off I got from Sally when I told her I had gone against her wishes and not dwelt on the move. I had been a Forest player all my life and I hadn't taken into account what it meant for a player to jump ship and join the arch enemy that Derby had always been. At the end of the day I was committing professional suicide. I was leaving a team fifth in the First Division and looking forward to being back in Europe to one that was in the Second and struggling financially.

I also confess that I was guilty of getting a bit too big for my boots and was believing in my own publicity. It was always said that 'When John Robertson plays well, Forest play well' and I allowed that to colour my thinking. When I realised that wasn't true it was too late. Despite all the changes we still had a good side at Forest and there were a number of young players like Colin Walsh, Gary Mills, Stuart Gray, Chris Fairclough and Peter Davenport beginning to make an impact. And with due respect to the players I was joining at Derby they were not in the same class. I learned the hard way, if you like, that I wasn't going to make much difference to any side on my own.

I don't want to lay any blame at the feet of anyone at Derby or the club in general but I can admit now that within a week of pre-season training I knew I had made a mistake.

My feelings were compounded by the fact that on 14 July my

Lining up for Scotland Schoolboys against England at White Hart Lane in 1968. That's me far right on the front row with Graeme Souness (third from left on back row) and Ally Robertson (sixth from left on back row). Maitland Pollock, who went with me to Forest, is on the far left of the front row. (© Kenneth Prater)

Slotting home the penalty that won us our first major trophy in 1978. John O'Hare (second from right) won the controversial spot-kick and I beat Ray Clemence in the Old Trafford replay that clinched the League Cup. (© *Nottingham Evening Post*)

The gaffer was always promoting us for international recognition and it was his idea to get us all in kilts before the Scottish squad was selected for the 1978 World Cup. Kenny Burns, Archie Gemmill and myself got the nod but John McGovern, who was so unlucky not to be picked for Scotland throughout his career, stayed at home.

Try that for size: my mum trying on one of my Scotland caps. And was she proud! Inset: my dad, Hughie. (Courtesy of the author)

Scottish pride: I felt on top of the world after scoring the winner for Scotland against England at Wembley.
(© Press Association)

The perfect pair: Peter Taylor and Brian Clough, to whom I owe so much.
(© *Nottingham Evening Post*)

Trevor Francis gets on the end of my cross and scores the goal that won Nottingham Forest the European Cup for the first time.
(© Press Association)

A night to remember: getting our hands on the European Cup for the first time after beating Malmö of Sweden 1–0 in Munich in 1979. (© *Nottingham Evening Post*)

An unforgettable moment: scoring the winning goal against Hamburg in Madrid. (© Press Association)

Hands up who's scored in a European Cup final. (© John Sumpter Photography)

In the dressing-room in Madrid after we had beaten Hamburg in 1980. I'm looking a bit glum and if memory serves me right it was because I had just been told we couldn't keep our shirts as souvenirs. (© John Sumpter Photography)

Who could give up the drink and the fags? That was the bet I had with the gaffer in 1982 but in truth we both cheated. (© John Sumpter Photography)

The downside of football – even if it means you are surrounded by nurses. I was recovering from a knee operation in 1983, a few months before I left Forest for Derby County. (© *Nottingham Evening Post*)

Cheers, lads: my Forest teammates join me at the start of my short career as a pub landlord. Ian Bowyer, Gary Mills, Garry Birtles, Gary Fleming, Franz Carr and Stuart Pearce behind the bar at The Old Greyhound in Aslockton. That's me in the middle, complete with what Sharyl calls 'the Tom Selleck moustache'.
(© *Nottingham Evening Post*)

Elisabeth's first photo shoot after her birth, with Sally, Jessica and me.
(© *Nottingham Evening Post*)

A bit of football glory after my professional days: winning the Nottingham District Spartan League Senior Cup in 1987.
(© *Nottingham Evening Post*)

Crimestoppers: Detective Constable Austin O'Driscoll (centre) and PC John Davis return my medals, which were stolen from my house in November 1992.
(© *Nottingham Evening Post*)

My mate Larry Lloyd and me in Griff Rhys Jones/Mel Smith pose during one of our speakers' evenings. Our debates and arguments in earlier years were nothing like as convivial at times but we always ended up as friends. (© *Nottingham Evening Post*)

Martin O'Neill and me celebrating one of our many successes at Parkhead. (© Press Association)

Never again: my one and only paragliding experience, on a holiday in Cyprus. Clenched fists and closed eyes tell the story. (Courtesy of the author)

Family pride: Sharyl and me with Elisabeth, Andrew and Mark. (Courtesy of the author)

first child Jessica was born severely disabled and right from the minute she came into the world, she was a very poorly girl. I didn't feel comfortable with the whole thing at Derby but it was overshadowed by Jessica's problems and without doubt it was the worst time of my life. I couldn't concentrate on football and it just seemed that every conceivable set of circumstances was conspiring against me.

Derby even ended up paying a lot more for me when a tribunal set the fee at £135,000, which was a lot of money back then for a 30-year-old. I'm sure Pete thought they could get me a lot cheaper but the tribunal was presented with documented proof that both Luton and Southampton had made sizeable bids for me and that jacked up the price. I certainly wasn't aware that bids had been made and if it were the case then I would have expected the gaffer to tell me.

When my first season at Derby got underway I tried my best to focus on the game as much as I could but it was very difficult and there were aspects of the football that just weren't right. At Forest I had benefited enormously from being fed the ball time and time again. I was the outlet and I loved it because the more possession I had the more confident I became. At Derby I didn't see anything like as much of the ball and when I did, I found myself almost trying too hard to make up for lost opportunities. It was a hopeless scenario and there were many times when I sat quietly, head in hands wondering what the hell I had done.

I had no one but myself to blame. Nobody else shook Pete's hand on a deal and nobody else put their signature on a transfer form. I want to make it abundantly clear that I was 100 per cent responsible for the entire episode – and it hurt.

To make matters worse the timing of it all could not have been worse. It just happened that when I was discussing things with Pete, the gaffer had gone on the Centurion Walk to raise money for an electric chair for a disabled girl in West Bridgford. He went with Alan Hill, who was Youth Development Officer at The City Ground at the time, Dr Mike Hutson, who was one of the club's doctors and Chief Inspector Tony Slater. Apparently they were halfway through the walk in the Yorkshire Dales when the gaffer rang home to speak to his wife Barbara who told him news had broken that I had signed for Derby.

145

Alan, who I still see these days, was prepared for the outburst because a little while earlier he had spoken to his wife Janice, who had filled him in on what had happened. Alan says he can remember Cloughie's reaction as if it were yesterday. The gaffer was breathing fire, bounced a bottle of Bell's whisky on the table and went on to demolish most of it in the following couple of hours. He vowed never to speak to Peter Taylor as long as he lived – a threat that he carried out – and evidently I was 'a fat little bastard that he wasn't going to speak to again'. I was banned from The City Ground and Alan said he kept up his rants not only for the rest of the walk but in the weeks that followed back in Nottingham.

I could totally understand his feelings – and actions. I should have been brave enough on the Thursday after the County Cup game to tell him I had arranged to meet Pete and at least then he would have known the full story. He made no attempt to contact me and I didn't expect him to. I'm sure his view was, 'The little sod has made his bed, now he can lie in it.'

You would think it could not have got any worse for me at Derby but sadly it did. They were relegated at the end of my first season, so there I was dropping down into the Third Division and it seemed that as every day passed I was paying a heavier rap for the terrible decision I made.

After I got to Derby Kenny Burns and Archie Gemmill also joined so I had players in the dressing-room who I knew really well, but being there just didn't sit easily with me. I was in a relegation battle with Derby and could have been in a Forest side that reached the UEFA Cup semi-final against Anderlecht.

Pete left the club to retire for good in April 1984, shortly before we were relegated – Arthur Cox took over after Roy McFarland had been in charge for a brief spell – and I felt as low as I possibly could with my football life.

Then during the following season Clough eventually relented and invited me back to see a game at The City Ground. I felt very uneasy about it but I was so keen to get back to Forest I was willing to go through anything. The last thing I anticipated was to get the opportunity to return to the club and play at The City Ground again but I was delighted when the gaffer threw out the olive branch and re-signed me in the summer of 1985. The Derby episode had effectively ended my career and I had to console myself with the thought that if it was the only mistake I made in my career, then it wasn't so bad after all.

I don't suppose I could have expected to return to The City Ground as if I had never been away. I was two years older, I didn't have the same confidence and I wasn't the automatic pick that I had always been. But I was always with the first team squad and went with them on a trip to Bermuda in January 1986 to play a friendly against Newcastle United at the Somerset Cricket Club ground. We won the game 3–0 but I could easily have received the biggest beating! Let me explain.

I'm honest enough to admit that when I've had a drink or two I do get a bit too loud for my own safety – and it nearly cost me a good hiding. I can remember Paul Gascoigne, who was just a young lad at the time and starting to get noticed at St James' Park, was in the Newcastle squad – as was Peter Beardsley. We stayed out there for a couple of days, and after a few drinks one night I was coming out of the hotel and letting my lip go in conversation with my team-mates, Ian Bowyer and Colin Walsh.

This big American guy – and I mean big – came up to me and said, 'Why don't you get your arse out of here and back to England?'

I couldn't let it rest at that, the drink gave me a bit of Dutch courage and I must have said something like, 'Who the hell do you think you are talking to?'

The argument escalated, one thing led to another and we ended up grappling like a couple of school kids outside the hotel. I got him in a headlock, started feeling really cocky and a bit pleased with myself for taming this monster. I must have been stupid really because he was nearly twice my size but I started sobering up quickly because it dawned on me that I might have bitten off more than I could chew. I thought I would quit while I was ahead and said to him, 'Do you give in?' It was said more in hope than anything else. At that point I let go and he took a swing and caught me a glancing blow. We then went into stand-off mode with him and his mate on one side and me, Bomber and Walshy on the other.

To be honest I didn't fancy the three of us against their two and in a bid to get away from it all I muttered, 'I'm sorry, we've had a few drinks and it's just me being loud.' We escaped without any damage being done but it went down as another episode when I got brave after I'd had a drink. It doesn't happen these days.

I only made a dozen appearances for Forest in that 1985–86 season and, towards the end of it, after a game against Liverpool Reserves, the gaffer told me he was going to release me. I was only on a year's contract and I was sitting in the bath when he came across and told me he wouldn't be offering me a new deal.

It was a bit ironic that my league career effectively came to an end at Anfield, where I had enjoyed so many good times battling it out in big games with Liverpool. But it was a decision that I was expecting because I knew in my heart of hearts that I was not the same player. Time had caught up with me and I had to move on. It was a sad moment but I had no complaints. Because of my own foolishness I had wasted two years of my career and I had to pay some price for that. That was the end of the road as far as my Forest life was concerned and it was obviously a sad time but one with lots of nostalgic memories.

I find it difficult to express in words just what it meant to me in 2005 when I was voted as Forest's best player of all time. I get slightly embarrassed by it but there is an underlying feeling of immense pride. I know it's all about opinion at the end of the day but I was humbled to be held in such high regard by Forest supporters. When you think of the names that came before me like Bob McKinlay, Jack Burkitt, Ian Storey-Moore, Joe Baker to name but a few, it puts it all into perspective. I would think that most of the supporters who voted for me were voting on reputation because it's 25 years or more since I pulled on a Forest shirt.

There are other players whose exploits are far more vivid and recent in the memory of fans. You only have to look at the immense popularity that Stuart Pearce achieved during his time at Forest to realise what an iconic figure he was and he had a rapport with supporters that was second to none. Des Walker is another who gained tremendous respect for his remarkable consistency and then, of course, there were the likes of Stan Collymore, who was an outstanding individual in the short time he was at the club.

But that was an accolade that meant an awful lot to me – much as any of the medals that I was so fortunate to win during my playing career.

11

Living the Scottish dream

AS A KID IN UDDINGSTON I used to lie in bed at night and think about nothing else but football. I swear I used to kick myself to sleep and when my dreams were at their very best I would imagine I was scoring the winning goal for Scotland against England – and probably just to add a little extra poignancy – at Wembley. Then I would wake up and realise that I was a million miles from reality. But you could always dream and there was no harm in that. Then in a Home International match on 23 May 1981 it all came very, very true.

I never used to have visions of scoring in a European Cup final, an FA Cup final or slotting in the goal that won the League Championship. No, as a wee Scottish lad brought up to believe that putting it across the auld enemy was everything, I wanted to beat the English. It might not have been in a major championship but for me playing for Scotland against England at Wembley was a major landmark in my playing career. To score the only goal of the game was very special and as footballing moments go, it is right up there with my European Cup successes.

The goal came from a penalty that was awarded after Davie Provan had played a superb ball into the heart of the English defence. Steve Archibald was after it and when he got into the area he was brought down by Bryan Robson. All our Scottish arms went up appealing for the penalty and it was duly given. But the euphoria of winning it was soon tinged with a bit of apprehension as I walked up to place the ball on the spot. We had a number of penalty takers in the side at the time but I was designated with the task and was up against big Joe Corrigan, who played for Manchester City, in the English goal.

I remember there was quite a wait while all the fuss had died down and during that time Trevor Francis, my team-mate at Forest, ran half the length of the field to tell Corrigan where he thought I would put the spot-kick. I knew what he was doing but I said to myself, 'Go to your normal side,' which, for me, meant hitting it to Corrigan's right. It was a case of bluff and double bluff because I stuck with my tried and trusted direction and Corrigan, on the advice of Trevor, thought I might switch sides. I had a quiet word with Corrigan afterwards and he confirmed what I had thought.

I didn't care, the ball was in the net and I had scored against England at Wembley. I was so excited, for some unknown reason I wanted to climb the fences that surrounded the ground to keep fans away from the playing area but, fortunately, Ray Stewart, who was a bit quicker than me, stopped me getting that far! What I was proposing to do I don't know because I was never any good at climbing but I was just so ecstatic I didn't know how to express myself.

Mind you I had to curb the celebrations after the game – when I was on the England team bus! Yes, I'd just scored the winner against England and I was hitching a lift on their coach back into London. I had arranged with Tony Woodcock, who was playing for England, to meet up in London that night and we eventually ended up at Stringfellows nightclub. I can't remember how I managed to get a lift on the bus – I can only imagine Tony organised it – but I can recall sitting as quiet as a mouse at the back. I didn't want to rub it in so I kept out of the way as much as possible.

It's amazing in the years since that game the number of Scottish fans who have come up to me and said how much that moment meant to them. But in turn I have often wondered that if I had missed the penalty, I probably wouldn't have been welcome north of the border again!

I was so proud and I was just saddened by the fact that my dad and my brother were not there to see it. For years they had travelled down to Scotland games at Wembley on a bus organised in the village and, through Forest, I had managed to get them the odd ticket for the game. But a year before my big day my dad had passed away and my brother Hughie had been killed in a car accident in 1979. I just hope they were up there cheering when the ball hit the back of the net. At least my dad saw me win the European Cup but they would both have been so thrilled to see their son and brother score a goal that beat England at Wembley. Victory over the English has always been so close to the hearts of Scottish people in all sports – but particularly football.

I actually made my Scotland debut at the end of the 1977–78 season after Forest had won the First Division title and League Cup. The Home International Championships were still running at the time and I was selected in the squad for the end of season games. It was the year of the Argentinian World Cup and Ally MacLeod, who was managing Scotland, had decided that he would pick his side for the finals in South America and that would also be his squad for the home internationals.

I had been called up for a previous game against Bulgaria but couldn't make it because it clashed with an important Forest fixture. And there was another occasion when I had been selected for a Scottish FA XI to play Rangers in a testimonial match for John Greig at Hampden Park. Although it was only a testimonial, that experience wasn't the best because we were beaten 5–0, so I was looking forward to making an impression when I got a chance in the Scotland team for real.

So I was named in the 22 for Argentina but when I look back now I honestly don't think I was ready for that particular challenge at that particular time. Obviously, I was delighted about it all but hindsight is a wonderful thing, and down the years I just felt that my selection came a bit too early – even though I had come off the back of probably the best season so far in Forest's history. I think I was a bit in awe of players like Kenny Dalglish, Bruce Rioch and Don Masson, who were all established international figures. At 24, I wasn't exactly a youngster but it was such a big stage to be entering and don't let anyone tell you that there is not a step up from club football to internationals.

My debut came against Northern Ireland at Hampden Park and Scotland were strong favourites to win the match . . . but it didn't work out that way and we drew the game 1–1. I was in direct opposition to Bryan Hamilton, who was normally a right-sided midfield-player-cum-winger but for some reason was playing at right-back. I doubt whether he had ever played there before or afterwards but he had an insurance policy called Martin O'Neill.

He was delegated to help Bryan out and, as Martin knew as much about my game as I did, I think I allowed myself to be psyched out of it before a ball was kicked.

I was obviously a bit nervous, walking into a Scotland dressing-room and pulling on the blue jersey for the first time. I probably let the occasion get to me . . . I'm not sure. Martin knew all my strengths and weaknesses, virtually coached Hamilton through the game, and he was largely responsible for me not getting a kick that day. In a nutshell I was very poor. To be perfectly frank it was probably the worst I ever played for Scotland and had the squad not been picked for Argentina, I doubt whether I would have gone.

I was so disappointed, not least because I had got tickets for my mum and dad and other members of the family. Talking to them outside the ground afterwards I remember saying, 'Well, I've done it – I've played for my country. It might be my first and last cap but nobody can take it away from me.' It was my way of consoling myself at the time and although I made a brief appearance as a substitute against Wales, that was effectively the end to my home international experience for that season.

My immediate prospects of actually playing in the World Cup were slim because Willie Johnston was first-choice left-winger in those days and a fixture in the side. He was doing very well for West Brom, was experienced and a very talented player so I assumed that I would be going along for the experience more than playing any significant part in Scotland's plans.

When it came to leaving for the World Cup the Scotland manager Ally MacLeod had clearly made up his mind that he was going to rouse the nation in support of the squad that was heading off to Buenos Aires. We were given the name of 'Ally's Tartan Army' after making a record of that name with Scottish comedian Andy Cameron. There was so much optimism in Scotland and most of it was as a result of MacLeod's determination to, one way or another, get the nation behind the players.

To be fair his team had done well on the field by qualifying for the finals from a group that included European champions Czechoslovakia as well as Wales and in the home internationals we had been given the extra boost of beating England 1–0 at Hampden. There was no doubt we had some good players in the squad and we were not short of creative or attacking talent.

Masson, Rioch and Asa Hartford were more or less the first choice midfield and up front we had what was generally accepted as the perfect blend with Joe Jordan and Dalglish with Johnston providing width. They were all top players.

We had a stage-managed send-off as an open-top bus went round Hampden before setting off to Prestwick Airport, where there were more crowds waiting to see us off. In fact, there were crowds en route down the Clyde coast. The hype was incredible and it's easy to say now but it might have been an awful lot better and less pressurised if we had just gone about our business quietly – as Cloughie used to insist at Forest.

But we seemed to leave all the euphoria and high spirits behind in Scotland because our base in Argentina left a lot to be desired and, footballers being footballers, the moaning began the moment we arrived at our hotel. It was in Alta Gracia, near Córdoba but the rooms were at best spartan and there wasn't even any water in the hotel pool – not that it bothered me much because I wasn't really into swimming. The facilities – or lack of them – certainly put a dampener on the mood after a long flight and I think it manifested itself in our performance in the first game against Peru.

I watched the game, which we lost 3–1, from the stand and we didn't play well even though Jordan gave us the lead. They had a boy called Cubillas, who had played in the previous World Cup and was supposed to be at the veteran stage of his career. But he took the game over, scored twice and with Masson missing a penalty with the score at 1–1 in the second half it all went horribly wrong for us.

We then suffered another bombshell when Johnston was found to have taken a banned substance. I think he had taken some medication called Fencamfamine that he had used at his club West Brom to combat a cold, but it was found to be banned and Johnston, who was a big player for us, was sent back to Scotland.

That meant yours truly was picked for the next game against Iran – a match that we were expected, and really had to, win. But we produced another inept performance in drawing 1–1. We went ahead with an own goal just before half-time but Iran deserved their equaliser on a bad, bad day for Scottish football. I was very disappointed in myself and as a team we were very much below par against a side we should really have beaten fairly comfortably. I had felt low enough after my debut but I got the same terrible, empty feeling after the Iran game and I thought that was definitely the end of the international road for me.

Our last qualifying game was against Holland, one of the best teams in the tournament, in Mendoza and after the Iran game the Scottish fans were shouting, 'No Mendoza! No Mendoza!' to indicate that they were not travelling to the match. We couldn't have blamed them one iota but Scottish fans being what they are, they still turned up in numbers for a game that we had to win by three clear goals to qualify for the final stages. I knew I wouldn't figure against Holland – I was an unused substitute – but our supporters were rewarded with a much-improved display.

Even so Holland took the lead with a penalty ten minutes before half-time but Dalglish got us level in the second half and then Archie Gemmill took centre stage. He was one of four changes in the side and, after putting us ahead from the penalty spot, he produced a wonder goal, which has been shown on television time and time again, as we turned on a bit of Scottish style to lead 3–1. With twenty minutes left we were amazingly in with a chance of qualifying, needing just one more goal, but our hopes were short-lived because Johnny Rep fired one in from twenty-five yards and getting another two goals was beyond us.

Holland went on to reach the final, where they lost to the hosts Argentina, but at least we were able to leave for home with a tiny bit of pride restored.

I don't know why it is but Scotland have a history of not doing well in games that we are expected to win comfortably and then defying all logic and causing problems for the best teams in the world. Many better judges than me have failed to come up with an answer to that question but we were heading back to Scotland to a totally different reception to the party atmosphere that accompanied our departure.

I was a bit fortunate really because we flew into Gatwick Airport and the England-based players made their way home from there. Unfortunately for the boys who lived in Scotland, they had to face the music when they arrived back and I did feel sorry for them.

MacLeod resigned after one more game in charge with Jock Stein taking over, but it was late in 1978 when I was next picked for a European Championship qualifying game against Portugal in Lisbon.

Stein was a great manager for what he achieved at Celtic. He had huge respect in the game, was recognised as a good tactician, he was a fair man and the players took to him. He wasn't really a shouter but he let you know when you had done well or badly and there was always a constructive element to what he said.

We didn't qualify for the 1980 European Championship finals but in 1982 we were on our way to the World Cup in Spain after clinching our place in a dull goalless draw against Northern Ireland at Windsor Park. I didn't play in the final qualifying game against Portugal because the manager wanted to try a few things out in what had become a meaningless match.

At one time I was a bit uneasy about whether or not I would be fit for the finals. In February 1982 Forest were playing Brighton at the old Goldstone Ground and beat them 1–0 with Peter Ward scoring the winner against his old club. But my big recollection of the match was getting a whack from Jimmy Case, who had moved on from Liverpool by then, and it left me in such pain that I thought my World Cup hopes would be in jeopardy. I got the injury to my ankle in the first minute of the game but, as he did from time to time, the gaffer decided to leave me on the field. I suppose he reasoned that I had got 89 minutes to run it off! I know I was never the most athletic of players but that day I hardly moved ten yards either side of the halfway line. I don't think I gave the ball away during the entire 90 minutes because I was content to play little short passes. Somehow I got through the game but I didn't play in the next half a dozen matches and to be honest the injury bothered me for the rest of the season.

The day after the Brighton game I was due to report with Scotland for a match and did so even though I had no chance of playing. Arrangements had been made for us to record 'We Have a Dream', which was to be Scotland's song for the World Cup finals. I was hobbling all weekend but was soon back at The City Ground receiving treatment and the gaffer sent me on holiday to Malta for a week to have a break. But at that stage I was still genuinely concerned about when I would be fully fit again. Fortunately, it cleared up in time but I think I made only one substitute appearance in the home internationals.

We set off for Spain with none of the razzmatazz that had accompanied our departure to Argentina four years earlier and we were based in a very nice hotel in Sotogrande, an area of the country renowned for its quality golf courses.

In our first game against New Zealand we started really well and were three goals up and coasting in the first half. But, typically I suppose, we let things slip. They scored twice and we started getting twitchy at the prospect of having another Scottish disaster on our hands. Then we got a free-kick just outside their box and came up with a routine from the practice ground . . . and one that worked. Graeme Souness, Frank Gray and myself were involved and it revolved around Graeme and Frank seemingly making a mess of it and bundling into each other and in the confusion I managed to get my shot over the wall and into the net. That gave us breathing space and we managed to get another goal before the end to get off to a pretty good start in the tournament.

In the next game we lost 4–1 to Brazil in Seville after playing really well on a blazing hot day. The conditions might have been more beneficial to Brazil than us but, to be honest, they didn't need any help at that time. They had the likes of Zico, Falcão, Socrates and Junior in their side. We got off to a flier against them when David Narey scored a superb goal. We couldn't believe it but I think us scoring first got them mad and Zico soon fired a superb free-kick past Alan Rough. It went downhill for us after that and left us facing Russia in our final group game and needing to beat them to go through.

We went one up but they scored twice before Graeme Souness came up with an equaliser, late on. After that we laid siege to their goal but couldn't come up with the extra breakthrough we needed and went out on goal difference. At the end of the day it all hinged on our result against Brazil and Russia had done better than us but at least we returned to Scotland after a much better experience than the one four years before.

Over the years I had some interesting experiences with Scotland squads – not least the occasion in 1979 when I thought I had forgotten to turn up for a game! It was the year that we won the European Cup for the first time at Forest after beating Malmö in Munich and on getting back home to Nottingham I was having a cup of coffee in a wine bar in the city and picked up a newspaper.

There was a headline on the back page, which read something like, 'Scotland stars go missing'. And I was named as one of them. I made a hurried phone call and was ready to apologise but then discovered that we had been given time off from reporting for a friendly against Argentina and had been asked to join up with the squad later for a European Championship qualifier against Norway. It just goes to show that you shouldn't always believe what you read in the press.

I remember the occasion well because I was really disappointed about not playing against Argentina, who had a certain Diego Maradona playing for them that day. He was still in his teens at the time and I would have loved to have played against him and seen him close up. I'm told he was excellent and Argentina won the game 3–1.

In April 1981 I had an episode to forget with Kenny Burns in the build-up to a World Cup qualifying tie against Israel at Hampden Park. We were playing a match for Forest against Crystal Palace at Selhurst Park but Jock Stein, who was manager at the time, wanted us to report to Glasgow as soon as possible on the Saturday night. Jim Cannon, a Glasgow boy who was playing for Palace, was also linking up with the squad so the three of us got together in the players' lounge after the game, which we won 3–1. We had an hour or so to wait for a taxi to the airport but that was long enough for Burnsy to get wrecked.

Contrary to common reputation Burnsy was never a big drinker and in truth it didn't take him long to get a bit tipsy and only a little bit longer to get utterly bladdered! He used to drink vodka and lime in those days and by the time the taxi arrived, Burnsy was well gone. I think he was physically sick out of the window but, fair play to the taxi driver, he took us all the way to Heathrow without any further mishap.

When I got out of the taxi I told Burnsy to hang on to me and I had a collection of my bag, his bag and a drunken Scotsman round my neck. We managed to get checked in but when we went through to board the plane we were stopped and the airport official, who was very friendly, basically said, 'I'm sorry but you're going nowhere tonight.' It left me in a right quandary so I rang Mr Stein to say we couldn't catch the plane because Burnsy wasn't feeling too well and could we get up in the morning? He was insistent that we got there that night and suggested getting on the sleeper train so that Burnsy could have a few hours' kip.

So Jim caught the plane while Burnsy and I jumped in another taxi heading for Euston railway station.

So far so good but when we got into Euston we found ourselves surrounded by Manchester United fans who had been in town that day. I told Burnsy to keep his head down but they spotted him and burst out into choruses of 'Kenny Burns is pissed, Kenny Burns is pissed . . .'.

I was thinking it couldn't get any worse at this stage but Burnsy, who was still considerably worse for wear, boomed out, 'I'll take any two of you on.' Thankfully he had no takers and we were able to limp off like two men in a three-legged race and get on the sleeper heading up north. We also got away with it with Mr Stein, who accepted the story that Burnsy had not been very well the night before.

And it all turned out well in the end because we beat Israel 3–1 and I scored the first two goals from penalties.

The next penalty I had to take for Scotland was in a World Cup qualifying match against Sweden at Hampden in September of that year. It was a game we desperately needed to win to stand a chance of going to Spain for the finals and that night I changed my mind from the spot. Instead of going hard to the keeper's right I thought that they had probably done some homework and noticed where I had put the two penalties against Israel and the one that beat England at Wembley. So I feinted to go right and then rolled the ball far too gently to the goalkeeper's left. Fortunately for me, he went the wrong way because if he had guessed right, he could have walked across his line and picked up the ball – it was that softly hit.

There's no doubt there is great psychology attached to penalties and I get great satisfaction from my record – I can't recall the exact stats but I missed only a handful out of around 70 taken – because both at club and international level I took them in some massive games. I can't help but snigger – and get a bit angry – at times when I hear so-called pundits talking about the decision making that goes with penalties, particularly when it comes to the shoot-outs that are in vogue these days. It's inevitable that somebody is going to fluff it at some stage because it is a very stressful, pressurised situation to be in. It's all right people harping on that practice makes perfect and all that sort of nonsense but when it comes to taking penalties the only constant is that you are shooting from 12 yards and you are facing a goalkeeper trying to stop the ball going in the net.

But no two penalties are the same and because of that I rarely used to practise them. For the life of me I cannot see how you can replicate those seconds when you have to stride up to the ball. It's different to other sports, and while the famous South African golfer Gary Player always said, 'The more I practise, the better I get,' it doesn't necessarily work when you are standing nervously over the penalty spot. For a start, the etiquette of the game of golf determines that you have hush when you are standing over a putt – you are certainly not accorded that sort of silence by a football crowd. Have you listened to the Kop baying for a player's blood when he is about to step forward? A golfer can take thirty or forty putts every time he goes out to play every day of his life while a penalty can only come along two or three times a season. And also there is not a little man in the hole waiting to pop up and stop it if it is on target. It's purely down to what you do at that time, but thankfully for me it's worked out a lot more times than I've failed.

My mishaps were mainly off the field, and there was another example of that when I could easily have got myself into real bother with Mr Stein around 1980. I could never resist chatting to a pretty girl, and the Scotland squad were ensconced in the Excelsior Hotel in Glasgow on one occasion and I was passing the time of day with this receptionist. I kept asking her what time she finished her shift and was trying to invite myself to have a late-night cup of tea with her. Eventually she gave in and said she was in room 402. About 20 minutes after she finished I went to the said room and knocked on the door. There was no answer so I tried again before thinking to myself that she had been winding me up.

I went back to my room and rang down to the night porter to ask him to ring Room 402 for me and to my horror he came back and said, 'You want to speak to Mr Stein at this time of night?'

I blurted out, 'No, no, no . . . goodbye.' And that was a lesson learned the hard way and one that could have caused me all sorts of trouble.

I sat on my bed, thinking, 'What if Mr Stein had answered the door? What would I have said . . . "Am I playing tomorrow, boss?"'

It was one that I got away with and, as someone told me afterwards, Mr Stein occasionally took a sleeping pill to help him get off at night. Thank goodness for that.

The story didn't end there because many years later when I had joined Celtic, this lad stopped me in a pub and recounted the story from some 20-odd years earlier.

'How do you know all about that?'

And he revealed, 'I was the hotel porter.'

It's a story I've repeated when I've done the odd after-dinner speech and it is a good tale even though I don't think my first wife Sally would exactly approve.

Then I was involved in another episode in 1982 when we went out to play in a European Championship qualifying match against Switzerland in Berne. We were staying in this hotel and every time we returned from training this girl, who was working in the hotel, gave me a bar of chocolate. One day I was in the room, which I was sharing with Frank Gray, and there was a knock on the door. There was no one there but a small package had been left on the floor just outside the door. I opened it up and couldn't believe that it was a watch and I couldn't wait to tell the boys that this girl, who was giving me all the chocolate, had now left me a watch.

I went to Graeme Souness's room because I knew one or two of the lads, including Frank, were in there and I had to recount the story.

I blurted out, 'I don't know what it is I've got but these Swiss girls all want it.'

I showed them the watch and added, 'Look what I've been left.'

Quick as a flash, Graeme opened a drawer and said, 'What, one like this?' At which point he had great delight in showing me a load of watches that had been presented to us from the Swiss FA. It's a story that all the Liverpool lads, like Souness and Alan Hansen, never tire of repeating.

In all I went on to play twenty-eight times for Scotland and scored eight goals, and although it doesn't sound that many I was very proud and honoured to represent my country on that many occasions. We didn't play anything like the number of international games that are played now and when I think that Jimmy Johnstone didn't play as many times for Scotland as I did, it proves the point because he was a really talented player.

Once I was selected by Jock Stein twenty-six of my twenty-eight caps came under him in pretty quick succession but they were still over a period of about four years. I've kept all the shirts, ironically apart from the one I wore when I scored the penalty against England because I swapped with Tony Woodcock after the game. But the others are still intact and I've also got the caps. We used to get one a season, not one for every match – you know how tight us Scots are – but they are all stashed safely away and I'll always treasure them.

12
Tragedies and tears

I PUT ON MY BEST suit, a white shirt and a tie . . . and went to see my daughter for the last time. It was September 1996 and my beautiful little girl had died at the age of 13; it was time to go and tell her how much she meant to me. She was finally at rest and rescued from what I can only imagine was 13 years of torment and frustration after being born into the world with a brutal handicap. The struggles that had been a permanent part of her life were finally over for my lovely daughter Jessica.

I went to the funeral home, where she lay in peace, with anguish in my mind, tears in my eyes but love and pride in my heart. I wrote her a letter in which I said how much I loved her and how proud I had been to be her dad. I slid the letter into the coffin where her frail little body lay and departed with a lump in my throat the size of the biggest football I had ever kicked.

A couple of days later she was buried at Wilford Hill, Nottingham in a ceremony that was as distressing an experience as it gets. You can't get your head around the fact that you are burying your own child but I consoled myself with thoughts that she was no longer in either pain or suffering.

I've lost count of the number of times I have asked myself down the years why, oh why, should she have been denied the quality and longevity of life that comes to most of us? I don't want to get into the philosophical side of things too much but I couldn't help but think why she had been here. For 13 years was pain and suffering all there was for her? Doesn't everyone deserve something better than that?

I reflected on the joy that Sally and I experienced when we first discovered that she was pregnant and we were to be parents for the first time. Ever since we were married we had tried for a baby because we were both keen to start a family as soon as possible. From day one contraception was out of the window. Sally just wanted to get pregnant and I was with her all the way. The months and years passed without any sign of us 'producing' and we both had tests to make sure neither of us had a fertility problem. We both discovered we were fine but with time creeping on we even considered having IVF treatment to see if that would help.

Then out of the blue Sally became pregnant in autumn 1982 and I doubt whether there were any happier prospective parents anywhere in the world. We were overjoyed to think that we had cracked it and were going to have our own child. Everything went well with the pregnancy until 36 weeks in when Sally went for an antenatal check-up. At the end of the appointment she happened to mention to the consultant that she had not felt the baby moving as much as normal and he asked her to get back on the couch to check the baby's heartbeat. He said that there was a heart deceleration and that Sally needed close observation in hospital; that concerned both of us because we didn't want to hear that there was the slightest little problem.

Sally stayed in the Queen's Medical Centre in Nottingham on the Monday of her appointment more as a precaution than anything else but nevertheless we were understandably getting more than a little anxious. I used to sit by Sally's bed looking at the monitors she was wired up to and see flashing numbers and beeps but not having a clue what any of them meant. Sally did because she was a newly qualified nurse and was working in the accident and emergency department at the same hospital where Jessica was born. We seemed to be left for hours on our own, wondering what was going to happen and hoping that everything was well inside.

On the Wednesday night I had just got home late after visiting her in hospital when I got a call from Sally to say, 'You had better get back. They are going to do a Caesarean section.' I had just switched on the television and was watching the Burt Reynolds movie *Deliverance*. If ever there was an omen that was it. I shot off back to the hospital, which was only three or four miles away, and Jessica was born at 1.25 on Thursday morning.

I was in the room at the time of the birth and remember them lifting her up by her little legs, showing her quickly to me and then whipping her away. It's a moment that I will never forget because what stuck in my mind – and has stuck in it ever since – was how grey Jessica was. She was very, very grey. Sally was still under sedation at this stage but I couldn't help but tell myself, 'This is not good – something is very wrong here.'

The next time we got to see her Jessica was in an incubator and Sally, who understandably knew much more about the medical side of things than I did, said our baby was sedated with an anticonvulsant. She said that Jessica had been fitting almost immediately after birth – a symptom of birth asphyxia.

We were a pair of very worried parents but although she was tiny she had beautiful eyes, lovely black hair and eyelashes.

After three weeks in the neonatal unit we were allowed to take Jessica home and were told that although she had had a bad start in life she had all the reflexes of a new-born baby and would be fine. As the weeks and months passed we just hoped against hope that Jessica would be like any normal fit and healthy child but all along there was a horrible nagging doubt in Sally's mind that our wonderful baby girl had some kind of serious problem. You look for things that babies do at certain times in their development and I remember willing myself to see her smile. I'm sure I did one day as she turned her head away but, in the fullness of time, I discovered that it had probably been a fit.

My recollections of Jessica's first few months were that she was always crying. She never seemed peaceful or happy, bless her. Believe it or not the only course of action that had any effect on calming her down was the noise of a vacuum cleaner. Whether the noise comforted her or not we will never know but we had the cleanest carpets in the village.

On one occasion Pat Serella, Dave's wife, visited us to give Sally a break from caring for Jessica but the constant crying went on and I think Pat was quite concerned at the levels of her unrest. We mentioned the problem to the local health visitor and as a result Jessica was given some form of valium to calm her down. All this added to our growing concern that there was a deep-seated problem.

Our feelings were shared by the health visitor who organised for Jessica to have more tests and she was about six months old when we got the dreadful news that she had cerebral palsy. Even then we didn't know the full extent of it. There are various degrees of cerebral palsy and on one occasion we saw a specialist who told us that Jessica might have problems walking. As time went on, if that had been her only handicap we would at least have been happier in the knowledge that she had some quality of life. The way it turned out our beautiful baby was eventually diagnosed as a spastic quadriplegic, which in layman's terms meant that she could do absolutely nothing for herself. And, sadly, I mean nothing.

Sally was a wonderful mother and, as she wrote in a touching short story about Jessica, her 'lioness instinct came to the fore'. We went everywhere to try and find a cure and we tried all kinds of therapists in a vain bid to give Jessica some relief and ourselves some hope. As Sally succinctly put it, 'These people had one thing in common – they charged you a whole heap of money for promising miracles and delivering nothing.' The money wasn't important but there was never the slightest indication that any of our visits to so-called experts would yield anything positive.

Our poor little girl was so severely handicapped there was no chance of any improvement in her condition, but despite all her massive problems, she was our daughter and we were so proud of her. She needed constant attention and we didn't even have the smallest crumb of satisfaction of seeing her interact with us in any way.

We were at a low ebb but on 22 September 1985 help was on its way to us in the shape of another daughter, Elisabeth. Following Jessica's arrival we were told that there was no reason to suspect that a second child would be anything other than 100 per cent healthy. Even so, the alarm bells were ringing once we found out in January of that year that Sally was pregnant again. Thankfully, everything did go well and we were blessed with a second daughter. When she was born and I heard her cry for the first time it was the most marvellous moment because Jessica had been taken straight from us when she came into the world.

To begin with Sally found it difficult accepting the fact that she had one wonderfully fit child and another who was, as she put it, in a 'broken body'. A few weeks went by before Sally fell totally in love with her new baby . . . a baby that somehow gave her the inspiration to fight for justice for Jessica. She was never happy with the events surrounding Jessica's birth and went to an independent obstetrician, who, after looking at the hospital notes, said that the treatment she had received would not have been expected in a third-world country – never mind a state-of-the-art teaching hospital.

Just over five years after Jessica was born and with Elisabeth three, Sally and I split up, but I can't blame the stress and strain we encountered for our parting. I'm sure it didn't help our relationship and my sympathies go to other couples who find themselves in similar situations but we were drifting apart and at that time I don't think I was the best husband around.

Sally continued the battle for justice and Paul Hackney, a solicitor who had helped me with some of my contracts with Forest, got himself interested in the case and Sally had total belief in what he was doing for us. Jessica was ten years old by the time Sally, with the considerable help of Paul, got the case to the High Court in London. Sally made sure she was heard – and why not – and at the end of a hearing, which lasted for four and a half weeks, it was found that there had been negligence, but because Jessica's injuries were so severe, the court decided that this could not have caused her brain damage.

Two years later the lawyers representing us found sufficient points of law for a further hearing in the Appeal Court . . . a hearing that lasted for one week. The evidence was all aired again but although the three judges decided to increase the amount of time in which there was negligence to 16 hours, it was once again decided that the negligence had not caused Jessica's brain damage. If Jessica was going to win any court case we had to prove things that were *impossible* to prove and it left us both, particularly Sally, who had fought so hard and passionately, with a terrible empty feeling.

Just a few weeks after that latest adjudication Jessica died. We always knew her life would end sooner rather than later but the weight of grief was still enormous. Everyone who went to her funeral walked behind the hearse from Sally's home in West Bridgford to the church and afterwards we had a celebration of Jessica's life at The City Ground. Although I don't know how much she knew about it, Jessica had attended the Ash Lea School in nearby Cotgrave and some of the other youngsters there came along to pay their own respects.

As you would imagine Sally and I received a lot of messages of sympathy and condolences – and one to me came from an unlikely source. The end for Jessica came when I was No. 2 to Martin at Leicester and the club chairman Martin George sent me the most lovely letter, which I've still got to this day. I always got the impression that Martin didn't like me too much – I always felt that he thought I was a bit of a rough and ready character – but the letter he wrote was very touching and I really appreciated his gesture.

I comforted myself – and I am sure Sally did – in the knowledge that whatever suffering and frustration Jessica had to endure throughout her 13 years was finally over. Five months before she died Jessica had been taken into hospital with severe breathing difficulties and I remember the doctor saying she might not make it through the night. I was in the hospital and looking at my beautiful helpless daughter and thinking on the one hand that I didn't want her to leave us. But on the other I just wanted someone to end her constant strife . . . and that's what it must have been. Amazingly she pulled through, but on the morning of 30 September Sally rang me to tell me that Jessica had gone.

She died without us ever knowing whether she knew who her mum and dad had been. I would love to think that there was some recognition of us down the line but I am doubtful even though Sally was adamant that Jessica was aware of who we were. She was convinced that Jessica could identify us, particularly our voices, and she had a little story that supported her theory.

While Jessica was attending the Ash Lea School she was taken on a trip to visit prisoners who the authorities were trying to reform and bring back into society as good, honest citizens. Apparently this big hulk of a bloke got talking to Jessica and although it was a totally one-way conversation, the prisoner spoke in a Scottish accent that was very much like mine. Sally was adamant that Jessica thought she was hearing my voice and had a big smile on her face. Sally was convinced there were other occasions when Jessica responded in a manner that suggested she knew who her mum and dad were and I would love to think she was right.

But despite the fact that she was so helpless, she left both Sally and myself with legacies . . . and good legacies.

For Sally's part Jessica's life and story inspired her to broaden her nursing experience and train as a midwife as a direct result of what happened to her first child. She now works as a co-ordinator in a hospital labour suite in Nuneaton, where she lived when I first met her. She swears that to the best of her ability, she will make sure that history does not repeat itself.

As for me, the privilege of being Jessica's father for 13 years made me a much more compassionate person. I think people who don't really know me view John Robertson the footballer as a bit of a lad, who liked a drink, liked a smoke and generally loved the existence that professional footballers are able to afford and enjoy. But being Jessica's father gave me a new outlook and perspective on life and, whether or not people agree with me, I know in my heart of hearts that I am a more caring and considerate person for the experiences she gave me.

Four years before Jessica was born I had to cope with the anger, sadness and grief of losing another loved one when my brother Hughie was killed in a car crash. He was only 35 and it seemed such a waste that someone so fit and healthy should be taken at such an early age amid tragic circumstances.

The accident happened on the Stirling Road out of Glasgow on 7 April 1979 – a wet and filthy Scottish night. Another car coming in the opposite direction had come across the central reservation on a dual carriageway and the impact was such that my sister-in-law Isobel was killed instantly. Hughie was cut out of the wreckage and taken to hospital but died later that night and my niece Jillian, who was in the back seat, was the only survivor.

After the crash she was in hospital for ten days suffering with internal bleeding, and the consequences of that terrible time affected her in later life. When she was married and wanting to have a family, she and her husband Dave were having problems conceiving because of the adhesions that had resulted from the accident. Jillian had two operations to try and rectify the problem and after the second she was told by the specialist that there was no hope of her ever getting pregnant naturally. She and Dave were on the waiting list for IVF when miraculously she found out she was pregnant. It brought them so much happiness but, going back to the accident, it was always going to be a long haul for her to overcome the whole episode mentally. Her task in life was to recover from the reality of being an orphan at the tender age of eight.

It was the days before mobile phones and I knew nothing about the crash or the horrific consequences for hours after the event. It happened on a Saturday and that afternoon I had played for Forest at Stamford Bridge, where we had beaten Chelsea 3–1 and put on a really good performance a matter of four days before our European Cup semi-final against Cologne. The win had put me in great spirits on the return journey from London and I was looking ahead to a nice night out with Dave Serella and his wife Pat, who got on really well with Sally.

When I got back to Nottingham we all went out for a meal in town and then on to a nightclub, where we passed the night and early hours away in our usual fashion. On the way back the taxi dropped Dave and Pat off before we headed home, and as soon as I got in the door the phone was ringing with Dave on the other end. He said that my brother-in-law Jimmy Rooney was trying to get hold of me and rang him because he thought we would be together on a Saturday night. He just said that I had to ring him as soon as possible.

I had my own ideas what it might be because when you get that kind of message it's bad news and my thoughts immediately went to my dad who had been having one or two problems with angina. It was about two o'clock in the morning by this time and when I rang Jimmy he simply said, 'I'm sorry, I've got some really bad news.' If memory serves me right I blurted out, 'It's my dad isn't it?'

Jimmy's voice got lower and lower and he said, 'No, it's Hughie . . . he's been killed in a car crash.'

'You're joking,' I answered in one of the most ridiculous comments I've ever made in my life – as if anybody would joke about such a terrible thing! But this was for real and it took time to sink in.

Apparently the crash had happened about 7.30 p.m. but by the time my relatives in Scotland had been informed and they had tried to get hold of me, we were out enjoying ourselves.

Hughie had been driving a car I had given him. After winning the First Division Championship the gaffer had arranged for all the players to get Toyota Celicas so I had a Vauxhall Viva that was going spare and thought that Hughie could put it to good use. I had only given it to him a couple of months beforehand and now he had lost his life in it. In some stupid way I felt a bit guilty because Hughie had not had a car in his earlier days and had only recently passed his test. The car I gave him was the first he had owned.

On getting the news my first thoughts were to get up to Scotland and be with my family as soon as possible but both Sally and I had been drinking and we couldn't go anywhere that night. We didn't sleep but the following morning we headed north by car and naturally the entire family was in bits. My mam and my dad took it really badly and I'm firmly of the opinion that Hughie's death played a big part in my dad passing away the following year because he never really recovered from the heartbreak of it all. It's not the sort of thing you can prepare yourself for. It was a massive shock and there was nothing anyone could say or do that would change the horror of it all. My parents were obviously distraught and could not find rhyme nor reason for the terrible events that had left their elder son and his wife dead and their grandchild in hospital. I tried to comfort them best I could but it was impossible.

Looking at it from their point of view it was just not meant to be. How could their son, in the prime of his life, be taken away from them? It wasn't the natural order of things and I'm sure they were thinking that they had lived a lot longer and were asking themselves why they were not taken instead of their son.

They loved us both very much but were closer to Hughie than me, largely because I had moved away to follow my football career while he had always lived nearby. But Hughie used to joke about their relationship and say things like, 'How about a cup of tea for your favourite son?' when he went to visit them.

I thought the world of Hughie but the logistics side of things – him being in Scotland and me in England – somehow made it a little bit easier for me to come to terms with the tragedy. Being removed from the family home I was able to compartmentalise the whole issue a lot better than my relatives on the spot could. Having said that, so many memories streamed through my mind about the times I had spent with Hughie . . . from singing to me at bedtime, spending hours playing football together in my earlier days and bugging me for Wembley tickets when Scotland came south. I remember sitting in my parents' house and thinking, 'I wish the hell he was in here now asking me for Wembley tickets – I'd get him as many as he wanted.' I had visions of him sitting in the local club – as he used to on a Saturday night – drinking his whisky and laughing and joking with his mates because he had a good sense of humour.

Then my mind wandered back to the car that I had given him and I still couldn't come to terms with that issue in the aftermath of the crash. He had not had a car before but providing him with transport led them to make a conscious decision to get out more as a family. I thought I was doing them a big favour. To this day I don't know where he was going the night of the crash but at the time I wished they were still travelling around on public transport. Had they done so, Hughie and Isobel would still be alive.

With me being a footballer, there was more media interest in the story than there might have been otherwise and journalists were hanging around outside my mum and dad's house hoping to speak to someone. But Sally dealt with the press really well. When anyone came to the door she took command and pleaded for them to give the family some peace in order to deal with their sudden grief.

In practical terms I had to contact the gaffer on the Monday morning to inform him of what had happened and why I wasn't in for normal training. This was two days before our European Cup semi-final first leg tie with Cologne at The City Ground but he was terrific about the whole thing . . . very sensitive and wanting to do anything he possibly could to help. He told me to take as long as I wanted with my family and whatever I decided to do he would respect the decision.

But as the hours passed my mum, dad and other members of the family told me that if I was up to it I should play in the game because it would have been what Hughie wanted. The funeral was fixed for the Thursday, which was the day after the match, so after much deliberation I decided to play and then get immediately back to Scotland for the service and cremation.

The weather was very poor at the time and at one stage there was a suggestion that the game might be postponed and put back 24 hours and that would have made it impossible for me to be available to play. So I returned to Nottingham, played in the game and then Sally and I caught an early flight up to Glasgow on Thursday morning to be at the funeral.

If it is not stating the obvious, it was a terribly sad affair. The funeral was a joint one for Hughie and Isobel and that seemed to add extra poignancy to the occasion. The one thing I do remember from that day to this, is that my cigarette smoking increased significantly. Up until that point I had nothing more than an occasional fag and never used to inhale. It's totally stupid but before then cigarettes had been more of a fashion accessory than an addiction. But, whether or not it was me trying to find something to deal with my stress and grief, I had more cigarettes the day of Hughie's funeral than ever before and from then on I suppose I became a much heavier smoker. Hughie used to like a smoke and I can remember justifying my actions by telling myself, 'They didn't kill him.' It was perhaps not the most sensible way to look at things but that was my pathetic interpretation of it.

Amid all the emotional upset we were constantly thinking of Hughie and Isobel's daughter Jillian, who had survived the crash. I'm so proud with the way she dealt with the situation in which she found herself after recovering from her injuries. She has gone on to be a wonderful woman with a lovely family all of her own. When we are together she likes nothing better than to reminisce about her mum and dad and we've spent many an hour talking about life before that fateful day.

I'd also like to say how much I've leaned on my sister Caroline and her husband Jimmy, particularly during the really sad times in my life. I even wrote them a letter when my mum passed away in 1994 thanking them both for everything they had done. Because I have spent so many years in England, they were the ones who were on the spot when tragedy hit the family in Scotland. They had to deal with the effects on my parents when Hughie and Isobel were killed and they were also the first ones on the spot when my mum and dad passed away.

I was across the Atlantic on a pre-season tour with Forest when my dad died in 1980. I knew he had not been well but I was certainly not expecting to hear the 'worst' when I got a phone call about four or five o'clock in the morning. I was sharing a room with Viv Anderson in Tampa Bay and it's never good news to get a phone call at that time of day. When Viv answered the phone, Jimmy was on the other end and he quickly passed it on to me. I didn't know what to do in the hours that followed so I got myself dressed and took a stroll along the beach in Florida to have a quiet time for myself. Cloughie wasn't on the trip but as soon as I could I had a word with Peter Taylor and he just said, 'Get yourself home as quickly as you can and we'll do everything we can for you.'

My mum's death came just as suddenly in November 1994. Earlier that year I was helping Martin O'Neill while he was at Wycombe Wanderers. They had reached the Third Division play-offs and were up against Carlisle United at Brunton Park. My mum came down to watch the match with Caroline and Jimmy and at the end of the game we were walking back to their car when she complained about having a terrible pain in her back. She used to witter on about things so we didn't pay too much attention but on this occasion it turned out to be serious. Soon afterwards she was diagnosed with ovarian cancer and within a matter of months had died.

Little things come into your mind when loved ones die and my mind went back to a day when she was down in Nottingham and I took her, my second wife Sharyl and Elisabeth to Drayton Manor Park for the day. I don't know why but during the trip I started singing Scottish songs – like 'Stop yer tickling, Jock' to her – and she was giggling away and joining in because she knew the words better than I did. The more I sang, the more she giggled and it was just one of those cherished memories that have stayed with me.

In her last hours she was topped up with morphine and began hallucinating and was very confused. Sharyl was pregnant with Andrew at the time and she knew she would not be around to see her grandchild born. But I remember her turning to Sharyl and in a broken voice saying, 'Look after that wean.'

Once more Caroline and Jimmy had the task of dealing with things and it's always appeared to me as if they have had a lot of responsibility on their shoulders. But it's not all been doom and gloom and we've also had some great times together – not least in 1999 when Sharyl and I were married. Jimmy was best man at my wedding – and that's how highly I value his friendship and the manner in which he and Caroline have supported me whenever I needed them. They even joined us on honeymoon! Sharyl and I went off to Cyprus for a week and then Caroline and Jimmy were among those who came out to join us and carry on the celebrations. Larry Lloyd and his wife also came, as did Sharyl's parents and family.

As well as being 'rocks' for me in my life, they can feel extremely proud of the four sons and daughters they have helped turn into brilliant people. Pauline, Jim, who acts as my accountant, Caroline and Alan have all done very well for themselves and that is due in no small part to the parental guidance they have had from two great people.

13
New love in my life

A LOT OF THE SELF-BELIEF that I had when my career was at a high with Forest had been knocked out of me following the Derby experience. And if there was anything left of my then fragile ego, it disappeared when I came to terms with the fact that my career was effectively over for good in the summer of 1986.

I genuinely felt that some club, somewhere would feel that at thirty-three I still had something to offer and would be interested in talking to me but I didn't get one phone call from a league club asking whether or not I was available. Not even a manager of a Fourth Division club was sufficiently interested in picking up the phone even to pass the time of day. It was all very surprising and disappointing. Maybe people felt that, because I had just been released by Forest I would be asking for signing-on fees and decent money, but I never got the slightest hint that a club was interested. I found it strange and a little bit dispiriting that someone who had played in as many games at the top level as I had was not worth at least an inquiry.

Then, out of the blue, came a call from former Mansfield Town player Colin Foster, who at the time was managing non-league Corby Town. With nothing else in the offing, I played a handful or so games for them but the new career path I was about to follow didn't accommodate dashing off to play semi-professional football all over the country.

When my days with Forest were over I didn't want to hang around feeling sorry for myself and Sally and I had long chats about what we could do. When football is your life and all you know as a means of earning a living, it can come as a bit of a rude awakening when it is all over. Too many footballers are ill-equipped to do anything else when their playing days are over and I was no exception. Our conversations invariably returned at some stage to the possibility of taking over a pub in the Nottingham area. It was the sort of thing that professional footballers did when their careers were over and I wasn't exactly qualified to take on a professional job of any kind. In readiness for going into a pub, Alan Hill and his wife Janice invited me – and one or two of the other lads who were interested – over to his place, the Rancliffe Arms in Bunny, a little village a few miles outside of Nottingham. I must admit I quite enjoyed the bit of an insight we got but that's what it was – a little taster.

The real thing demanded a lot more effort, commitment and time. We had two children by that stage – Elisabeth was born in the season I was back at Forest – and Jessica, bless her, continued to need round-the-clock care. Looking back now I wonder how we could imagine that we could take on a new venture like a pub, with all the hard work and unsociable hours it entailed, as well as looking after two young children, one of whom was severely disabled.

But, perhaps without too much in the way of reasoned thinking to back up the decision, we took over the tenancy of a pub at Aslockton, near Nottingham, called The Old Greyhound. It was a nice, typical village pub where the locals met at the end of a day's work to sort out the world's problems over a pint or two. But almost immediately I could tell we were going to have problems over time, logistics and every other factor you care to mention.

We had lived in Plumtree, a village just four miles from The City Ground, since we married, before moving to West Bridgford in 1985, and Sally spent the days looking after the kids at home there and then got a babysitter so that she could help me out at night. In truth Sally had got her hands full with the children, particularly the demands that accompanied Jessica's health. She must have been whacked out by the time she made her way to the pub at night even though it must have provided her with a welcome break.

It didn't take me long to realise that I wasn't cut out for the pub business but thank goodness I had great help from a lady called Barbara Porter, who had run The Old Greyhound in previous years. She was still around the place, helping out as a cleaner and such like and she realised that I was in need of help and advice from someone with a bit of nous in the trade. I couldn't have got by without her guidance and encouragement and she brought all her old landlady skills to the table in a bid to help me along and, indeed, bail me out. I also got a lot of help from John Hodgkinson, a drinking pal we always referred to as 'Mungo' and without him and Barbara I would have been in a right mess.

For a time we got by and one of the plusses for me was that I got to play for the pub football team on a Sunday morning and I also joined a local team called Whatton, who played on Saturday afternoons. Most of the players represented both teams and it was a good way for me to get away from the pub and clear my head at what was a difficult time in my life.

So many things were different in 'Sunday' football compared with the professional game, of course, and you literally couldn't swing a cat in some of the dressing-rooms I went into. The banter was good and it was interesting listening to lads who went out on a Friday and Saturday night and got bladdered on the eve of a game. I was more tuned in to being tucked up in a hotel room preparing to give your best the following day at Anfield or Old Trafford. But it was a good experience and for someone who had won two European Cups I can't tell you how much pleasure I got in helping the pub team win a knock-out cup competition called the Willie Hall Trophy.

There was always plenty of chat flying around from opposition players but I can honestly say that the lads I came up against were very fair and for the most part friendly. I'm sure it came into the minds of one or two opponents that they could have gone home on a Sunday afternoon and boasted about 'kicking John Robertson up in the air'. I'm not sure why, but I played centre-forward and I'll be the first to admit I was no Peter Withe or Garry Birtles. I was a bit of a sitting target – I didn't move around much by then – but I got away quite lightly. On the rare occasions when I sensed I might get a bit of a whack thankfully I still had the brains to get out of the way.

I had more trouble with referees, who seemed to take great relish in booking me, but I've got to admit there were times when my arguing and dissent justified a yellow card or two. On one occasion I went too far and got myself the second – and final – red card of my career. I was taking a bit of stick in this game and wasn't happy about a challenge from behind that the referee didn't even see as a free-kick. I had a right go at the referee, wouldn't let it lie and eventually his patience snapped and he pulled out the red card. He muttered something about the FA as I trooped off the field and rather pettily I came back with, 'It doesn't make much difference to me at my time of life.' But I was bang out of order and if he's reading this now, I would like to apologise to him.

I stayed in the pub for eighteen months, leaving in March 1988 and over the last two or three months I was there I became very disillusioned with just about everything. I knew I was doing the wrong job and the whole business was beginning to get on top of me. I was tired, wasn't eating very sensibly and felt really run down. It certainly wasn't the healthiest or happiest time for me.

Soon after I left the pub Sally and I split up, and in all honesty I didn't really anticipate meeting up with someone else and getting married for a second time. Life had not been easy for either of us but particularly Sally who was a great mum and took most of the responsibility for looking after Jessica and Elisabeth. Almost inevitably, there was a lot of strain and stress in our relationship and in the end we just drifted apart and became totally incompatible. But we still had one very important factor in common – we adored our daughters and we were determined not to pass by responsibilities on that score. They meant the world to both of us. I often had the girls at weekends and other occasions to fit in with Sally's shift patterns. Sometimes I would go round early in the morning and get them ready for school or alternatively pick them up from school and stay with them until Sally returned from work.

It was at that time that Martin O'Neill took his first strides in management with Grantham Town and he rang to ask if I fancied the idea of playing for him. Although the travelling was going to be difficult, he convinced me to give it a go and I played seven or eight matches for them. He also recruited Kenny Burns, Mick Maguire, former Liverpool full-back Alan Kennedy and Terry Curran so it was a bit of a former All Stars XI. We just went along for the pleasure of it and to help Martin out because Grantham were not exactly a prosperous outfit.

You could instantly see the enthusiasm and thoroughness that Martin brought to the job and even dealing with seasoned pros, many of whom had been his former team-mates, he wasn't afraid to dish out bollockings when they were needed. We struggled for a while but Martin was as professional as he could possibly be in the circumstances. He spent hours driving around watching local league football in an effort to uncover a hidden gem. And he found one in Gary Crosby, who was a wiry little winger who went on to join Forest and had a great career under the gaffer.

I was invited to go and watch Forest play at Manchester United one day and, although it was perhaps not very fair of me, I opted out of playing for Grantham that weekend. I know Martin felt a little bit let down but it gave him the chance to give Crosby, or 'Bing' as everyone knew him, an opportunity to show what he had to offer as my replacement. Martin had seen Bing playing for a team in Lincoln and liked what he saw. With me going off to Old Trafford it gave him the opportunity to have a look and Bing duly impressed.

I decided after that to stop playing for Grantham and told Martin that I would be more than happy to sit alongside him on the bench if he wanted me to. And that's really how our partnership began. We left Grantham and had a few months in charge of Shepshed but it was at a time when we were both very undecided about the future and trying to make a living away from football.

Martin and I went to work for life assurance company Save & Prosper – he was working inside the office as a manager and I was out on the road trying to drum up business as an agent. We attempted to combine that with managing Shepshed but we rapidly discovered that we couldn't be in two places at once. On one occasion we were almost late getting to a midweek match against Frickley Colliery in South Yorkshire and I think it was at that point that we knew we couldn't carry on. The football wasn't going too well so we decided between us that it wasn't possible to do both jobs and it was sadly time to concentrate on the insurance world.

By his own admission Martin's knowledge of the financial services products we were trying to sell wasn't the best but in the meetings we had he came across as though he knew the business inside out. That's how he got a manager's job. People responded to his leadership and it just goes to show that if you have a talent for man-management it can come to the fore in any walk of life.

Despite our family responsibilities and commitments, whenever Martin and I met the conversation always turned to football and I think we both hankered after another opening. Then, right out of the blue, Martin was offered his first really big break as manager of Wycombe Wanderers in 1990. He had been working for ITV as a co-commentator with Alan Parry on a match between his old club Norwich City and Liverpool. Alan was passionate about Wycombe, was on their board of directors and at the time they were looking for a new manager. One thing rapidly led to another and it transpired that Wycombe were about to appoint Alan Harris, the brother of former Chelsea legend Ron, in the very near future. Martin made it clear that he would be interested in the job, went down to Wycombe the following day for an interview and was appointed soon afterwards – I would assume much to Harris's annoyance.

That same week Grantham had got back in touch with Martin to ask if he fancied returning to the club. He told them that he was taking the Wycombe job but recommended that they ring me because Wycombe were still a non-league club at that stage and the finances were not available for me to join him. I duly got the call from Grantham, was asked if I fancied giving it a go and I said, 'Why not?' John Robertson, the manager, was something new in my life because I had always been one to sit in the background and let others take on the worries and decisions that came with being No. 1. I wasn't sure how it would go but I stayed there for about 18 months and really enjoyed it.

They were playing in the Beazer Homes League and were in trouble when I first went there. In fact, we could have been relegated with five or six games to go but we managed to scramble enough points together to stay up and I got a bit of a kick out of that. I took to the task of being the boss surprisingly well and I was fortunate in that Martin had left a bit of a legacy from his days in charge. One or two of the players he had signed were still around and by Grantham standards they weren't bad. I was happy being in control and if I had to bend a few ears in the dressing-room and on the pitch then so be it.

The actual running of the team on matchdays came quite naturally to me but it was the other aspects of the job that I found difficult. I didn't fancy trekking around the country watching crap football matches in the hope of spotting a potential signing here and there. I quickly discovered there was a lot more to the job than 90-odd minutes on matchday and I wasn't really prepared for that. Martin was far more industrious and thorough when it came to that side of the job and it's probably an indication of why he became so successful.

As part of the agreement with Grantham, they created a job for me looking after the commercial side of the club during the week and I was given a van to get me around. It was all about raising as much money as I could from schemes like lotteries and raffles and it was hard work, persuading people to hand over their hard-earned cash.

After leaving the pub I was living the life of a single man again and Jimmy McCann, who had remained a big friend since our Forest days, got me fixed up at a place where he was staying in West Bridgford. He was living with a lad called Dave Howard, whose house it was, and they kindly put a roof over my head. They had the bedrooms, I curled up to sleep on the sofa and the van came in handy because it was my mobile wardrobe!

You might not think it was the basis of a happy and fulfilling life but it suited me for a while. I did my job, went to The Willow Tree pub at night and met up with the old Forest club doctor Bill Heathcote – a lovely man who just enjoyed talking non-stop football. He is sadly no longer with us but we spent many a happy hour together – did the *Telegraph* crossword and then I went home to kip on the couch.

I suppose you could say I was a bit of a hobo really and after staying with Jimmy and Dave I moved in with a lad called Cameron Miles, who had been a goalkeeper in local football. Gary Charles, who had been an exciting young full-back with Forest in his earlier days, was also staying with him. I had my own bed so at least things were looking up with the sleeping arrangements.

Even though I was reasonably happy I was still badly in need of some stability in my life and the best thing that could have happened to me was meeting Sharyl. We actually first met at the end of 1988 but it was over a year later before we finally got together and became 'an item' in 1990 in the middle of the days when I was footloose but not very fancy!

We still disagree about how we met. I think the first time was in a Nottingham bar called No. 10 but Sharyl insists it was at a Save & Prosper Christmas 'do' at The Royal Hotel in the city centre with our meeting at No. 10 coming later. Sharyl worked for a company called Business and Commercial Insurance and it was one of those Christmas functions when groups of people from different companies came together to make one big party. Their table was very close to ours and, as you do, I had a good look around to eye up the talent. I caught Sharyl's eye and sent a match box over to her with a note inside saying, 'I love you.' It wasn't the most original chat-up line you've ever heard, particularly when you bear in mind that I had never even met her before. Sharyl says we met in No. 10 after that but we didn't properly get talking until I was in Jallons bar one lunch-time and Sharyl came in. Our eyes crossed again and we had a brief chat. I'm sure I said, 'What did you say your name was again?' Sharyl replied, 'I didn't,' so we were off to a good start! But at least she went on to ask where I used to go for a drink and we sort of developed a relationship from there.

We kept bumping into each other at various places and I think it's fair to say that we both ended up chasing each other. It was amazing how we both kept ending up at the same bar in town. I remember one night our paths crossed in The Stage Door, a pub in Nottingham city centre where Larry Lloyd was landlord. As I walked past her in the pub I came out with the line: 'Can I take you to bed tonight?' It was a bit of tongue in cheek but to my utter amazement Sharyl said 'Yes' but then proceeded to run out of the pub, laughing as she went, and disappeared quickly into the night.

The romance, however, grew and grew and there was a certain inevitability that we would get together on a permanent basis. Sharyl is fifteen years younger than me and an attractive girl – she's also got the best pair of legs I've ever seen – and I've always joked to her that one day she would want to trade me in and get a newer model!

I can't stress how important she has been. She came along when I was probably at my lowest ebb and most vulnerable but she played a huge part in me getting my life back together. It's at times when you are not expecting something to happen that it invariably does and Sharyl coming into my life gave me a totally different perspective on things. She's also been very supportive with Jessica and Elisabeth and regularly looked after them when I was away on football business.

When I first met Sharyl she had her own house in Arnold and here I was dossing down with various mates. Eventually I decided to sort myself out and rented a house in Mapperley, not too far away from where Sharyl was living. Having a 'home' also meant I was able to have the girls stay overnight with me occasionally – something I'd not really been able to do before. When Sally and I were divorced in 1992 I bought myself a house in Compton Acres, West Bridgford, so I had a place to call my own again.

Soon after I had moved in I was left devastated when the house was broken into and I lost a lot of the medals that I had won during my playing career. The medals had been out of harm's way in an old cardboard box and, quite rightly, Sharyl thought they should be on display so she made a place for them in the house where everyone could see them. I was so proud of them, I was devastated by the break-in, and I thought there was absolutely no chance of getting them back. I thought the person who had stolen the medals would have great difficulty selling them because there were so few around and they could be easily traced. So I imagined that the medals would be just left in some burglar's house to gather dust when I should have had the pleasure of looking at them for the rest of my life.

Then right out of the blue I received a phone call from the police saying that the thief had owned up to stealing the medals when being questioned over another matter. What a stroke of good fortune! Apparently the police officers in charge of the inquiry had been speaking to this suspect and said words to the effect of, 'You can imagine how John Robertson felt after having his European Cup medals stolen.' I'm not sure whether or not the thief was overcome with guilt or just wanted to confess but the upshot was that I got the medals back in December 1992 and I couldn't have had a better Christmas present. Apparently he had kept them in his girlfriend's laundry basket. They were returned to me by Detective Constable Austin O'Driscoll and PC John Davis and I'd like to thank them publicly now for helping me get the medals back. And just in case anyone is thinking of having another go at nicking them, let me stress that they are now very safely under lock and key.

Despite having my own place I used to stay with Sharyl a lot in her house in Arnold and it wasn't long before we took the next step and I moved in with her. We were very much in love, were settled in a great relationship by that stage and in February 1995 Andrew, our first child – and my first son – was born. Sharyl and I could not have been happier. Eventually we both sold our houses and moved to a bigger one near to where I had been living in Compton Acres. We've kept the same home to this day – no matter where I've been working – and we've been very content together there.

Martin was doing very well by this stage. He had got Wycombe moving forward and had brought in Steve Walford and Paul Franklin, men who were to play a big part in his backroom team in subsequent years. Unlike me at Grantham, he had put his heart and soul into management and was getting the rewards. He got Wycombe into the Football League and by that time I had agreed with Grantham that we were not making as much progress as we all had hoped and left by mutual consent.

Wycombe weren't exactly awash with money so Martin couldn't offer me a full-time job but he did ask me to be his scout and I realised that if I was going to be serious about working in football I had to do it properly. Martin paid me £7,000 a year plus expenses but I knew full well that I had to prove myself and get off my backside and be a lot more positive. I actually worked really hard, travelling a lot of miles watching matches and players. I was out most days of the week and spent a lot of time eyeing up league clubs' reserve sides in the hope of picking up a talented player who had slipped through the net.

I must have done something right because Martin managed to up my salary to £12,000 a year but in return he wanted me to spend a bit more time with him in Wycombe. I actually moved down there for about six months, went to games with him and generally got a lot more involved in day-to-day matters.

He had become a hugely popular figure at Wycombe and with his record you could understand why. It was a homely sort of club with a lot of nice people in and around it and it was an ideal club for Martin to get a grounding in league management. Despite reaching 94 points Wycombe had unbelievably missed out to Colchester United in getting into the Football League on goal difference in his first full season, 1991–92, then the following season he succeeded in getting them into the Football League for the first time in their history. They continued their forward march and 12 months further on he got them into the third tier of English football following a 4–2 play-off victory over Preston North End. In addition to their unprecedented success in the league Martin also led Wycombe to two FA Trophy successes in 1991 and 1993. It was a tremendous run and he went on to consolidate Wycombe in the third tier of English football before leaving in 1995 to go to Norwich City.

He took Paul and Steve with him as first team and reserve coaches respectively and I carried on doing the same scouting role but we were only there for a matter of six months. Everything looked very promising. Norwich had been relegated from the Premier League under John Deehan but Martin had turned things around very quickly and the whiff of an immediate return to the Premiership was certainly in the air. The Carrow Road fans responded to Martin but behind the scenes there were differences of opinion with chairman Robert Chase. The problem that reached a head and led to Martin's departure revolved around promises being made about possible signings. Martin was keen on buying Dean Windass but at the end of the day he had to pull out of the deal because the finances were not available.

But as one door closed, another opened and there was a new inviting challenge awaiting Martin back in the East Midlands.

14
Mixing it with the best

THE NORWICH EXPERIENCE, WHICH SEEMED to come and go very quickly, in no way damaged Martin O'Neill's burgeoning reputation as one of the top young managers in the game. And in December 1995 he got the platform he needed to show that he could go on and mix it with the big boys like Sir Alex Ferguson and Arsène Wenger in the years that followed.

It was a case of second time lucky for Leicester City, whose chairman Martin George had courted Martin before he took on the Norwich job. But when Martin left Carrow Road, Mr George moved swiftly to make sure he was in pole position to get his man at the second time of asking. Mark McGhee had just left to take on the Wolves job so it fitted neatly into Leicester's plans when Martin became available.

At the time Paul Franklin initially indicated that he wanted to stay on at Norwich because he had moved his family to East Anglia and didn't want to uproot again. Steve Walford was keen to step up as first team coach so when things didn't work out as Paul had hoped at Norwich, he eventually ended up at Filbert Street looking after the reserves. It was role reversal for those two but I carried on doing very much what I had been doing before but spent a lot more time sitting next to Martin.

Our first task within hours of going to Leicester was to watch them play at Grimsby Town and, when they were two goals down at one stage, the immediate future didn't look too clever from where we were sitting. We managed to get back to 2–2 but it didn't camouflage what we were thinking. Let's just say we knew straight away there was considerable work to be done.

It would take time for Martin to knock things into shape and he wasn't helped by the parting shot of McGhee as he left for Molineux. He said something like, 'This team that I am leaving is good enough to win the First Division by a stretch.' That didn't make any sense to me because he had gone to Wolves, who were well below Leicester in the table at that time. Why, then, was he leaving a club with what he perceived as having an excellent chance of promotion for one with a lot more ground to make up? Why didn't he stay at Filbert Street, see the job through into the Premier League and see his own reputation enhanced?

What his comments did, of course, was to raise the expectation levels among Leicester supporters and it wasn't easy managing those aspirations the minute we arrived at the club. To make matters considerably worse we couldn't buy a victory. The harder we tried, the worse it seemed to get and it was ages before we managed to get a win to bring a bit of belief to the players. Ironically, the victory came against Wolves at Molineux. We beat them 3–2 and, in view of McGhee's comments when he departed Leicester, it gave us a bit of extra satisfaction.

We needed to make changes and the finances to do that became available when we sold Julian Joachim and Steve Corica before the transfer deadline in March 1996. Joachim, who had come through the ranks at Leicester, moved to Aston Villa in a deal that brought us £1.5m. Corica made it clear that he wanted to leave Leicester and link up with McGhee again at Wolves and we ended up getting a similar figure for him. Corica was a nice footballer but we thought we were getting good money and as he made it clear he wanted off, there was no point in keeping a player whose heart wasn't in it.

Crucially for us, the outgoing transfers enabled us to buy Neil Lennon from Crewe Alexandra . . . and what a huge signing he turned out to be. We had seen Neil on a couple of occasions and had gone down to Southampton to watch him play in one match. Everything about him suggested he would be a great buy for us so Martin spoke to Crewe manager Dario Gradi and asked to be kept informed if Neil became available. Crewe wanted to keep the player while they were in the FA Cup but they went out in a replay to Southampton and we immediately approached Dario to try and set up a deal. You can imagine how we felt when we were told that a transfer had been put in place for Neil to move to Coventry City, who were managed at the time by Ron Atkinson. Martin didn't want to end our interest there and said if we could match the £750,000 fee, could we speak to the player?

We did that and set off to meet Jim Melrose, who was Neil's agent at the time. Jim told us about the Coventry deal but we said, 'We've come up to Crewe, we've agreed a fee so can we at least have a word with the player?' He had no problems with that and off we went to Neil's house, which made my worst living conditions look like a palace . . . in fact I felt very much at home there! Neil won't mind me saying this but his place resembled a hovel – it looked as if it had been taken over by squatters – but we weren't there to buy the property. We wanted the player and didn't want to leave without him agreeing to join us. Once Martin got talking he weaved his Irish magic and Neil decided he would come. Jim was quite cute because I think he told a few porkies about how much Coventry had offered in terms of wages and if we wanted Neil we would have to match the figures he had already been offered. But we viewed it as an important capture and convinced the lad that there was a good future for him at Leicester.

Neil was a great reader of the game and never gave the ball away. You always got the impression with him that he thought the possession of the ball was priceless and that's very much how I used to value it when I was playing. He didn't score as many goals as he might but he was great at winning the ball back and with his ability to use it, we felt as though we had a real player on our hands.

I don't think Big Ron was too happy about what took place but he had been around a long time and won more than he had lost in the transfer game.

As the 28 March transfer deadline loomed Martin was frantically trying to add players to the squad in a bid to give us a chance of figuring in the play-offs. And just before the deadline we made another two significant captures when we bought Steve Claridge from Birmingham for £1.2m and then did a deal with Chelsea to bring in Muzzy Izzet on loan.

In addition to Steve having bags of experience, he was a player who always worked his socks off. In fact, they did often end up around his ankles. He was happy playing with his back to goal and could be a real handful on his day so he gave us a lot of attacking options. He did a great job for us, scoring some vitally important goals, and he went on to have a fantastic career with what seemed like a million and one football clubs before retiring. Nobody knew much about Muzzy, but during his Wycombe days Martin used to watch Chelsea reserves quite a lot and he always had a sneaking fancy for the boy, who wasn't making as much headway as he might at Stamford Bridge.

Our success at signing players was not reflected on the field and results were still not good – the Wolves game had produced our only victory – and we were under severe pressure to improve and get into the top six, where we were expected to be. The Leicester fans were getting impatient and it all came to an unpleasant head on a day when we lost 2–0 to Sheffield United at Filbert Street. Neil was suspended, we weren't very good at all – in fact we were bloody hopeless – and the crowd really turned against us. I was standing beside Martin in the dugout area and all I kept hearing was, 'Fuck off, O'Neill.' I remember Martin taking a deep breath and saying to me, 'It's wild, isn't it?' We were clutching at straws in terms of what to do to provide a lift and Muzzy went on for the last 20 minutes to give us a brief indication of his ability. He didn't change the course of the game but in his short time on the pitch he had shown Martin and me that he had something to offer.

The protests continued after the final whistle and it got so bad that a delegation of fans came forward to the reception area wanting to put forward their point of view. And that's when Martin really earned his corn. There were about a dozen or more supporters involved and he agreed for them to come into a room inside the ground and I went along with him to face the music and give him some support. Martin spoke really well and basically asked them to give him a chance. He reasoned that he had not been at the club long – barely four months in fact – and if nothing changed over a period of time then by all means call for his head. They went away feeling a little bit better about things if only because he had given them an opportunity to vent their feelings.

But Martin had grasped the nettle by this stage and agreed to go on a local radio phone-in the following Monday night to front up and answer more criticism. He got a barrage of pointed questions and it wasn't very pleasant for him. But he stood up to be counted and I think he drew a lot of praise and respect for doing so.

But as Brian Clough always used to say, nothing changes things in football like results. The following night we were playing Charlton at The Valley with Neil back from suspension and, after what he had shown us against Sheffield United, we decided to give Muzzy his full debut. Charlton were doing quite well themselves but we ended up winning 1–0 with a goal by Steve Claridge and for a few hours at least the air around the place seemed a bit clearer.

The following Saturday we were back in South London to face Crystal Palace and again we won 1–0 with a goal from Iwan Roberts and from that moment we were on our way. We did have a hiccup when we lost 2–1 at home to West Brom but our results picked up and we went to Watford on the final day of the season with a chance of creeping into the play-offs.

Millwall and Ipswich were also in the reckoning and the promotion issue was right up in the air but we just had to concentrate on winning our game and see what happened elsewhere. It was a bit like the situation we were in at Forest in 1977 when Cloughie told us, 'We'll do our job and worry about what others do after that.' We beat Watford thanks to a goal by Muzzy, other results fortunately went our way, and suddenly there was a real sense of optimism around the place when a few weeks earlier there had only been anger and frustration. We were in the play-offs and now we wanted to make the most of the opportunity.

Stoke were our opponents in the play-off semi-final. We drew the first leg at Filbert Street 0–0 and Kevin Poole pulled off a wonder save from a far post header by Mike Sheron to keep the scoreline blank and give us a chance in the return game. The clean sheet was vital, and when Garry Parker fired in a brilliant volley early in the second half at the Victoria Ground, we were through to Wembley.

Only Crystal Palace stood between us and going up. Unfortunately, despite playing well, we found ourselves a goal down when Andy Roberts scored after just 14 minutes. But we kept plugging away and in the second half Muzzy latched on to a ball over the top down the left and got into the box, where he was pulled down. Garry Parker made it 1–1 from the spot. We had an Australian goalkeeper on the bench called Zeljko Kalac, who almost joined Mark McGhee at Wolves but eventually went on to play for AC Milan. He was a really big lad who we thought could prove daunting in a penalty shoot-out. So, with a view to him facing the penalties, we sent him on with a couple of minutes to go but it didn't get to that because in the last seconds of the game we got a dramatic winner. It came from a volley by Steve Claridge, who was always capable of producing the wonderfully unexpected at a vital time. It was a great feeling and I remember saying to Martin soon after the final whistle, 'God, you're going to manage in the Premier League.'

Considering the strife and stress we had gone through when we first moved to Filbert Street, it was a fantastic achievement . . . and we celebrated accordingly. We had a bus tour round Leicester and the idea was that we would report to the training ground before boarding the bus that would travel through the city centre. 'Lenny' (Neil Lennon) was missing and there was still no sign of him when the bus trundled off. We were on this road into the centre when amid the mass of blue and white colours we could see this red-haired person bouncing up and down. It was Lenny, who had decided to start the celebrations a bit earlier. But we managed to drag him onto the bus and he joined us on our way to the Town Hall.

Under normal circumstances being late would have warranted a fine but on that occasion Martin let him off and that was only right because nobody had played a bigger part in the club's promotion. His partnership in the centre of midfield with Muzzy was so important to us and if anybody deserved to have a good time it was those two.

We were so pleased with Muzzy that making his signing from Chelsea a permanent one was one of our priorities when Martin got down to shaping a side ready for the Premier League. Just a few days before the start of the new season we also signed American goalkeeper Kasey Keller from Millwall for around £900,000 and Spencer Prior, who was Norwich's Player of the Year in the previous season, for around £600,000. Ian Marshall, who could play up front or at the back, was also brought in from Ipswich Town as we got underway in the Premiership.

It turned out to be the start of a wonderful era in Leicester's history and Martin deserves every credit for masterminding the success we had there. For a start we had four top-ten finishes and, with due respect to them, for a club of Leicester's size and spending power that was a remarkable achievement.

But that was only part of the story. We went to three League Cup finals and won two of them, in 1997 and 2000, ending the club's long search for silverware in emphatic style. We won the League Cup in our first full season by beating Middlesbrough in a Hillsborough replay after drawing at Wembley. And something we had experimented with against Liverpool on Boxing Day helped us overcome Middlesbrough. Steve McManaman was a huge threat for Liverpool at the time and although we were not really in the business of man-to-man marking we decided to put a lad called Colin Hill on him for the entire 90 minutes. It worked a treat and we got a 0–0 draw at Anfield, where anyone was happy to come away with a point.

I distinctly remember Ronnie Moran, who was a key figure in the Liverpool backroom in those days, complimenting us after the game. He said words to the effect of, 'There's no secrets in the game – it's all about working your socks off, play and move and having no time for fancy Dans.' It meant a lot to us that he had taken the trouble to say that and how impressed he was with our performance. Having said that, it's worth mentioning that we had a superb record against Liverpool in the four years we were at Leicester, winning twice and drawing twice. How many teams could boast that kind of Anfield record?

But back to the man-marking. When it came to the League Cup final, we knew that the little Brazilian Juninho was capable of causing us a bucketload of problems. He was a real box of tricks. There wasn't much to him but he was a slippery little player, with good pace, exceptional skill and, of course, he had a track record of scoring goals. We had played Middlesbrough at Filbert Street about two or three weeks before the final and Juninho had absolutely run riot. We just could not afford to let him do the same in the final so we detailed Pontus Kaamark to do the same man-to-man marking job on him that Hill had done on McManaman and it proved just as successful. We had to restrict Juninho's space so Kaamark, who had recovered from an injury he had when Martin and I came to the club, was given the man-marking role.

He did a great job in what was a very tight Wembley final that went into extra-time. Just five minutes into the extra period we went a goal down when Italian striker Fabrizio Ravanelli scored but Emile Heskey equalised with just a couple of minutes left to earn us a draw and a replay in Sheffield.

We still had it all to do because Middlesbrough had a very good side at the time. It wasn't as if Juninho made them a one-man team because in addition to him and Ravanelli being in the same side they also had Brazilian midfielder Emerson who was a very talented player. Middlesbrough also got to the final of the FA Cup that year before losing to Chelsea. However, we won the replay 1–0 with another goal by Claridge, who was making a very useful habit of scoring big goals for us.

Winning the League Cup meant we were in European football and that was only the second time in Leicester's history that had happened. The only previous occasion was 36 years before. We had hopes of making an impact in the UEFA Cup but we unfortunately drew Atlético Madrid in the first round and they were one of the strongest sides in the competition.

The first leg was in Spain and despite playing very well we lost 2–1 – Ian Marshall gave us an early lead and we held on until they came back to score twice in the last 20 minutes. But we were quite happy with the result because the away goal was always a massive bonus and we knew that a 1–0 win at Filbert Street would be enough to get us through.

On the night our performance justified a victory and, without being biased, I remember us having what looked like three stonewall penalty appeals turned down. Had we been awarded just one of those penalties it could easily have changed the course of the tie because it was so delicately poised, but after putting them under pressure for much of the game they delivered two sucker punches in the last twenty minutes. Juninho, who had moved to Madrid from Middlesbrough by this stage, scored the first goal and we went out on a 4–1 aggregate and that was very harsh on us because the result of the tie had been in the balance for so long. Ironically, Atlético Madrid were the team that had put Leicester out of Europe 36 years before.

Two years later we were back in the League Cup final but lost to Tottenham, who at the time were managed by George Graham.

We had a bit of an upset on the eve of the match because we lost the services of Frank Sinclair, who Martin left out for a breach of discipline. On the Friday before the game at Wembley Martin had given the players the afternoon off to go and relax and Frank reported back an hour later than he was told to. Martin was very big on discipline and told Frank that he had let everyone, including himself, down and he was going to leave him out. He must have been gutted because he would probably have played as one of three central defenders or as a wing-back but he paid the price for his misdemeanour.

Like all George Graham sides, Tottenham were well organised but they had match-winners, too, and the Danish striker Allan Nielsen got a late goal with a diving header to deny us.

Although it was really disappointing to lose the final, I had a lot of happiness coming my way a couple of months later in May 1999 when Sharyl and I were married. Our relationship was well and truly cemented by that stage and I cannot stress how delighted I was that it worked out between us. She's made a huge contribution to the kind of person I am these days and, of course, she presented me with two wonderful sons. I thought my days of fatherhood were over but the boys coming along has just made my immediate family complete.

I actually proposed to Sharyl on Christmas Eve 1997 at The Ferryboat in Wilford after we had gone out for dinner. Larry Lloyd was with us and I remember him mischievously asking Sharyl what she wanted for Christmas, thinking she would say an engagement ring but Sharyl played it cool by saying 'a new coat'. But all along I had told Sharyl that I would marry her before Andrew went to school. I didn't tell her that I really meant university!

Back on the field we continued to thrive at Filbert Street as we built up a side that was capable of competing with the best. We might not have had the financial muscle of the big clubs but Martin had been very shrewd in the transfer market and there was always a great spirit about the squad.

But if Frank Sinclair's time-keeping had caused us a problem before the 1999 final, it was nothing compared with the commotion that was heading our way in the build-up to the following year's Wembley showdown with Tranmere Rovers. Even now, every time I hear mention of La Manga it makes me want to cringe. I suppose it's a lifetime punishment I'll just have to accept. Ever since that fateful day all I wanted was the chance to turn back the clock and totally obliterate the experience from my memory.

It all began when Martin decided it would be a good idea to get the players away for a bit of sun and La Manga, a purpose-built resort in Spain, was the ideal venue. The training facilities there were superb and with plenty of golf courses, tennis courts and swimming pools, you wanted for nothing. It seemed the perfect venue to get away from it all – but it wasn't as straightforward as that.

We flew to La Manga without Martin, who was due out the following day, and I was happy for us all, including me of course, to have a few drinks on the way out to Spain. I wasn't the best of fliers by then and liked a drink anyway because it helped me relax. I might even have taken a valium to calm me down a bit.

As soon as we arrived at La Manga most of the lads went for a game of golf while the coaching staff and I went off to watch Norwegian side Rosenborg, who were also out there at the time, play in a practice match. We didn't last long because quite frankly it wasn't worth watching and we returned to the Piano Bar to have another drink or two. The lads had been out golfing and after changing and having a meal they were clearly up for a good night. We had all knocked back a few because we had started on the plane and carried on drinking when we got to the resort.

Martin's last words were to impose a midnight curfew, which was very reasonable, but footballers being footballers a few of them weren't satisfied with that and wanted a bit more action. We were sitting round in the hotel when the players were yapping on about extending the curfew and they just wouldn't drop the subject. I told them that there was no way I was going to go against what Martin had ordered but they kept nibbling away at me and it was at that point that I made one of the worst decisions of my life.

Ian Marshall said to me, 'If you won't give us permission, can we give the boss a call and ask him?' And for some reason that I can never explain I eventually relented and gave Martin's number to Ian so that he could pose the question. It was fairly late by this stage so Martin was probably in his own bed and let's say he was far from pleased. He was fuming with Ian and, understandably, he was less than happy with me for giving out his telephone number. Martin had laid down the ground rules and that should have been that as far as he was concerned.

But that phone call paled into insignificance compared with the internal call I received in my bedroom from Paul Franklin at 7.30 the following morning. Quite simply he announced that 'All hell had broken loose' after I had gone to bed. It appeared that everything had been fairly quiet for a while with people milling about in the bar having a last drink. Then Stan Collymore, who had only been with us for a week or two after joining us from Aston Villa, found himself again the centre of attention at a time when he was doing everything to keep his nose clean.

Stan had been in a number of scrapes off the field and when he joined us Martin had stressed in no uncertain terms that he had to do his utmost to keep out of any trouble. But that night in La Manga he was sitting in the corner by the door, when he decided it was time to have a bit of fun with a nearby fire extinguisher. He pointed it at our physio Mick Yeomans and, from what I heard later, genuinely had no idea what was about to happen next. But it turned out to be a prank that went horribly wrong. Stan expected the extinguisher to stop spraying when he released his finger on it but it didn't work out that way and the entire contents were sprayed not only all over Mick but most of the bar.

After Paul had alerted me I dashed down to the bar area and the evidence was still there in all its foamy glory. It was just like a sea of white paint had swept into the place. It certainly wasn't very funny at the time but the lads christened Mick 'Casper' after the friendly ghost and it was a nickname he struggled to get rid of as time went on.

Obviously, the other hotel guests were very upset about the whole episode and I had to face one or two of them to apologise the best I could in really difficult circumstances. There was some talk of the police being notified but, thankfully, it didn't get to that stage. But I still had other issues to deal with – like the hotel management and, of course, I had to face the music with Martin.

The hotel management had decided their priority was to get us all out of there as soon as possible. They certainly didn't intend us staying in La Manga for another night. I've often wondered since that had it been any other player than Stan who was involved in the incident, would the hotel have treated it any differently? By that time Stan had picked up a reputation off the field that stuck to him like glue. But there was no placating them and they were so keen to get us out of the country – never mind the hotel – that they had made checks to find out whether or not flights were available. Had there not been I think they would have hired a plane such was their determination to see the back of us.

Speaking to Martin was far from easy. He wasn't too chuffed with me anyway because I had given Ian Marshall his number the night before. When this lot came showering down on top of that I was prepared for the biggest bollocking of my life. But he was more concerned with getting the group home and trying to sort out the mess when we all got back to Leicester. There was no suggestion of trying to find another hotel out there – that just wasn't an option.

So we left La Manga and, as we got ready to board the bus for the airport, Ian Marshall came out with the line, 'I've had such a good time I feel as though I've only been here a day.' It was very funny but I could have done without any quips from him, bearing in mind the initial problem he had caused by ringing Martin. One of the last instructions Martin gave me before we left was that nobody was to have any drink on the way back. Considering my feelings about flying, I wasn't personally too happy about that but I fully understood and gritted my teeth and got on with it.

We flew back into Gatwick Airport and avoided the waiting press by boarding a bus on the tarmac and getting straight onto the M25 and back up to Leicester. We met up with Martin in a hotel in Hinckley that we used a lot and, as you can imagine, the mood was very prickly to say the least. Soon after we met, I had a quiet word with Martin and said, 'Listen, I'll resign if that's what you want.' I had been in charge of the trip at the time of the incident and was rightly getting the flak but to be fair to Martin he said, 'Not at all.' To say he was unhappy about the events in Spain was a huge understatement, however. In private he spelt out that I should have known better but in public he backed me up and tried his best to calm the situation.

It was big news in the media for a couple of days and every time we arrived at the training ground there was a lot of flashing cameras and journalists desperate to get interviews, but somehow we managed to dampen things down. In the days that followed an article appeared in Norwegian newspapers and filtered back into England about Rosenborg's view of it all. Apparently the Rosenborg coach had called me 'Whisky John' but where he got that from I don't know because I've never touched a drop of whisky in my life. As footballers do, the players picked up on it and for a few weeks afterwards I was referred to as 'Whisky John' around the club.

With another League Cup final coming up we had to get back to normality as quickly as possible and find a way of switching the emphasis back onto football matters. On the field we were flying at the time, doing well in the league and League Cup but had we been struggling, it was the sort of damaging episode that could easily have led to heads rolling. And I was well aware that mine might have been one of the first!

We had reached the final thanks to a goal by Matt Elliott, who we had signed in a £1.6m deal from Oxford in 1997. Martin had been on his trail for a long time but we heard on the grapevine that Southampton, who were managed by Graeme Souness, were also very keen. On the night that we discovered that he was about to sign for Southampton we were playing in an FA Cup match against Southend at Filbert Street. We won the game and we were sitting in the dressing-room afterwards discussing the disappointment of having seemingly missed out on Matt.

Right out of the blue Martin said, 'I'm going to ring his agent and see if we can do something.' By this time it was well after 10 o'clock but Martin came off the phone to announce that he was on his way. We were all in it together so Martin, myself and Steve Walford all set off in separate cars – Martin and Steve were still living in the south – to try and clinch a deal. Martin had arranged to meet Matt and his agent in the early hours of the morning and when we got there Matt had come along with his wife Kath. She liked a smoke so we had a common interest straight away. We soon found out that she was a Birmingham girl and we kept plugging the fact that Leicester was only a short journey away from her family. I can't remember whether it was daylight by the time the talks ended but the fact that we had all taken the trouble to drive south at a ridiculous hour had clearly meant something to Matt and his wife.

Martin eventually got him to agree to the move and the following day I think Matt went to Southampton to tell them the bad news that he was joining us. He was a great signing. Essentially a central defender, he had the ability to play as a striker and he had a lot of attributes. He maybe lacked a bit of pace but he would go through a brick wall for the cause, was excellent in the air in both boxes and had very good technique and control.

We were up against Aston Villa in the semi-final and held on for a goalless draw at Villa Park in the first leg and Matt, who was playing up front at the time, grabbed the winner at Filbert Street seconds before half-time.

When the La Manga dust had settled and we got round to the final, Matt again came up with the goods. He scored both goals in our 2–1 win over Tranmere which was the last League Cup final to be played at the old Wembley Stadium. Matt gave us a first-half lead with a header from Steve Guppy's cross and although Tranmere were reduced to ten men following the sending off of Clint Hill, they equalised through David Kelly. But Matt, who was captaining the side, produced another magnificent header to score the winner from a Guppy corner.

With another trophy won, we were keen to finish the season on as high a note as possible – and Stan came back from the La Manga debacle to more than play his part. By this stage of his career Stan had moved to Aston Villa but no club were showing any interest in him because of the scrapes he had been in. But Martin had always liked him as a player and took a chance when he got the opportunity to sign him on a free transfer from Villa Park.

He made his debut in a draw at Watford but in the game after that he really showed us the ability he possessed. It was his home debut against a Sunderland side doing very well under Peter Reid but that day they couldn't live with Stan and Emile Heskey. They were sensational – Stan got a hat-trick and the pair of them tore Sunderland's defence to bits in a 5–2 win.

It would have been very interesting to see how the partnership would have prospered because they were two highly talented and powerful boys. They were great individual strikers but a fearsome pair and I'm sure it was a huge disappointment to Leicester fans that they never got a chance to see them develop together.

Emile didn't get as many goals as he should for someone with his ability but he was never short of admirers and when Liverpool came in with a £12m bid, it was only a matter of time before he left for Anfield. It was a lot of money and once Emile was aware of Liverpool's interest nobody could blame him for wanting to see the transfer reach a conclusion.

But he wasn't the only one leaving the club and after five happy and very successful years at Filbert Street, a huge new challenge awaited Martin and me in Scotland.

15
The pleasures of Parkhead

THE IDEA OF RETURNING TO Scotland at some stage of my life always appealed to me. But little did I know that when it happened I would get so much pleasure and reward from what was undoubtedly the highlight of my time working alongside Martin O'Neill in management. We had enjoyed so much success at Filbert Street that it was going to be a sad occasion when we left Leicester City but it was tempered by the huge anticipation of joining one of the world's biggest club sides in Glasgow Celtic.

We were looking forward to another season with Leicester in Europe, having won the League Cup for a second time, when Celtic came calling for Martin in the summer of 2000. Celtic were managed by John Barnes and Kenny Dalglish up until that point but in February they lost 3–1 to Inverness Caledonian Thistle at Parkhead and that brought about an end to their spell in Glasgow.

I could tell by Martin's reaction that it immediately appealed to him because he had always had a soft spot for Celtic as he was growing up in Northern Ireland. Once discussions and negotiations got underway I knew we would be heading north of the border. Leicester were obviously disappointed that Martin was leaving but they also realised it was a wonderful opportunity for him to go and manage on such a big stage. He had earned that right.

I didn't join Martin at the outset because I still had matters to deal with at Leicester and I don't mind admitting that I was a wee bit apprehensive about how people would react to me, having been brought up as essentially a Rangers fan. I soon came to terms with that and in hindsight I should not have had any doubts because the welcome I received at Parkhead was so warm and sincere. After all,

Jock Stein and Kenny Dalglish were both brought up as Protestants but became legendary figures at Parkhead.

It was something of a homecoming for me. I got to return to my Scottish roots, Sharyl was quite happy taking the family north and we bought a house back in the same Uddingston village where I had been brought up. This time we had four bedrooms and were living in the posher end of the village but it was a pleasure for me to be back home. It was still the same and the people were still as friendly as I had known them to be 30-odd years before. For the first time in my life most of my close and extended family were nearby and I loved it. We even added to the family because during the time we were living in Scotland our second son Mark was born.

The great pity was that my mum and dad were no longer around because I am sure they would have taken great pleasure in me returning 'home'. That would have meant a lot to me. But there were still a lot of family members in the vicinity, including my dad's sister Auntie Jeanette, who I had hardly met up with in all the years I had been in England. But we saw a lot more of each other and Jeanette actually became our regular babysitter during the time we spent in Glasgow.

My brother-in-law Jimmy Rooney, who had had such an influence on me when I was younger, was able to come to home matches as my guest and he loved being on the 'inside' of a club that meant so much to him. I christened him 'King of Parkhead' and he liked that because he used to lap up every minute of watching Celtic in those days, sitting in the directors' box with my sister Caroline.

One of the pleasing factors of returning to Scotland was that I could spend more time with my niece Jillian, who had been orphaned in the car crash that claimed the lives of my brother Hughie and his wife Isobel in 1979. Thankfully she couldn't remember anything about the horrendous events of the day. She was only eight years old at the time of the accident and sometimes you wonder if people get a feeling of what fate has in store for them. Some time before the crash Isobel had asked her cousin Iris Suckle that should anything happen to Hughie and her, would she take care of Jillian. When the accident first happened my first wife Sally and I talked about the possibility of bringing Jillian south until we heard about the request that Isobel had made. In view of that and the fact that it would have meant taking an eight-year-old child out of the environment that she knew and was comfortable in, it was quickly decided it was best for Jillian to stay in Scotland.

So Iris and her husband Andy, who also lived in Uddingston, had no hesitation in taking Jillian under their wing and she became very much a daughter to them. They instantly became as close as any child–parent relationship could be. Iris and Andy can take enormous credit for the way that Jillian has turned out to be a fine young woman in her own right. She is happily married to Dave and has two lovely children, Rhys and Neve.

Sadly, there was more heartache for her in August 2011 when Andy passed away. Sharyl and I were on holiday with the kids when Jill rang with the news. Unfortunately, it meant we couldn't attend the funeral, which was a great shame. We would really have liked to have been able to pay our respects to a man who had done a fantastic job of bring up my niece – obviously with more than a little help from Iris.

It was a massive bonus to be back among my family, and knowing that Sharyl loved it from day one and got on with my family extremely well helped me settle down straight away. We were so comfortable living back in Uddingston that my elder son Andrew has never really forgiven me for coming back south. He was very happy in his school and had made a lot of friends in Scotland.

As a young boy myself I had gone into Glasgow on the bus with my mum and looked on in awe at Parkhead, seeing the huge floodlights rise up into the sky. I had been brought up to follow Glasgow Rangers but I could listen for hours to my brother-in-law Jimmy talking about the institution that was Celtic. He used to take me to the odd game at Parkhead and, because of Jimmy's influence, my loyalties were torn between blue and green-and-white.

But it was a pleasure and a privilege to be asked to go and work at Parkhead and you don't get the full realisation of what the club means to people until you are actually right there in the thick of it.

After I had moved back to Scotland and settled into the job, Sharyl and I used to drive into Glasgow city centre on my day off. We used to pass Parkhead on the way and Sharyl used to get fed up of me saying, 'Do you know what, I've got a say in what goes on in there.' Sharyl used to go around the shops and I spent time in Borders, a famous book shop in Buchanan Street which, sadly, is no longer there. I loved going for a cup of tea in Princes Square but wherever I went I couldn't get away from all things Celtic.

There were a lot of good people at Parkhead and one of the finest was John Clark, who has spent more than fifty years at the club. He was one of the famous Lisbon Lions and he's been a player, assistant manager, coach and now kitman at a club he adores.

It was such a happy place to be and we had a lot of laughs during our time in Glasgow. One of the best came at the expense of Jim Hone, who was contracts manager at Parkhead. He was always on the Internet, checking on players and gossip and we decided one day to wind him up. It was transfer deadline day and we were hanging around waiting to see if anything was happening with players and asked Jim if he had heard of a player we were being linked with called Panini. What could we give him as a Christian name? I know, 'Jamón' (we pronounced it as 'hamon'). And which club did he play for? It had to be Parma. So Jim set about trawling the Internet and spent a good few minutes searching before the penny dropped and he slowly picked up his eyes and announced, 'Someone is having yous boys on.' It was even funnier because he thought we had been set up ourselves instead of just having a laugh at him.

Jim and thousands like him just wanted to talk about the club, the last match, the next match and all the hopes and dreams that made Celtic so special. Nobody had to tell me about the great rivalry between Celtic and Rangers but until you are living the intensity of that day in, day out, you don't really get a true perception of what it means to so many people. When we went to Parkhead, Celtic had only won the Championship once in ten years – but it had been a hugely significant title win in the eyes of the fans. Back in the glorious '60s and early '70s Celtic had won the Scottish Championship nine times in a row and when Wim Jansen steered them to the title in 1998 it prevented Rangers overtaking Celtic's record by registering ten on the trot. Celtic fans did not want that to be beaten and although Scottish football involves far more than what goes on within Glasgow, you cannot get away from the pressure of beating the other half of the 'Old Firm'.

Coming second counts for nothing in Scotland and although the side that comes out on top in the Celtic–Rangers battles wins most of the honours, you have to understand what it means to other clubs who are competing against them. Every time Celtic or Rangers play

Hibernian, Hearts, St Mirren or any other side, it is their cup final, and because of that players joining the Big Two have to have a special kind of understanding of what it is all about and they have to possess the character to deal with it week by week. To put into perspective what it means to teams beating Celtic or Rangers, we once lost 2–0 in a league match at Aberdeen and after the game their players all joined in a duck walk on their knees and were going around the pitch in conga fashion. We weren't very happy about it and the next time we played Aberdeen there was no great need for a team talk. But deep down we knew their reaction had come from what it meant to put one across Celtic.

As soon as he arrived at the club Martin supplemented what was already a very good squad and his first signing was one of the best in Chris Sutton. Mark Viduka had made it clear that summer that he wanted a move at a time when Martin was just arriving so there was an immediate void to fill. Martin paid Chelsea £6m for Sutton, who had not settled in London after leaving Blackburn Rovers. But from our days at Leicester, we always fancied Chris, who had figured in such a brilliant partnership with Alan Shearer when Blackburn won the Premier League in 1995.

I always liked what I had seen of Chris from a distance but when we got to work with him he was an even better player than I thought. He had a fantastic touch, a great football brain, superb control, vision . . . a very clever player. As a striker he reminded me a lot of a taller version of Nigel Clough and I can pay him no bigger compliment in saying that. He could play in a variety of positions too. He filled in at centre-half for us one day at Ibrox when we beat Rangers 1–0 and he was nothing short of sensational. Then when John Hartson joined us, Chris dropped into midfield to show that he was just as comfortable and effective playing there.

Henrik Larsson was truly world class and when Wim Jansen took him to Parkhead for a mere £650,000 in 1997 it must rank as one of Celtic's greatest ever signings. He had the air of a top-quality player – he knew he had great attributes – but not for one second did he come across as a prima donna. He was a wonderful professional and even if he disagreed with managerial decisions that were made – as every player does from time to time – he just went out every game and performed to a consistently high standard. That is the mark of a great player. They don't let anything get in the way of their football and they don't make excuses. He had two great feet, was superb in the air, his work rate was unbelievable and, of course, he was a fantastic goalscorer.

It was really fitting that he ended his career with Barcelona and then had a brief spell at Manchester United. Henrik was already a top-drawer striker when Martin and I arrived at Parkhead but I think he would agree that over time we brought in other quality players that enhanced his own game and I think he appreciated that.

Eventually in 2004 he got the move and the Champions League medal that his talents deserved when he went off to Barcelona, but before then he was a tremendous player in green and white. As fate would have it we were drawn with Barcelona in the same Champions League group in his first season in Spain. He scored one of their goals in a 3–1 win at Parkhead and he was quoted after the game as saying it was very difficult to celebrate the goal because 'I had so many great times at the club'.

Paul Lambert had already won the European Cup with Borussia Dortmund and he was another player who was so easy to work with. He did a holding role in Dortmund but when we lured Neil Lennon up to Scotland from Leicester, Paul became more of an attacking force and adapted to playing outside of Neil in a more advanced role. He was a fantastic professional, looked after himself and had the understanding of the game that explains why he has gone on to do very well in management.

I dwell on the quality of players we had because for a period of time I genuinely believe that the Celtic side that Martin and I had were good enough to compete in the Premier League in England. I don't know whether that scenario will ever come about in the future but I am convinced that that team would have been capable of challenging for honours south of the border. I think we proved that when we beat Blackburn and Liverpool in the UEFA Cup to reach the final against Porto in 2003.

The expectation levels are so high at Celtic that players have no hiding place. You are in the shop window all the time and have to front up to the challenges that are always staring you in the face. The same applies to Celtic managers but Martin's win record throughout his time at Parkhead was nothing short of phenomenal. The record books show that he won 213 of the 282 games that Celtic played during his time as manager. In his first season he won

97 points and won the treble. In his second season he got 103 and won the league. In his third season he got ninety-seven and lost the league by one goal. In his fourth season he got 98 and won the double. In his last season he got ninety-two and lost the league by one point.

The first three points we won after I had linked up with Martin came in the shape of a memorable 6–2 win at Parkhead over Rangers on 27 August. I had sat in the stands in midweek when we had played a team from Luxembourg in a European tie but the Rangers game was some way to start. I will never forget the game and the fantastic atmosphere as long as I live. We went 3–0 up after just ten or eleven minutes but in management you never get the feeling that a game is over until the final whistle goes. Rangers got a goal back before half-time and that put doubts in our minds because the next goal was always going to be massive. We got it thanks to the very special talents of Larsson, who chipped the ball over the Rangers keeper in a manner that came so naturally to him. Rangers got a penalty to bring the gap back to two goals and we were fidgeting again until Henrik made it five and then Chris Sutton scored a sixth to give us a truly magnificent start to life at Parkhead. We couldn't have written the script better for a way to announce ourselves in our first Old Firm clash.

It wasn't all plain sailing, however, and that same season Rangers beat us 5–1 at Ibrox on a day when we were reduced to ten men after Alan Thompson had been sent off. We were well beaten and when it got to four and five I was praying it didn't get to six because it would have meant they had matched our goal tally from the game at Parkhead. Upon such thin dividing lines bragging rights are claimed – such is the immense rivalry between the clubs.

At the end of that first season we had won the Scottish treble and Martin was the only other manager outside of Jock Stein to achieve that feat. What was really remarkable was the points swing that took place between Rangers and ourselves. In the 1999–2000 season Rangers had enjoyed a 21-point winning margin but a year later we had finished 15 points ahead of them. A thirty-six-point turnaround was, by any stretch of the imagination, a staggering one. It just showed the quality and spirit that was evident among the players and the successful changes that had been made.

We had already won the league by the time we went to Ibrox for the second time that season with four games remaining. It can be incredibly hostile and intimidating coming off the Celtic bus and onto the steps entering the ground and there were deafening boos coming from Rangers fans who had assembled to give us the usual abuse. Cool as you like, Martin stopped on his way up the steps, turned slowly around and simply said, 'Champions.' It didn't silence the hordes but he got his message across all the same.

We won that day 3–0, our first win at Ibrox, and it made up for the thumping we had received when we had gone there in the previous November. L'ubomír Moravcík, a Czechoslovakian midfielder with great skills and shooting ability who had become a huge favourite, scored two of the goals that day and Larsson got his almost inevitable goal as we ran out very comfortable winners. Moravcik, who had played most of his earlier football with Saint-Étienne in France, was apparently Zinedine Zidane's favourite player . . . such was his calibre and technique.

Over the five seasons we were there we played Rangers twenty times in Scottish league games and our record was superb. It read: P 20; W 13; D 3; L 4; F 35; A 22; Pts 45.

Winning three trophies in our first season was a tremendous way to announce ourselves at Parkhead. The League Cup was the first trophy we won, beating Kilmarnock 3–0 in the final with a Larsson hat-trick. He had also scored twice in the semi-final when we beat Rangers 3–1 and in that season scored two more when we defeated Hibernian in the Scottish Cup final. The Swedish international was a goal machine and he accumulated an astonishing 53 goals in all competitions that season.

We lost only one game – at Aberdeen in December – as we won the title by twenty-one points the following season. We virtually led from start to finish and it was a remarkable achievement. It was just a shame we missed out on the double that year. We reached the final against Rangers but a last-minute goal by Peter Løvenkrands meant they lifted the trophy – as they did the League Cup after beating us after extra-time in the Hampden Park semi-final.

In 2002–03 we won nothing but I've had so many people come up to me and say that it was their favourite season because we got to the final of the UEFA Cup. In the first round we beat a Lithuanian side Sudova 10–1 on aggregate and that put us through for an Anglo-Scottish clash with Blackburn, who were managed by Graeme

Souness. With Graeme having spent some time with Rangers, the press were really interested in the tie for obvious reasons. Any England–Scotland match-up attracts intense publicity north of the border.

We might not have been at our best in the first leg at Parkhead but Larsson – who else? – gave us a valuable one-goal lead with a goal five minutes from time. In fairness to them Blackburn had played quite well but there were a lot of comments flying around afterwards to the tune that we did not deserve to take a lead with us to England. Someone actually said it had been like 'men against boys' but the boys had somehow come out on top.

What it did was to make Martin's team talk almost irrelevant for the second leg because our players were so determined to prove a point at Ewood Park. Larsson chipped Brad Friedel, who we were later to sign for Aston Villa, for the first goal after about 15 minutes. And Chris Sutton, who had revelled in playing against his former club, produced the kind of header that Blackburn fans had known so well during his time at the club to complete an excellent win. By the end of the game Blackburn fans were reduced to a taunt of 'You'll never play in England' and perhaps the way we had played on the night, they should have been somewhat grateful for that.

In round three we played Spanish side Celta Vigo and again led from the first leg with Larsson getting his customary goal. It was tough for us in the away leg but John Hartson, who we had signed for £6.5m from Coventry in 2001, scored a priceless goal. We lost the game 2–1 but the away goal was enough to see us through.

German side Stuttgart barred our path to the last eight and we were up against it in the first leg when they opened the scoring at Parkhead. But our fans were once again magnificent as we clawed our way level and went on to win 3–1 on the night. We stretched that to a 5–1 aggregate lead when Alan Thompson and Chris Sutton scored in the first 15 minutes of the second leg but Stuttgart had nothing to lose and threw everything at us as they came back to win 3–2. It was too little too late though.

It really was billed as a Battle of Britain in the quarter-final when we were drawn against a Liverpool side under the management of Gérard Houllier. We were again at home for the first leg and went a goal up after just three minutes through Larsson but Emile

Heskey, who we had sold to Liverpool just before we departed Leicester, came back to haunt us with an equaliser. With a 1–1 draw and a game to come at Anfield, Liverpool had the edge but it was a night when we proved that we could match the very best in England. Alan Thompson put us ahead with a free-kick on the stroke of half-time and ten minutes from the end Hartson played a one-two with Larsson, side-stepped a defender and blasted his shot into the roof of the net. We knew then that Liverpool didn't have the time to come back at us and it was a truly memorable night in Celtic's recent history.

The semi-final against Portuguese side Boavista was another Larsson success story. An own goal by Belgian defender Joos Valgaeren put us behind just after half-time and Larsson equalised and then missed a penalty that would have given us the edge for the return. But you could never keep Larsson down for long and ten minutes from the end of the second leg he came up with the winner that sent us off to the final in Seville.

We lost the game to José Mourinho's Porto but the experience of going to Seville and being among the throng of Celtic fans is something that will stay with me until the day I die. It was estimated that there were around 80,000 Celtic fans in the Spanish city that night and when we made our way to the ground from our base in Jerez, it was just an unbelievable sea of green and white that awaited us on the approach to the stadium. Larry Lloyd, who was living in Spain, came to the game and one of his mates asked if we could fix him up with tickets. On the day he told Lloydy, in all seriousness, that he would be 'the one wearing green and white' and Lloyd wasted no time in telling him, 'So will thousands of other fuckers.' Celtic fans have always had a reputation for going away from home in vast numbers to support their team and I doubt that any team has gone anywhere with so much support as we had that night. It was just a pity they couldn't all get tickets for the game and we would have loved to have brought the trophy home for them because the fans deserved it.

Mourinho wasn't as well known as he is now but he had a very talented team with Deco, the midfielder who went on to play for Barcelona and Chelsea, very much at the heart of their operations. There was never very much in the final and although Porto twice took the lead Larsson got us level on both occasions. But we were reduced to ten men when Bobo Balde was sent off and Porto got the winner five minutes from the end of extra-time.

After the disappointment of Seville we had to return home and play our final league game and were still in with a chance of pipping Rangers for the title. They were at home to Dunfermline while we were away at Kilmarnock and we had to better Rangers' score by a goal to lift the title. Despite the agony of the UEFA Cup final defeat, the players got themselves up for the match against a side who had always caused us a few problems on their own pitch. Our players' application was spot-on and we won the game 4–0 but Rangers beat Dunfermline 6–1. We finished level on points but their goal difference was 73 to our 72.

I'll always remember that in the dressing-room at Kilmarnock after the game Martin spoke superbly to the players. He said, 'Lads, you've been absolutely brilliant and you've deserved much better than what's happened. But I tell you what, you are such a great bunch of players you'll come back and win the league by 20 points next season.' He wasn't quite right but we did win the title with a 17-point winning margin . . . and that made a big enough statement in itself.

During our time at Parkhead we established some incredible records – like beating Rangers in seven successive Old Firm games. To be perfectly honest I didn't really enjoy the games against Rangers while they were happening because there was always so much tension and pressure involved. Sometimes I could feel my stomach churning over with the stress of it all and I was just glad when they were over and, more often than not, we were able to enjoy a victory afterwards.

Although Dick Advocaat was manager of Rangers when we first went there he moved on to coach the Holland side after the 2002 World Cup and for the last three years our opposite number at Ibrox was Alex McLeish. Alex always struck me as a very genuine sort and that was underlined by the way he greeted Martin and me before and after games. During Advocaat's reign there was none of the after-match football tradition of inviting the opposition manager in for a drink, but immediately Alex came along it was something we did as a matter of course. Sometimes it is very difficult when you lose games and all you want to do is get away as quickly as possible but although we had the upper hand over him at the time, I always found Alex very welcoming and gracious. So too were his assistant Andy Watson, who had been with Alex since their playing days at Aberdeen, and Dutch coach Jan Wouters, who was another decent man.

I regarded Alex as a very good manager and he has gone on to prove that by the success he had in taking Birmingham back into the Premier League and lifting the Carling Cup by beating Arsenal in 2011. It surprised me greatly that Birmingham were relegated at the end of last season when Alex seemed to have consolidated their position in the Premiership. It came as an added surprise to me when he opted to take the short journey from St Andrew's to Villa Park during the course of last summer.

One of the other records we broke during our time in Glasgow – and one of the proudest – was winning twenty-five consecutive games during the 2003–04 season. That is a staggering achievement and gave us immense satisfaction – very much like the 42-match unbeaten run we had during our playing days with Forest. To boast a record of 25 outright victories in any grade of football is a wonderful statistic, particularly when you are up against teams who desperately want your scalp.

The Celtic boys were winners as players and the in-bred determination they had then has shown itself again since some of them have moved into management in recent years. Although I know Neil Lennon was massively disappointed not to win the Scottish Premier League in 2011 I think he has done a tremendous job at Celtic in far from the easiest circumstances. And Paul Lambert deserves enormous credit for what he has achieved at Norwich with promotions in successive seasons. I got a lot of pleasure ringing him to offer my congratulations when Norwich had clinched their place in the top flight at the end of the 2010–11 season. To take a club from League One to the Premier League in two years is an incredible achievement but it does not surprise me because he's got that inner steel and determination to succeed at whatever task he takes on.

Although it was mostly unbroken success for Martin and me at Parkhead there was one huge disappointment just before we left. In fact, it was probably the worst moment I've had in the game because we knew we had to beat Motherwell to win the Scottish League title again in 2004–05.

Victory would have guaranteed us the title in four out of the five years we were there and by that stage we knew we were leaving at the end of the season. Martin had made the decision that he wanted to take time out of football to look after his wife Geraldine, who was very poorly, and I was desperately keen for him to finish on a high note by winning the league.

Rangers were playing Hibernian at Easter Road that day and we were a goal up against Motherwell thanks to a Chris Sutton strike. But Scott McDonald scored twice against us in the last three minutes to leave us absolutely devastated. While we were on the receiving end at Fir Park, Spanish striker Nacho Novo was scoring the crucial goal for Rangers and they ended up pipping us for the title by one point. You could have heard the proverbial pin drop in our dressing-room afterwards because we were shell-shocked. We knew we should have won the league but it had been snatched away from us in the final minutes of the season.

A week later we were involved in our final match in the Scottish Cup final against Dundee United and a goal by Alan Thompson early in the game made sure we left by putting another trophy in the cabinet. What made me really pleased and proud that day at Hampden Park was that the players pushed Martin, myself and Steve Walford up to receive the cup. Jackie McNamara was the captain but he insisted that we went forward before him to hold the cup up to the Celtic fans and it was a lovely touch and something I will never forget.

Losing the league still hurt though. It was a sickening feeling and an awful way to bow out of Parkhead, bearing in mind all the success we had enjoyed. But although it was tough to take it didn't cloud all the good and memorable times we had in Glasgow.

It was also very sad because I knew I would be leaving Scotland for the second time in my life. I had loved every minute of the five years I had been back but I knew that if Martin was going to return to management it would be back in England. Martin wanted to have the break at that time but if Geraldine improved, which thankfully she did, it was only a matter of time before he got a new club.

We both felt that after Celtic nothing could compare with that experience in Scotland so I knew it was time to leave . . . with plenty of wonderful memories.

16
The dressing-room lawyer

THERE IS NO DOUBT AT all in my mind that Martin O'Neill has earned the right to manage one of the country's top clubs. It used to be a 'closed shop' of four but with Manchester City's Middle East billions it seems only a matter of time before the riches produce dividends beyond their 2011 FA Cup success. But because of the manner in which he has taken on the challenges at Leicester City, Glasgow Celtic and Aston Villa I believe that Martin has proved himself a worthy candidate for a place at English football's top table.

In 2004 I was very surprised that Liverpool did not come calling at Martin's door when they were looking for a replacement for Gérard Houllier. There was speculation in the press that Martin was a candidate but that was as far as it got and Rafa Benítez was eventually appointed. The demands of managing one of the elite clubs in English football would not have fazed him and he would have applied the same ideals and principles to managing Liverpool as he did at Wycombe.

Managing players at that level would not have been a problem. He's dealt with plenty of big players in the past and, generally speaking with players, the bigger they are the less trouble you have with them.

Martin certainly has the experience required to take on a top job and he's also got the qualities and characteristics that are needed. There's no doubting his intelligence and had he not pursued a wonderful career as a football player and manager he would no doubt have become a very successful lawyer. He was studying law at college in Belfast when he got the chance to join Nottingham

Forest from Distillery at a time when he was a highly promising teenager making his first waves in the game. I'm sure there were voices in the O'Neill family that encouraged him to continue his studies and treat football as a secondary issue – he was also a very good Gaelic footballer – but I can understand why the lure of football won the day despite the academic background he was coming from.

Brian Clough did not have that same education behind him but they are very similar in many ways. Not least is that they can enter a conversation, debate or argument with anyone at any level and put forward a constructive point of view. If Martin knows he is right he can fight his corner as well as anyone and that's one of the qualities he would have needed in abundance had he gone ahead with a future in the law.

I've not talked to him about whether he had regrets at not having a legal career but it's not prevented him carrying on a big interest in the subject. When the Yorkshire Ripper case was on in 1981, for example, he was so fascinated by the way it unfolded in court that he took time out to go and watch the proceedings.

But football was his No. 1 choice and once he had made up his mind that it was the track he was going down it captured his 100 per cent focus. I remember in his early days at Forest when we were midfield players vying for the same attention and opportunity at The City Ground. He had an inner determination to make the most of his talents and a self-belief that certainly overshadowed my own.

We became friends soon after his arrival from Northern Ireland but while we had an instant rapport off the field, there was rivalry between us on it. For a few years we both thought of ourselves as central midfield players, strutting our stuff and believing we could spray passes to all corners of a football field. And, as such, we were often candidates for the same position in the side. I remember on a couple of occasions Martin coming off the bench to take my place and making an impact and I didn't take too kindly to it. But it was a healthy sort of competition between us and when the gaffer came along and sorted everything out at the club from top to bottom I'm delighted to say he found room for the both of us in his first team.

Martin is very much his own man and on the occasions when his development wasn't moving along at the rate he had hoped he was never slow at making sure his opinion was heard. He's always possessed the ability to put forward reasoned arguments, however, and that part of his make-up has shown itself down the years in his dealings with the press – and that is such an important facet in the life of a modern-day football manager. He's perfected the essential art of saying a lot of words to the media without divulging too much and he's got a great command of the English language and the ability to deliver it in a telling fashion. He usually manages to put across his point of view in an interesting manner and, like Clough, he has the knack of being able to treat even the most complicated issues on a basic level that people can understand.

It sounds like I am building up a case for Martin being a mirror image of the great man and he also has Clough's capacity to charm the hind legs off a donkey. It's probably got much to do with his wonderful way with words but Martin certainly possesses a charming nature that can often be very persuasive and influential. I'm convinced that every football club we have been at became a better place for his presence. They were happy places when he was there and it wasn't a manufactured 'feel good' factor that he created. It came naturally and I would like to think that the staff we came across on our travels viewed Martin, myself and other members of his management staff as decent people and that the general atmosphere was a product of that. We tended to treat people the way we wanted to be treated ourselves. There were no bull-shitters or big-time Charlies among us – just grounded people attempting to do an honest job. He treated everyone on the same level and whether it be cleaners, security, maintenance men, office staff or whatever he always had time for them. People might not think it is important but there are times in football when things don't go your way and it is during sticky periods that you need folk to rally round for the cause. And it's on those occasions that the benefits of having a happy and contented ship show themselves.

Right at the outset of his management career at Wycombe Martin worked at building a team ethic and camaraderie. It was all about building a side and I'll always remember a comment that was made to Martin after his Wycombe side had gone to Boston United and beaten them 4–0. Then Boston manager Dave Cusack said to Martin after the game, 'I could get promotion with your team.' I don't think he meant it in any disparaging way but in my book it wasn't a very clever thing to say because those players he was talking about didn't just suddenly appear from the heavens. They were assembled, moulded and brought together in unison to make a good team. It didn't happen by flicking a switch!

Martin is top class when it comes to man-management and, also like 'you know who', he has this innate ability to get players to want to play for him. It's a basic requirement, I know, but you would be amazed at how many players simply don't want to perform to their full potential for a given manager. Throughout my time with Martin he has always told players exactly how it is with no attempt to hide the truth in a bid to pander to anyone no matter how big a name he was dealing with. If they have played well he will tell them, if they have played badly he will also tell them and it's all about being honest and truthful with everyone. That way you can gain respect for each other and know that any criticism that comes along is constructive, well meant and in the best interests of the team as well as the individual. Some players can't accept that but good players do.

Martin has never been afraid to dish out bollockings. He did so when I was a player under him at Grantham and at the other end of the football spectrum there were times when he handed out criticism to a world-class talent like Henrik Larsson when we were at Celtic. But, being a very top player, Henrik had the nous to take it on board and move on.

Martin has this talent to turn average players into good ones, good players into excellent and excellent ones into the very best. There are many examples of how he turned careers around but the way he got Stan Collymore playing again when his career had hit the buffers best illustrates what I mean. Stan was a prodigious talent, who I remember watching in his Forest days and thinking there's nothing to stop him going all the way to the very top. His off-the-field antics put a great strain on that special ability when he moved away from The City Ground and, when he was in his final days at Aston Villa he looked a pale shadow of the player that got spectators out of their seats earlier in his career. But Martin looked beyond Stan's reputation, was willing to take a gamble, got him on board at Leicester and for a little period he was back to his unplayable best. His career was on fire again until he broke his leg in a match at Derby. That also coincided with us leaving Leicester to move to Celtic and that was a great pity from Stan's point of view because he had regenerated himself as one of the game's top strikers.

Martin was also very tactically aware and conducted all the research and preparation that goes into today's football but he didn't allow it to colour his belief that at the end of the day it is all about players . . . and how they perform. We had great success, for instance, at Leicester by playing with a back three and wing-backs pushing on and when we moved to Celtic for the most part we continued with the same system. We both share the same belief that tactics only work if players produce within them. I've got the perfect example to illustrate what I mean.

When we were at Celtic we had just come back from playing Boavista against whom we had gone with three at the back. But the Saturday afterwards we were facing Rangers at Ibrox and at the time they had a system of playing one up front and two men in wide positions. We had had the odd problem with it but for that game we decided we would switch to a back four because we could cope better with what Rangers were trying to do. We won the game 2–1 and afterwards we were hailed for being tactical geniuses in having the foresight to change a system that had got us through to a European final. But the truth of the matter is that Ronald de Boer missed three great chances in the first ten minutes of the game and had he taken them Rangers could have ended up comfortable winners. If that had happened we could easily have been slaughtered in the press for changing a winning system!

If you make an honest decision – as we did in that instance – you can't fault yourself. You might be proved right or you might be found to be wrong but you should be able to accept the consequences if you have been straight with yourself. The way I tend to look at it, you are not the biggest genius when you get it right but neither are you the biggest numpty on earth if things go wrong. At the end of the day you just have to accept in football that sometimes it goes for you and sometimes it doesn't.

I've mentioned so many similarities in the way that Martin and Cloughie went about their jobs but I genuinely don't think there was any considered effort on Martin's part to manufacture that likeness. They shared the same principles about the game but I don't think anyone could replicate the characteristics that made Clough such a great manager.

One other thing they have got in common though – and for once this is not complimentary – is their total disregard for time-keeping. The gaffer had been known for keeping people waiting for hours, never mind minutes, and there were occasions when he just didn't turn up at all. I'm not suggesting Martin is that bad but punctuality is certainly not one of his strongest suits. When Martin was a player he was never on time for anything. I'm sure he used to think, 'If we say eight o'clock and get there for half past we'll be OK.' I think he actually used to set his watch fast to make sure that he had a bit of leeway and it's surprising that he didn't pick up more Red Trees in his playing days at Forest.

He was a much underrated member of the side that brought so much success to Forest in the late '70s and early '80s. And he had a competitive streak that was second to none – on and off the field. He even took it on holiday with him!

In 1980 Martin, Tony Woodcock, myself and all our wives went to Crete on holiday. We all got on together very well and had a great time. While we were there we met up with this lad called Peter, who lived in London and was a Crystal Palace supporter. The four of us ended up having a table tennis match and, unfortunately for him, Martin was paired off with Pete, who let's just say wasn't very good. We played one game, which Tony and I won very easily, and Martin wasn't particularly happy with the team set-up or the result. At the beginning of the second game Tony and I hatched a little plot between us that when we were poised to start we would hop around on one leg and put our spare hand over our eyes to indicate that we could win blind on one leg! Tony and I were rolling about with laughter but Martin was not a happy bunny. It was an indication of how much he wanted to be a winner whatever he was doing.

I've got a lot to thank Martin for and without him I would have had none of the marvellous experiences I've enjoyed at Wycombe, Leicester, Celtic and Villa. I know I've got a reputation for getting up to a few things, enjoying a drink, loving a fag and dressing like a tramp. But, fortunately for me, Martin looked beyond those perceived 'stains' on my character and saw that deep down I was an OK sort of bloke with a reasonably good knowledge of football and someone he could trust. I know I let him down over the La Manga episode during our days at Leicester City but he stayed loyal with me then and he's been nothing short of supportive all the way down the line.

Some people, like Martin, are meant to be a No. 1 but I don't think I could ever take the responsibilities, commitment and 24/7 nature of the job. I know myself well. I want to do a job to the best of my ability and then go home to relax – but management doesn't really allow you to do that. Managers have to deal with directors, press and the running of the club, whereas it suited me to be in the dressing-room and out on the training ground with the lads.

With us Martin has always been the boss. Yes, we've disagreed at times but what was said has always remained private. That's the way it was with the likes of Steve Walford, Ian Storey-Moore and Seamus McDonagh, who have been part of Martin's backroom staff down the years. It's important to have a tight-knit group who stay loyal to one another and Martin and I have been fortunate to work with people whose honesty, trust and integrity you could rely upon.

That's not always the case in football and I remember not too long ago chatting to an assistant manager at another club and asking him how a particular player was doing. His answer was, 'Well, let's put it this way – I wouldn't have signed him in the first place.' That was bang out of order to say the least and almost a betrayal of the trust that should be evident between a manager and his No. 2. It was also a sign to me that something wasn't right in that relationship but fortunately that's never been the case with Martin and me.

I've lost count of the number of times people in Nottingham have asked me whether Martin and I would have liked to have come back to Forest. I think a lot of Forest supporters would have seen it as something of a dream ticket but I'm not too disappointed that it didn't happen. There was a lot of talk about Martin and me going back to Forest after they had been relegated in 1999 under Dave Bassett. But I would have hated to do anything to spoil my reputation as a player at The City Ground.

It's a matter of immense pride to me that I was held in such regard during my playing days at the club and I wouldn't have wanted to have tarnished that in any way by things not working out in management. It might be a cowardly way of looking at it but it's an honest assessment of how I feel. I'm not a great believer in going back to where you were successful and I know that I went against that theory when I returned to Forest in 1985 for a season. But at that time I needed to leave Derby and there was comfort to be had in returning 'home' to Forest. I know I wasn't the same player but I managed to keep my reputation intact and that was important to me.

I thought Frank Clark, for example, was very brave in taking on the manager's role at Forest in 1993, particularly when he was succeeding the gaffer, who was an impossible act to follow. He was on a hiding to nothing but, fortunately, the club backed him in the transfer market, and he did a wonderful job in taking Forest straight back into the Premier League. I've got nothing but admiration for Frank's achievements in not only winning promotion but taking Forest to third in the table the following season when they qualified for Europe.

But I had my time at Forest and I'm well thought of in Nottingham because of my playing days and I would very much like to leave it at that.

17

Some you admire, some you don't

HAVING SEEN HIS UNIQUE STYLE and excellence at close hand for so many years at Nottingham Forest, I would always put Brian Clough at the top of any football manager's pile I was constructing. He also had success with two clubs who could hardly be described as being big city outfits in football terms.

To do what he did with Derby in taking them to the First Division title and the semi-final of the European Cup was a monumental achievement. More significantly, he went on to have the most amazing success at Forest – the kind you cannot ever imagine being repeated by a provincial city club in today's game. To take on the might of Liverpool as he did in the late 1970s and take away their English and European crowns was nothing short of incredible.

Before he took us to the top in 1978 Liverpool had reigned supreme under the management of Bill Shankly and Bob Paisley, who were very different men but were united in one major way – they were unbelievably successful at Anfield. Liverpool were a Second Division team when Shankly arrived at the club and lifted them to incredible heights with his amazing charisma, enthusiasm and knowledge of the game. I've chatted to Larry Lloyd a lot about Shankly and he speaks as highly about him as we all did about Cloughie. It's not surprising that Shankly and Clough got on very well and when we played at Anfield in the glory days, Shankly was a regular and welcome visitor to our dressing-room before matches.

I've also got a lovely testimony from Shankly at home. Some years ago I was stopped in the street by a guy in West Bridgford and he told me he had a vinyl record about me during my playing days. I thought it must be the 'We've Got the Whole World In Our

Hands' offering that we put together at Forest when things were going so well. 'No, it's a record of Bill Shankly being interviewed and talking about you,' he said. He let me have the record and in it Shankly was very complimentary about my ability and that meant a lot to me.

I was delighted when he penned a few words for my testimonial programme in 1980. He wrote: 'When I see John Robertson play he excites me. It excites me to think about what he can do for Scotland in years to come. No Scottish side should take the field now without his name on the team-sheet. It would be absolute nonsense to leave him out. I know the area where he was brought up. I know that it can never have been easy for him there and the environment in which he was brought up is seen in his play today.

'He has a cute footballing brain which gives him a yard start on opponents and that first yard is the most important in football. That's where he excels. He's a thickset, powerfully built lad but he's nimble too. He's also one of the most accurate passers of the ball in the game today . . . and with either foot. He can thread a ball up the touchline like a snooker player and he's such a good user of space that to give him an inch is to give him an inch too much.

'He gives Nottingham Forest options. They can attack the opponents' by-line with him or they can sit back and slow it down and keep possession through him. He's several different players in one shirt. Everybody is important to Forest's success but John Robertson has an extra special importance.'

I hope you don't mind me repeating that because I'm not one for blowing my own bagpipes but I was humbled by what such a great manager had said about me.

It was a surprise to a lot of people in the game when Shankly decided to call it a day in 1974 but the Liverpool Board of Directors had enough trust to appoint Paisley as his successor. Paisley wasn't a character in the Shankly mould, he didn't seek publicity and was a real quiet man of football but his record became phenomenal.

In the days of Shankly and Paisley, Liverpool had a very successful habit of buying good players and then letting them slowly bed into the Anfield way of things before being introduced to the expectation levels of first team football at the club. They had great continuity and although they have not won too much in recent years, they are still one of the major forces in the English game – thanks to the efforts years ago of Shankly, Paisley, Joe Fagan and Kenny Dalglish. It's almost like a dynasty but when Cloughie dragged Forest out of the doldrums he had to build all the foundations himself.

Aside from the gaffer's wonderfully unique success, I have got the utmost admiration for the remarkable record that Sir Alex Ferguson has built up with Manchester United. There will be no shortage of takers but I really feel for the man who eventually has the task of taking over from him at Old Trafford. When the day comes it will need very special handling because United and all that it stands for has been ingrained by Alex's influence all down the years. When you think of all the success he has had at the club, it's hard to imagine that he went through his first four years without winning a trophy. And it was widely reported that had it not been for an FA Cup third round goal by Mark Robins against Forest at The City Ground in January 1990 he would have been on his way from Old Trafford. But the United board stuck with him and got unprecedented levels of success for doing so. His achievements stand favourable comparison with anyone's.

I know Sir Alex has had all the financial backing and support that comes from one of football's great institutions but nothing guarantees silverware. He has made it all possible and year after year he has delivered. He's had to reinvent the wheel several times but his record since winning his first trophy is nothing short of staggering. To maintain the hunger and desire over such a long period is amazing because he's at an age now when most blokes are tending the roses and playing with their grandkids. But he's maximised and nurtured a bunch of players from the mid 1980s who have formed the basis of all that he has achieved.

To my mind there has never been a better player in the Premier League than Ryan Giggs. It's not just his ability but the way he applies himself, his sportsmanship and general demeanour on a football field that make him just about the perfect package. At the end of the day, you also have to look at the trophies and medals he has won to realise that he is a very special footballer and nothing that has happened in his private life should detract from his achievements on the field.

He's been the No. 1 icon for United but in that same group were the likes of Paul Scholes, David Beckham, Nicky Butt, Gary and Phil Neville . . . players who were brought up together and formed the solid base around which so much of United's success was built. It's almost as if the determination and application that they have all possessed is in their DNA – such is the remarkable consistency they have shown at the highest level of the game. To have the length and quality of careers that they have enjoyed is nothing short of amazing. They would all have been brilliant players anywhere they plied their trade but they are even better individuals and have reached greater heights because they had the benefit of Sir Alex's influence.

Martin and I have been in opposition to Sir Alex on many occasions, of course, and I've always found him to be gracious in victory and magnanimous in defeat. He's always been very complimentary and respectful, which I can't say is the case with all his contemporaries.

There is something about Arsène Wenger's manner that I have never been able to come to terms with – whatever our results have been against his Arsenal sides. I've always found him to be aloof and arrogant and the way he behaves on a touchline with his arm-waving antics is what you get away from the action.

Television cameras picked up what I can only describe as his totally unacceptable behaviour in April 2011 when Liverpool were at the Emirates for a game that Arsenal desperately needed to win to keep in touch with Manchester United at the head of the Premier League. There was a load of time added on because of an injury to Jamie Carragher and right at the end of it Arsenal won a penalty from which Robin van Persie gave them the lead. But Liverpool still had time to get down the other end and win a penalty of their own and Dirk Kuyt stepped up to score, earn his side a draw and send Wenger into the kind of eccentric poses that would have done justice to John Cleese! The Liverpool manager Kenny Dalglish clearly didn't take kindly to Wenger's remonstrations but where that scenario is concerned many others have gone before him and many more will undoubtedly follow.

I don't know whether it's a cultural issue or not but I've never seen Wenger go out of his way to give another team credit. He's never been slow to reveal his contempt when teams face Arsenal and put men behind the ball. But I watched with interest when he took Arsenal to Barcelona in the Champions League in 2011 and got players back into defensive positions at the merest hint of danger. In that instance it was almost as if it was acceptable because his Arsenal side were doing it.

And at the end of the game he spent most of his time moaning about the sending off of van Persie when he would have gathered a lot more credit and respect had he paid tribute to the quality of an extremely gifted Barcelona side who had won the game fairly and squarely. There's no harm in admitting that you have been beaten by a far better side and I think you can gain personally and attract respect by adopting that kind of stance. There are ways to enjoy winning and there are ways to accept defeats and in my eyes Wenger has always had a problem with this. It's customary in football for managers to meet after a game and share a drink, whether it be a glass of wine or a cup of tea but I've never had that experience with him . . . and never really wanted to.

Don't get me wrong, I am not totally against Wenger and you have to admire the honours he has won in the past. You also have to acknowledge the quality and style of football that his current Arsenal side produces. There is no doubt their passing game is very pleasing on the eye and has provided some great entertainment. But the game, more than ever before, is about winning. Arsenal under Wenger have now gone six years without winning a trophy and I don't know any manager from the so-called top four or five who would have survived as long without putting some silverware on the table. Carlo Ancelotti won the double at Chelsea in 2009–10 but he went through the majority of the following season with continuous speculation about how long he would survive at Stamford Bridge and in May 2011 he was sacked for finishing second!

But in the eyes of the press it seems that Wenger can do nothing wrong and in my opinion he gets away very lightly for his part in a lot of incidents. I just wish he could bring himself to be more courteous and more respectful. He would win himself a lot more friends in the game if he did.

Because of Sir Alex's amazing reign at Old Trafford and Wenger's long stint with Arsenal, very few jobs become available at the very top of the English game. Those that do invariably go to foreigners. Chelsea's last home-based manager, for example, was Glenn

Hoddle, who was at Stamford Bridge first as player and then manager from 1993–96.

The money that is in the higher echelons of the English game now dictates that the best are always seeking the very best. In a lot of cases, certainly as far as the directors of the top football clubs are concerned, that means going abroad to get managers and players alike.

The game has gone down a road where the players are so powerful and I must admit that the average football supporter cannot relate to footballers earning upwards of £150,000 a week. I'm all for the very best individuals in any industry earning top salaries but it's now reached the stage where very average players are picking up sums of money that have no reflection on their ability levels. There are some very ordinary players in English football earning £30,000 a week plus and are multimillionaires in their early twenties, and you have got to question whether that is morally right.

Money has been a problem in the game for a long time and there is no doubt that there are players in football who just want to earn as much as quickly as humanly possible. But I once had a long conversation with Des Walker, who was arriving on the first team scene at Forest just as my professional career was ending in the mid 1980s. Des and I were having a chat one day about money and he was horrified at the attitude of one of his Forest team-mates who couldn't wait to milk the club for all it was worth – all he was interested in was when the next pay rise was coming – and then move on. Des's attitude was that if he went out and did the best he could game after game, season after season, the rewards and riches that football had to offer would follow as a matter of course. I thought it was quite refreshing to hear that viewpoint from someone who went on to win 59 caps for England and was regarded as one of the finest defenders of his generation.

The money issue is very much one that takes care of itself. Can you imagine that the pound signs were flashing in the eyes of players like Bryan Robson and Roy Keane when they set foot on a football field? Not likely. All that bothered them was winning matches, collecting trophies, picking up caps . . . and letting their financial aspirations take care of themselves.

But as long as we have Sky and the multimillion-pound

sponsorships that swill around football, players will prosper. We all have to be thankful for the money that television has put into the game but it doesn't make it any easier for me to accept some of the clap-trap that we have to endure from so-called pundits. It really rankles with me when I listen to them blathering on about the rights and wrongs of what managers should be doing. So much so that nowadays, as soon as it is half-time or full-time in a game I am watching on television, I make no excuses for turning off the sound. If I don't I end up arguing with a screen and getting wound up about the way that alleged experts spend their lives pontificating.

It really does rile me when I hear former players or former managers sitting in the comfort of a television studio telling all and sundry that it is 'time for change'. Have they not got the common sense to realise that managers, bursting blood vessels on the bench, have not had the very same thought? I think there is so much disrespect shown to managers who are striving to do their job but at the end of the day the views are swept under the carpet as a 'matter of opinion'.

A lot of people who sit in front of a television camera giving their opinions don't know whether they want to be a manager or a pundit. I've never been one for wanting to sit in front of a TV camera but Martin O'Neill has worked for television at a couple of World Cups. First and foremost he's a manager and a pundit second but I get the impression a lot of so-called experts are not sure which hat to wear. And I think that has been reflected in the views Martin has given when he has been on television panels. He's imagined himself in the situation that a manager has been in and given his opinion in a way that shows respect to the individual. Martin is entertaining and his opinion is well respected and if he wanted to make a career out of television punditry I am sure he could. Maybe one day he will.

18
Stats tell the story

I CAN'T PRETEND THAT THE Aston Villa experience was the happiest of my career but the bottom line in football is often statistics – and to that extent Martin O'Neill could consider himself extremely successful during his time in the West Midlands. During the four years (2006–2010) we spent at Villa Park we stabilised the club in mid-table in the first season, had three successive sixth place finishes, reached a cup final and flirted with the prospect of getting the club into the Champions League. In these days when you are competing with clubs of the stature and financial clout of Manchester United, Chelsea, Arsenal, Manchester City, Liverpool and Tottenham, I reckon Villa supporters would have been happy with the performances and achievements of the side during that four-year period.

Martin had more or less taken a year out after leaving Celtic to spend more time with his wife as she slowly recovered from serious illness when he was offered the opportunity of succeeding David O'Leary at Villa Park. They had finished 16th in the Premier League in his final season – 2005–06 – and Villa were desperate to compete with the bigger teams who seem to be nowadays competing in a league within a league at the top.

To an extent Villa, like Nottingham Forest before them, were still dreaming about hopes of repeating their European Cup-winning days but memories of our old team-mate Peter Withe scoring the winner against Bayern Munich in Rotterdam in 1982 were becoming more and more distant. Even so, traditionally Villa are one of the major clubs in English football and I am sure Martin viewed them as having immense potential and being one of the few outfits capable of breaking into the elite group at the top – if he was given the right kind of backing from the boardroom. We knew there was talk of a takeover in the air at Villa Park but it was Doug Ellis who was in charge when Martin was offered the position in early August 2006.

With Steve Walford and myself immediately joining Martin, he had people around him that he knew and trusted. Down the years it has been a threesome between us rather than a partnership, and both Martin and myself would never underestimate the contribution 'Wally' has made. He's a top-class coach, an excellent organiser and someone who pays a lot of attention to detail. On top of that he's got a great sense of humour and around players and in a dressing-room environment you have to have that. Soon after we arrived at Villa Park Martin brought in a couple of other recruits he was keen on to his backroom staff. Seamus McDonagh arrived as goalkeeping coach. He had been with us at Leicester City and although there wasn't the opportunity to take him to Celtic, Martin was delighted to get him back on board at Villa Park. And he also wasted no time in appointing Ian Storey-Moore as chief scout. Ian had been a close friend of Martin's for many years – since their days together at The City Ground – and his knowledge of the game was always held in high regard. Muggsy had lost his job as chief scout at Forest when they embarked on a cost-cutting exercise after going down to League One so it was a timely opening for him. We were going to lean on his experience in bringing new players into the club but one of the first arrivals was a player we knew well from our Parkhead days.

Stiliyan Petrov had been a great player for us at Celtic – he was signed from his native Bulgaria before we arrived in Glasgow – and we were delighted to bring him south in a deal that cost the club an initial £6.5m. He was superb on his debut against West Ham but took time to settle after that and the fact that we had to utilise him on the right-hand side didn't help him to acclimatise. The crowd got on his back for a time and after toiling to make an impression he battled through to prove himself the quality individual and footballer he is. So much so that he eventually became club captain and certainly led by example.

Other major transfer activity had to wait because with the

season just around the corner there wasn't really time to make big inroads into the market and we had to hit the ground running. In fact, within 24 hours of Martin being appointed as manager we were on a plane out to Hanover in Germany where the players we had inherited were taking part in their build-up to the new season. One player who was missing from Villa's squad at the time was Gareth Barry, who had been left at home to recover from injury. But, fortunately for us, he was fit for the start of the Premier League programme.

When it got underway we couldn't have wished for a better start to our first season. A goal by big Swedish defender Olof Mellberg gave us the lead against Arsenal at The Emirates and we looked to be heading for a memorable opening day win until Gilberto Silva equalised with just a few minutes left. Nevertheless, it was the start of an unbeaten run that stretched for nine games. In fact, we didn't suffer defeat until the end of October against Liverpool at Anfield and we continued to hover around the top six until Christmas time.

In the January 2007 transfer window we made a significant capture when we signed Norwegian striker John Carew from top French club Lyon. Czech striker Milan Baros, who Villa had signed from Liverpool, went to Lyon as part of the deal and we were convinced that Carew would make an impact. John had all the attributes to be as successful as he wanted to be in the game – two good feet, excellent in the air and very skilful.

As he settled in we had an indifferent spell midway through the season but finished as we had started with a nine-match unbeaten run that earned Martin the Manager of the Month accolade for April. We ended the season in eleventh position – five places and eight points higher than in the campaign before we arrived.

As time went on one of the changes we made concerned Gareth Barry, who before we arrived had flitted between playing left-back and left side of midfield and didn't really have a permanent position. We felt very strongly that he was more than capable of playing in a more central midfield position, where he had greater scope to influence a game . . . and it worked a treat. Before we arrived I think Gareth had won just one cap but his conversion into an out-and-out central midfield player not only led to him making a major impact in the Villa side but to establishing himself in the England set-up. It was a move that greatly enhanced us as a side and sometimes decisions like that can have as much of a bearing on a club's fortunes as a big-name signing.

That also proved to be the case with James Milner, who we signed from Newcastle United in August 2008 for £12m. James had been on loan at Villa during O'Leary's time at the club and had clearly enjoyed the experience. But he had gone back to Newcastle and settled down for a while as his stock as an out-out-winger improved. We still felt there was a chance of getting him out of St James' Park and although a lot of people questioned the size of the fee, we were delighted to bring the boy to Villa Park. I like to think that we worked on and improved his game to such an extent that, like Gareth before him, he was more than capable of holding his own in a more central role. After we had brought Stewart Downing to the club from Middlesbrough in the summer of 2009, it opened up the way for James to move into midfield and he immediately showed the quality and know-how expected of someone playing in that position.

Sadly, Villa were not able to hold on to James but those people who doubted his value when we bought him from Newcastle were forced to think again when he joined Manchester City just days after Martin and I left Villa Park in August 2010. The deal that took him to The City of Manchester Stadium – Stephen Ireland moved in the opposite direction – was reported to be worth £26m and that's some return on the £12m investment Martin made in him just two years before.

One of the other major buys Martin made was to get Ashley Young from Watford in the 2007 January transfer window for a fee that added up to nearly £10m. A lot of clubs looked at Ashley and were very interested but the majority of them were put off by the kind of fee that Watford were suggesting they wanted for him. In the end I think it got down to a straight battle between West Ham and ourselves and we were very happy to get a player whose best days were clearly ahead of him. He was only twenty-one at the time he moved from Vicarage Road but we knew we were getting a player with pace and skill and one who was capable of delivering quality balls with either foot. Like Milner, his value increased significantly – and that's a great return on another player whose transfer fee raised a few eyebrows.

In the 2007–08 season we were in contention for a UEFA Cup spot for much of the time but picked up only two points from our last three games. We missed out on the final day of the season when Everton won and we drew and had to settle for a place in the Intertoto Cup, which meant a short summer break for the players. We won the Intertoto by defeating Danish side Odense in the final and because of that earned a place in the UEFA Cup . . . and made progress into the third round, where we were paired with CSKA Moscow.

The side had also been performing really well in the new league season and, come February 2009, we were sitting third in the table following a 2–0 away win over Blackburn Rovers. We had lost only four league games up until that point of the season, the team were understandably playing with a lot of confidence and we genuinely felt we had an opportunity to finish in the top four.

The carrot of Champions League football was standing right in front of our eyes at that stage and Martin thought long and hard about his priorities. There was no doubt in his mind that if he could get Villa into the Champions League with all the financial rewards that it brought, it was worth giving our Premier League games maximum focus at the expense of our European ambitions. It was probably a decision that split the feelings of Villa supporters. I am sure a lot of them understood Martin's belief that with a relatively small squad, he had to put one target ahead of the other and to get Villa into the Champions League would have been a magnificent achievement. But there was an element who felt that a European prize was within our grasp and we should go in there with our strongest team and suffer the consequences with our league form.

We had drawn 1–1 with CSKA at home but Martin opted to rest several players for the return and we went out of the competition following a 2–0 defeat. It was one of those instances in football when you cannot win but the great pity for us was that we lost our way in the Premier League after that and ended up having to settle for another sixth place finish in a season that had promised so much more. We were slaughtered in some quarters for the CSKA business but hindsight is a wonderful thing and at the time we were making the decisions that we felt were in the best interests of Aston Villa Football Club.

At the end of that 2008–09 season we suffered another major blow – and one that sadly had been coming for some time – when big Danish defender Martin Laursen had to give up his battle against a serious knee injury. Martin was at the club when we got there. He had been signed from Milan in 2004 for just £3m and I've not come across too many more determined footballers, starting with my fearsome mates Larry Lloyd and Kenny Burns at Forest. I've played with and worked with many top-class defenders in my time but I don't think I've ever seen anyone more committed to heading the ball as the big man. Scandinavians generally don't mind the physical aspect of the British game but Martin was one who positively thrived on it and it was such a tragedy that he had to call time on his career because his knees could no long stand up to the demands of professional football. Had he been fit throughout our time at the club I have absolutely no doubt that we would have done better than we did because he had the kind of will to win that makes very good players great ones. It was an emotional moment when he grabbed the microphone before our final game of the season – a 1–0 win over Newcastle that put the Geordies down – and addressed the Villa fans. My heart went out to him because you never want to see a genuine football man like he was denied the chance of pursuing a career that he enjoyed so much. He was a lovely bloke and that just added to the sadness of it all.

We were again in the reckoning for a Champions League place in 2009–10 – our final season at Villa Park – and we had some excellent wins against Manchester United, Chelsea and Liverpool to support the belief that we could make that breakthrough. But again it was not to be. We dropped a lot of points, particularly at Villa Park, where we drew a lot of games we should really have been winning, and for the third consecutive season had to settle for sixth place. It was no mean achievement but we had not given up hope that we would take that extra stride and it was frustrating that we never quite managed it.

We were tantalisingly close to winning silverware in 2010 – and but for a poor refereeing decision I am sure we would have won the Carling Cup that year. We beat Cardiff City, Sunderland, Portsmouth and Blackburn Rovers on our way to the final against Manchester United at Wembley. It was Villa's first final in ten years and we started the game superbly and should have taken a bigger grip on the game than we did after just six minutes. Ashley Young knocked a ball into the United box for Gabby Agbonlahor to chase and he was through on goal when he was tugged back and brought down by Nemanja Vidic.

It was a clear penalty and an even clearer red card but we had to settle for the penalty that was tucked away by James Milner. Let me say here and now that I am dead against players being haphazardly sent off but we were playing under rules that dictated that any player denying a goalscoring chance by an illegal challenge had to be shown a red card. And it was as clear as day that Vidic had committed a crime that more than justified a sending-off offence. To add insult to injury the referee Phil Dowd didn't even book Vidic and I can only assume that it was a human reaction of not wanting to spoil a Wembley showpiece by reducing one of the sides to ten men so early in the contest. I must admit the decision left a really bad taste and you could sense even from United's players and Sir Alex Ferguson that they realised they had got away with one in that flashpoint incident. Even United, with all their talent, would have found it very difficult being a goal down and playing 85 minutes with a man short.

It's history now that Michael Owen equalised and then Wayne Rooney, who was in a rich goalscoring vein at the time, headed the winner. We did all we could to get back on level terms and Downing and Richard Dunne both went close to taking the game into extra-time. Sadly, we will never know what the outcome would have been had Vidic taken the long walk early in the game but we wouldn't have minded finding out!

Had things gone our way at Wembley and we had managed to lift the Carling Cup you never know where that might have taken us. The first trophy is always the most difficult to win and it often leads to more silverware. But when Martin resigned from Villa in August 2010 we departed with a feeling of what might have been. Obviously, events of the cup final still rankled with us but we genuinely felt that we were within touching distance of bringing Villa fans the success they yearned for.

It's not possible for me to say too much more about what happened at Villa for legal reasons but on a personal level I can say that I have enjoyed my time since away from the intensity of day-to-day football. It is such a pressurised business, particularly for managers who have to deal with all manner of things, and my sympathies go to those whose health has suffered as a result of the stresses that go with the territory. As someone once said, the highs in football are never as high as the lows are low. It's quite a profound statement but I totally understand the sentiments of the person who originated it. When you win a game of football, it's amazing how quickly the joy and elation disappear and you have to focus on the next match. When you lose a game, it takes days to get it out of your system and normally it sticks with you until the next good day comes along.

As Martin's No. 2 I have had nothing like the worries that confronted him day in, day out and to be perfectly frank I am more than ever convinced in my own mind that I could not have coped with being a No. 1. I've thoroughly enjoyed the break I have had from the game and over the last 18 months I've been able to take a step back from football and appreciate some of the other things in life that sometimes pass you by.

One of the first things I did was to set my stall out to play a lot more tennis. It's a game I love from a spectator point of view as well as playing and to be honest I've spent more time watching Roger Federer and Rafael Nadal on television than I have football matches. I've taken a great interest in Federer down the years and I've had the fullest admiration for the way he kept himself in the forefront of the game for so long as well as conducting himself in an impeccable manner. It was Martin who first told me to watch Federer and appreciate his talent and admire his demeanour. That was years ago but ever since I've marvelled at the way he played the game with such style and charisma as well as dealing with his rare lapses with such great dignity. To my mind he's an example not just to all budding tennis players but to sportsmen and women whatever their game. I've been desperately keen to see him play live and I was fortunate to be at Wimbledon in 2011 to watch him beat David Nalbandian in straight sets on Centre Court. But back home in front of the television I was majorly disappointed when he went out to Jo-Wilfried Tsonga in the quarter finals.

At one time my tennis interest and capabilities were restricted to the odd game on holiday with friends when inevitably you spend more time retrieving and picking up balls following wayward shots than actually hitting them. By playing so much I'd like to say my game has come on leaps and bounds. In reality I've still got a lot of weaknesses and I can tell you my net play leaves a lot to be desired. But it keeps me reasonably fit and I love the type of game it is. You have to think a lot and work your position and when it all comes to fruition with a 'winner' it gives me as much pleasure as I used to get when leaving a full-back on his backside.

Fortunately, I've got some mates from my football days who all enjoy a game so I'm not often short of an opponent. When I finished at Celtic I was having a drink with former Forest player and manager Paul Hart one day. The conversation somehow got round to tennis and I asked him if he fancied having a game some time. He did and whenever he's had his spells out of management over the last year or so he's certainly been up for a game. Also Liam O'Kane, who I played with at Forest all those years ago, fancies himself as a bit of a player. So too does Garry Birtles who arrived on the scene more recently and between us we have had a lot of pleasure – and hopefully there is a lot more to come. It's like we have a little club going between us and we all love it. I try and play two or three times a week.

The extra time that I have had away from football has also enabled me to spend more priceless time with my wife Sharyl and the boys. We enjoy our holidays but I must confess to getting too brave for my own good on one family break in Cyprus. We had been enjoying a few drinks watching people paragliding along the coastline when, galvanised by a bit of Dutch courage, I suddenly announced, 'I could do that.' I shocked myself but everyone was stunned because it is a well-known fact in the family that I'm not the bravest, particularly when it comes to heights. I start getting wobbly on the second rung of a ladder! On top of that I can't swim so the very thought of drifting along with water underneath should have filled me with horror. My son Andrew immediately said he would go up with me and once I had said 'Yes' there was no turning back.

The sweat was pouring out of me as I was getting strapped in but up we went and I can honestly say I was petrified with a capital P. I hung on to the harness so tightly that my arms ached for days afterwards. Andrew, bless him, talked me through it to give me some token courage but when we were up there my throat was so dry I felt like I was at the dentist. You know that feeling you get when the dentist is inside your mouth and you want to swallow and can't? That was me. I had my eyes closed most of the time, was hanging on to the straps for dear life and there was not a happier man in Cyprus than me when I touched down. Mind you, I felt pretty pleased with myself afterwards. I was presented with a certificate as evidence that I had actually done it and I was flushed with pride.

My bravery was all put into perspective a few minutes later, however, when my other son Mark, my daughter Elisabeth and a friend went up and they were waving and having a laugh as they sailed through the air without a care in the world. It was only when I was back in the safety of the boat and saw them up in the air with both hands free that I realised you could let go of the harness.

We've recently enjoyed more breaks away than we would have been able to had I been in football and we've had one or two great holidays in caravans which is something I could probably never have seen me doing twenty-odd years ago.

It's been great being able to relax and spend time doing not an awful lot.

My daughter Elisabeth still lives at home with Sally although she has a long-standing boyfriend, who I'm loathe to admit is probably the most important man in her life. But I still see a lot of her and I couldn't be more proud of her as a person or for what she has achieved. Considering I failed the 11-plus and was devoid of any academic qualifications, I was absolutely thrilled when Elisabeth went to Manchester University to study philosophy. She came away with a 2:1 and I soaked up every minute of her graduation. Since then she has gone into teaching and is now working at a school in Nuneaton. It wasn't easy for her in her early days because Jessica's condition demanded so much of our time, particularly Sally's. But even though Elisabeth was very young, she loved her sister dearly, was very understanding about it all and still talks lovingly about Jessica now.

Having had the two girls with Sally, I was delighted when Sharyl and I had a baby boy in February 1995. The arrival of Andrew and more recently Mark has made sure the Robertson name will continue in the family because I was the last male in the line and my mum and dad would have been happy about that.

Andrew is 16 now and has just gone through his GCSEs and is

starting to think of what he will do in the future. He's really knuckled down with his studies and although, like me, he enjoys tennis, he's shown no inclination to develop as a footballer. I think he might have had a bit of peer pressure at school because most of the kids will know that I'm his dad.

But it doesn't worry me one bit that either Andrew or Mark, who is now nine, are not particularly interested in football. It's no real surprise or concern to me either because it's a very small percentage of lads who follow their dads into the professional game. Nigel Clough, Scot Gemmill, Frank Lampard and Jamie Redknapp spring obviously to mind as examples of players who have followed in their fathers' footsteps but it's not a given thing. My only wish is that Andrew and Mark are happy in what they do and at the moment I think they are.

Andrew has talked to me about teaching and I would be very happy if he followed his sister into the profession but that's very much for the future. For the time being he's been very happy with the help that Elisabeth has been able to give him before taking his GCSE exams. Andrew is a good talker, can argue any point and perhaps there is a politician inside him waiting to come out. I often say that he can argue a black crow white! Mark is more interested in dinosaurs than footballers – he can tell you anything you need to know about them. He's the comedian in the family and often makes us laugh with his one-liners and facial expressions. He was born in Glasgow in 2002 during my time at Celtic and being a Scotsman I quite liked that. The boys certainly look up to Elisabeth as their big sister and I'm really fortunate that all of my three children get on so well and are so fond of each other.

When I'm not doing things with the family and get time to myself I still love having a crack at *The Times* crossword even though more often than not I still don't finish it. And I'm never far away from a Sudoku challenge – I carry a book of them around with me in the car.

With one thing or another I can honestly say I have not missed football too much but it's still obviously very dear to my heart. It might not be the game it was when I was dawdling my way down the left wing at Forest but it has been a huge and rewarding part of my life and it has given me some wonderful moments and memories that will stay with me forever.

Acknowledgements

It's given me a lot of pleasure to have retraced in words the steps I have made since my infant days in Uddingston.

Having an autobiography that Bill Campbell at Mainstream Publishing felt was worthy of setting down in print, I am indebted to John Lawson for putting it together in some constructive and readable order.

I've known John for almost 40 years and he did me a huge favour in the early Brian Clough days by telling the great man that he thought I could play. I've never forgotten that and when eventually I decided to go ahead with the book, there was only one person I wanted to do it.

My thanks also go to Fraser Nicholson for proofreading, providing an inspired suggestion for a title and for being one of the few people who bought a pension policy from me when my football days were over.

But without the help and influence of two men who are sadly no longer with us I would probably not have had a story to tell at all . . . and certainly not one that included so much success.

I owe so much to Brian Clough and Peter Taylor for nurturing the talent with which I was blessed and without their equal measures of grief and guidance, who knows what direction my journey would have taken. I will be eternally grateful to the gaffer and Pete for helping me realise my potential as a footballer. And I'm not the first one to say that.

By the same token I would like to end by thanking my mate of 40 years Martin O'Neill for the friendship and opportunities he has given me. It's been a pleasure and a privilege to be at his side for so long, enjoying experiences that I will never forget.